DOCUMENTING AND AUDITING FOR ISO 9000 AND QS-9000

DOCUMENTING AND AUDITING FOR ISO 9000 AND QS-9000

TOOLS FOR ENSURING CERTIFICATION OR REGISTRATION

D. H. STAMATIS

Central Michigan University
Contemporary Consultants Co.

IRWIN
Professional Publishing®
Chicago • London • Singapore

▼▼ Times Mirror
Ⓜ Higher Education Group

Library of Congress Cataloging-in Publication Data

Stamatis, D. H., 1947–
    Documenting and auditing for ISO 9000 and QS-9000 : tools for ensuring certification or registration / D.H. Stamatis.
        p.   cm.
    Includes bibliographical references and index.
    ISBN 0-7863-0862-1
    1. ISO 9000 Series Standards.   2.   Quality control—Standards.
    I. Title
    TS156.6.S714   1996
    658.5'62'0218—dc20   96–3180

Printed in the United States of America
1 2 3 4 5 6 7 8 9 0 Q B P 3 2 1 0 9 8 7 6

In memory of my uncle

Nickolaos

*who taught me at an early age how to plan,
document, and audit in the apiary business
before quality was in vogue and before ISO/QS
was even thought of.*

PREFACE

The international standards known as the ISO 9000 series offer a basic system of quality and the opportunity to build that quality throughout the organization. The standards, indeed, become the blocks of quality by which the organization can achieve total quality management (TQM) and World Class Quality. The standards offer a common foundation for all to work from and at the same time allow for individuality.

This book is about how to implement the ISO 9000 series in the organization. It addresses the structure and the requirements of documentation as well as auditing for the ISO 9000 series. It discusses a detailed approach to fulfilling the requirements of the documentation process for the ISO 9001 (ISO 9002 and ISO 9003 are part of the ISO 9001). Furthermore, it addresses the issues of auditing from both the auditee's and auditor's perspective.

This book also addresses one of the most recent developments in the world of customer requirements (standards), that is, the QS-9000. Specifically, documentation and auditing considerations will be discussed as they relate to the QS-9000.

The book has two basic objectives. The first objective is to provide a reference and a manual for the ISO 9000/QS-9000 documentation material. As a result the target audience is anyone who is interested in or involved with documenting quality issues. The second objective is to explain the methods and tools of the ISO/QS auditing process to help an organization attain the certification as well as keep it. Thus the target audience is the individual(s) in any organization who is responsible for the implementation of the ISO/QS-9000. The book also identifies the process of auditing and what is expected from the auditee's perspective.

This book may be used as a college text or as a reference for undergraduate- or graduate-level courses dealing with documentation and/or auditing.

WHAT THIS BOOK IS NOT

This book is NOT a primer on either the ISO 9000 or the QS-9000. This book is also NOT an interpretive guide to every element of the ISO 9000 or the QS-9000. Furthermore, this book is NOT designed to give the reader a historical perspective of the development of either the international standard or the automotive requirement. Finally, this book is NOT a handbook to answer all the pertinent questions one may have for either the ISO 9000 or the QS-9000.

HOW THIS BOOK MAY BE USED

This book is very specific in its purpose—to guide, demonstrate, and facilitate the reader, and more precisely the practitioner of the ISO 9000 and QS-9000, in understanding and implementing the appropriate and applicable documentation so that his or her organization will attain and keep the appropriate certification. Towards that end we have designed each chapter and appendix to be totally independent. We also have provided a plethora of generic examples from a variety of industries to show the wide applicability of the standards and requirements.

Chapter 1 introduces the quality standards with a general overview of the ISO 9000 and the QS-9000, third-party assessments, and the surveillance method.

Chapter 2 gives the reader an overview of the documentation process and a generic structure of the documents.

Chapter 3 details the documentation requirements on an element-by-element basis and explains in detail the structure of the documentation and the requirements of a quality manual.

Chapter 4 details the documentation requirements for procedures and instructions and discusses the issues of cost, quality plans, quality records, document control, and production as they relate to documentation.

Chapter 5 reviews the audit and gives the practitioner some general insight into the audit process. The inclusion of this section, we hope, will help the auditee prepare for the audit with the appropriate documentation. This chapter also covers some of the current issues and concerns that affect both the auditor and the auditee.

Chapter 6 addresses the automotive requirements. In this chapter we treat only the additional requirements of the QS-9000, and we explain the documentation and the evaluation process. The reader who is working for an automotive supplier must be remember that the requirements in this chapter are in addition to the requirements in Chapters 3, 4, and 5.

Appendix A provides the reader with a cursory overview of a documentation matrix, tools used in the process of documentation, and a typical preassessment survey.

Appendix B provides sample quality policies from eight different organizations (not all of them automotive).

Appendix C contains two complete samples of quality manuals. One is chosen from the medical device industry, and the second is from the automotive industry. Our rationale for this selection is that the medical device industry is quite complex and must comply with much more stringent requirements than those of the ISO 9001. The automotive industry also presents additional requirements. Of importance in this appendix is the issue of length. The reader will notice that both manuals are much longer than the length that is recommended in the text of Chapter 3. The reason for this unusual length is that we have tried to include many possibilities in both documents. In reality, however, the individual organization may not have all these requirements and the length of a typical quality manual is likely to be in the 30- to 60-page range. The reader will also notice that the quality manuals differ in form as well as in text description. This is done by design to demonstrate the different ways one may prepare the manual and still fulfill the ISO 9001 standard and the QS-9000 requirement.

The book concludes with five more appendixes. Appendix D provides the reader with a summary of procedures and instructions, records and procedures that are required by the ISO 9001, and six examples from a variety of industries; Appendix E provides the reader with a generic checklist and certificate of accreditation (laboratory); Appendix F provides samples of checklists for the ISO 9002, ISO 9001, BS 7750, and ISO 14000 to demonstrate the diversity of checklists; Appendix G provides miscellaneous information for both auditors and auditees; and Appendix H provides a typical training curriculum for internal auditors and lead auditors.

ACKNOWLEDGMENTS

In writing this book, I want to express both my thank you and gratitude to the people who directly or indirectly contributed to this book. Special thanks go to

> Carla for her support and valuable suggestions throughout this project.
>
> The Chrysler, Ford, and GM Task Force and the A.I.A.G. for allowing me to use some of their materials on evaluation from the *Quality System Assessment.*
>
> The American Society for Quality Control for allowing me to summarize the intoduction of the ISO 9000, the QS-9000 and third-party certification from the book *Integrating QS-9000 with Your Automotive Quality System.*
>
> Mr. K. Wolfe for sharing with me some of the concerns in auditing.
>
> Mr. N. Abunab for his continual support and help with the computer graphics. Without his support, I would have been lost in the maze of hardware and software.
>
> Mr. E. Mann from Transamerica Leasing and Mr. R. Williams from Positronic Industries for sharing their thoughs about auditing and registration.
>
> Mr. W. Harral and Mr. Doug Burg for introducing me on a formal basis to the concept and the application of ISO.

Furthermore, I want to thank all the participants in my public seminars over the years; I have tried to incorporate as many of their suggestions and specific recommendations as I could. Their comments and input made this book possible.

Finally, I want to thank the editors at Irwin Professional for their constant support, encouragement, and suggestions for improvement.

D. H. Stamatis
Southgate, Michigan
November, 1995

CONTENTS

Chapter 5

Audits   77

FIGURES

TABLES

CHAPTER 1

Introduction to Quality Standards

Rising customer expectations around the world and increasing competition are setting new benchmarks for quality in every sector. In the case of the ISO, the intent is to harmonize the global variation of many individual standards. In the case of the QS-9000, the intent is to harmonize automotive requirements. This chapter introduces the ISO/QS standards and discusses the need for such standards.

INTRODUCTION OF THE ISO 9000 STANDARDS

The ISO standards were developed by the International Organization for Standardization, a Geneva, Switzerland, organization founded in 1946 to promote the development of international standards and related activities, including conformity assessment, to facilitate the exchange of goods and services within the European Union (EU) (then known as the European Community) and worldwide. Testing, inspection, laboratory accreditation, certification, quality system assessment, and other activities intended to assure the conformity of products to a set of standards or technical specifications are all constituents of conformity assessment.

The ISO is composed of nearly 200 technical committees, and its members come from more than 90 countries. The U.S. member is the American National Standards Institute (ANSI). The jurisdiction of the standards extends to all areas except those related to electrical and electronics engineering, which are covered by the International

1

Electrotechnical Commission (IEC). The results of ISO's technical work are published as international standards or guides. Technical Committee 176 (ISO/TC176) on Quality Management and Quality Assurance began to work on the ISO 9000 standards in 1979, and they were first approved in 1987. The first revision was implemented in 1994, and this book is based on that revision.

The detailed description of the development of the standards has been given elsewhere in the literature (Stamatis 1995, 1995c; Voehl 1994; MacLean 1993; Cottman 1993; Peach 1994; Lamprecht 1992), and in this section we are giving a very limited overview of the subject.

The parents of ISO 9000 series were the British Standards BS 5750, the Canadian Standards CSA Z2999, and a variety of other standards from defense and nuclear facilities. The final product is the following family of standards:

ISO 9000 guideline to help in the selection of the certifiable standards.

ISO 9001 certifiable standard dealing with design, manufacturing, and assembly.

ISO 9002 certifiable standard dealing with manufacturing and assembly.

ISO 9003 certifiable standard dealing with assembly.

ISO 9004 guideline defining a quality system and helping in the selection of the appropriate certifiable standard.

The ISO 9000 series is the result of an evolutionary process and is composed primarily of five documents (ISO 9000–9004). The series describes three quality standards, defines quality concepts, and gives guidelines for using international standards on quality systems. Contrary to what many believe, ISO 9000 does not apply to specific products and does not guarantee that a manufacturer will produce a quality product (Stamatis 1992). The standards are generic and enable a company to assure (by means of internal, external, and third-party audits) that its quality system meets one of the three published standards for a quality system.

The reasons for the great success of the ISO are that (1) the EU used it to achieve harmonization in the newly created market as opposed to individual quality standards for each separate country before the EU; (2) for the first time, a standard was developed to deal with the way of doing things, as opposed to emphasizing the end product; (3) communication increased, since "quality" developed its own common language; (4) quality was defined with generic, comprehensive, and implementable standards; and (5) third-party auditing and certification helped to eliminate biases.

In the United States the movement for standardization has gained ground in industries such as steel, chemical, automotive, electronics and within the federal government. The goal of this fast-paced movement is to allow individual organizations and governmental agencies to

- Define a quality system that is appropriate and applicable.
- Demonstrate their commitment and management system to maintain quality to the customers.
- Compete in international markets.
- Follow standard safety and product liability regulations and procedures.
- Reduce cost and provide a practical results oriented target(s).
- Help themselves maintain quality improvement gains.
- Minimize supplier surveillance—through second-party audits.
- Provide a platform from which to launch a "continual improvement" program such as total quality management (TQM) or Malcolm Baldrige.
- Involve ALL employees by stimulating understanding of quality systems and their effect on the organization and its customers.

QS-9000 AUTOMOTIVE REQUIREMENTS

Effective September 1994 the automotive industry of the United States released a harmonized requirement (standard) to compete in the world markets as well as to send a signal to its supplier base that indeed the automotive world is very conscious of the plethora of individualized standards and unique requirements in the industry. This requirement, called Quality System Requirements: QS-9000, referred to as QS-9000, was revised in February 1995. The purpose of the revision was primarily to clarify the original requirement rather than to add more requirements (Stamatis 1995a, 1995b). The introduction of this standard was the culmination of years of trying to standardize the individual standards that each of the big three automakers (Chrysler, Ford, and General Motors) used to control their internal and external quality.

As a result of this harmonization, the Task Force replaced the following individual programs with the QS-9000.

- Chrysler's *Supplier Quality Assurance Manual.*
- Ford's Q-101 quality system standard.
- General Motors's NAO *Targets for Excellence.*
- General Motors's Europe General Quality Standard for Purchased Materials.
- Truck Manufacturers' quality system manuals.

The actual QS-9000 standard is based on three items. They are

The ISO 9001

Sector-specific requirements

Customer-specific requirements

The significance of this replacement is of great concern to the individuals who are responsible for both documentation and auditing. In addition to reading the actual requirement, the reader is strongly encouraged to read Stamatis (1995c) for the details of the actual standard and what is really covered under its jurisdiction. For more details on the documentation and auditing see Chapter 6.

THIRD-PARTY ASSESSMENT

A third-party assessment is undertaken by an independent body to establish the extent to which an organization meets the requirements of an applicable standard or set of regulations. Third-party assessment bodies can assess against any required standard. The independent auditing body—the Registrar—issues a certificate of registration that indicates acceptance of the organization as *a company of assessed capability,* or something similar. The registrar issues this certification after a review of the quality system and a physical audit of the organization.

The original certification takes approximately 10 to 24 months (from preparation to submitting the application to certification). After the certification is achieved, the certification body visits the assessed organization once or twice a year for surveillance purposes and every three years for a major recertification assessment. Generally, the cycle of surveillance and recertification depends upon the policy of the Registrar. On the other hand, the QS-9000 requires a surveillance every six months and a major recertification every three years.

The certification bears witness that the assessed organization complies with all of the requirements of the applicable standard. Certification does not guarantee product or service quality. It guarantees only that a quality system has been defined and exists.

ASSESSMENT METHODS

Each certification body has its own method of assessment and certification. However, all of them base their assessments on the current documentation of the organization and the site-audit results. The routine events of the certification procedure follow.

1. *Initial contact from the organization to the Registrar.* General information is exchanged and appointments are set for the preassessment meeting.

2. *Preassessment visit.* Either a questionnaire or an actual visit takes place to establish the amount of work needed. For a self-assessment, see Appendix A.

3. *Quotation from the Registrar.* A formal quote for the certification and surveillance services is given to the organization.

4. *Acceptance of the quote.* The organization signs the quote or a legal contract for the certification and surveillance procedure as well as the price.

5. *Review of the quality system.* The registrar requests the quality system—sometimes called the documented system—for a review. This review compares the written system (quality manual, procedures, instructions) of the company with the specific ISO standard elements that the company is seeking certification in. Sometimes this audit is called a desk audit. The purpose of this audit is to identify any omissions, ambiguities or major nonconformities prior to the physical (site) compliance audit.

6. *Resolution on the desk audit.* When the quality system is accepted, a request for the site compliance audit is made.

7. *The compliance audit occurs.* It is generally undertaken with a team of auditors (assessors). The team is made up of one lead auditor and three or four auditors. The time is usually no more than five days. A typical audit has the following elements:

- Opening meeting
- Audit
- Closing meeting

8a. *Certification is issued.* If everything goes well and no nonconformities are found, then certification is issued. Although the actual certificate arrives four to eight weeks after the assessment, the organization is now certified.

8b. *Certification is denied.* Denial is caused by either minor noncompliances or major noncompliances. In either case the organization might be reassessed when the noncompliances are corrected.

Any nonconformity must be recorded and its effect assessed by the lead auditor. Some Registrars have a guidance procedure to assist in the ultimate decision.

A *major* noncompliance is the absence or the complete breakdown of a required element of the system. A required element is any of the sub-sections of section 4 of the applicable standard. Sometimes the term *major noncompliance* is used interchangeably with s*erious noncompliances* or *hold points.*

A *minor* noncompliance is an isolated failure to comply with specified requirements. A single *minor* noncompliance would not normally be reason to deny certification. However, a series of related minor nonconformities may, in the judgment of the lead auditor, constitute a breakdown of a procedure or of the entire system. At this point, all related minor nonconformities are classified as major.

For example, suppose the auditor finds a document without the appropriate signature as defined in the quality manual, certainly a nonconformance item. The auditor makes a note of it and completes the audit. The auditor finds no more infractions of any kind, reports the lapse as a minor noncompliance and asks for a follow-up to assure that it does not happen again. On the other hand, if the auditor finds unsigned documentation in other departments of the auditee, that infraction may be viewed as a major noncompliance, since it indicates a system breakdown.

9. *Surveillance.* The ongoing program of making sure that the organization maintains the quality system.

10. *Appeals.* If during the audit an auditor does not conduct himself/herself in a professional manner or some other complaint is justified by the auditee, the auditee has the right of appeal to the Registrar. The actual process depends on the specific Registrar. The Registrar will investigate the complaint always with an independent third party. If the Registrar is unable to satisfy the customer, the auditee has the right to complain to the certification body. The certification body may review the complaint by asking for additional information and authorize a new audit. In any case, the decision of the certification body is final.

The Registrars have the right to decertify an organization that fails to maintain an adequate standard or misuses the logo of the Registrar and the certification.

SURVEILLANCE

To receive certification from a Registrar is only the beginning commitment to a quality system that needs monitoring to ensure continued compliance with the standard. The actual monitoring varies from Registrar to Registrar; however, all Registrars have some kind of monitoring system. Some rely on regular, unannounced audits; others reassess at regular intervals (three years is common) with one minor audit every six months.

Since one of the objectives of the certification is to assure confidence in the system, the idea of the surveillance is to make sure that the assessed organization continues to maintain its quality program. A typical surveillance may cover the following:

- Maintenance of the internal audit program and appropriate corrective action.
- Customer complaints and their follow-up.
- Satisfactory completion of all corrective actions agreed upon at the previous audit (internal or third party).
- Appropriate use of the Registrar's logo.
- Follow-up on all nonconformance items.
- Aspects of the quality system, possibly guided by the recorded nonconformities and minor nonconformities from the last audit.
- Whether top management utilizes internal audits for continual improvement purposes.

SUMMARY

In this chapter we gave a cursory historical perspective of the ISO/QS and addressed some issues concerning the ISO/QS standards. These issues were the third-party assessment, the method of assessment, and surveillance. In the next chapter we give an overview of the documentation process.

REFERENCES

Bureau of Business Practices. (1992). *ISO 9000: Handbook of Quality Standards and Compliance.* Needham Heights, MA: Allyn and Bacon.

Cottman, R. J. (1993). *A Guidebook to ISO 9000 and ANSI/ASQC Q90.* Milwaukee, WI: Quality Press.

Hagigh, S. (February 24, 1992). "Obtaining EC Product Approvals after 1992: What American Manufacturers Need to Know." *Business America.*

Lamprecht, J. L. (1992). *ISO 9000: Preparing for Registration.* Milwaukee, WI: Quality Press.

Linville, D. (February 24, 1992). "Exporting to the European Community." *Business America,* pp. 11–13.

MacLean, G. E. (1993). *Documenting Quality for ISO 9000 and Other Industry Standards.* Milwaukee, WI: Quality Press.

Military Specification. (1956). *MIL-Q-9858A: Quality Control System Requirements.* Washington, DC: Superintendent of Documents.

Peach, R. W. (ed.). (1994). *The ISO 9000 Handbook.* 2nd ed. Burr Ridge, IL: Irwin Professional Publishing.

Stamatis, D. H. (August 1992). "ISO 9000 Standards: Are They for Real?" *ESD Technology,* pp. 13–17.

Stamatis, D. H. (1995). *Understanding ISO 9000 and Implementing the Basics to Quality.* New York: Marcel Dekker.

Stamatis, D. H. (November 1995a). "Toward an Automotive Quality Standard: Revisions of the QS-9000 Fall Short of Expectations." *Sensors: The Journal of Applied Sensing Technology,* pp. 4–5.

Stamatis, D. H. (December 1995b). "QS-9000 Revisions: Not Far Enough?" *Quality Digest,* pp. 12–14.

Stamatis, D. H. (1995c). *QS-9000 the Automotive Standard.* Milwaukee, WI: Quality Press.

Voehl, F.; Jackson, P.; and D. Ashton. (1994). *ISO 9000: An Implementation Guide for Small to Mid-Sized Business.* Delray, FL: Lucie Press.

CHAPTER 2

Documentation Overview

This chapter presents an overview of the development and ongoing maintenance of (1) the documentation of standards and procedures and (2) the documentation of records from the results of inspections, reviews, and audits.

Our focus is the ISO 9001 since it is the most demanding standard of the ISO family and it is the basis for the QS-9000 as well. The additional specific items dealing with QS-9000 will be addressed in Chapter 6.

OVERVIEW

The ISO standards enable firms involved in international trade to obtain a degree of confidence in the quality of the work done by current and potential suppliers. Furthermore, the assumption on which they operate is that if the process is effective, the product and/or service will more likely than not be of high quality.

This effectiveness, however, involves compliance with a set of standards and procedures, which the organization has defined based on its products or services. Compliance, on the other hand, is assured through a formal system of inspection and audits.

This formality is addressed in the ISO 9000 as a requirement that a firm must document its processes and conform to the statements of its own process.

Where the certifiable—contractual—standards (1987 versions of ISO 9001, ISO 9002, ISO 9003) did not require much in writing, the new revised standards of 1994 require documentation and maintenance of the documentation for the quality manual and all quality records. This requirement is very specific in ISO 9001, ISO 9004, and QS-9000 and this presents a major problem: Unless something is in writing, it cannot be documented. In fact, the problem is so great that the most common reason for failure during registration is related to inadequate documentation (Irwin; "How to Prepare" 1993).

The ISO 9001:1994 clause 4.2.1 states:

> The supplier shall establish, document and maintain a quality system as a means of insuring that product conforms to specific requirements. The supplier shall prepare a quality manual covering the requirements of this American National Standard. The quality manual shall include or make reference to the quality system procedures and outline the structure of the documentation used in the quality system.

In addition, ISO 9004 section 5.3.1 states:

> All the elements, requirements and provisions adopted by a company for its quality management system should be documented in a systematic and orderly and understandable manner in the form of **policies and procedures. However, care should be taken to limit documentation to the extent pertinent to the application.**
>
> The quality management system should include adequate provision for the proper identification, distribution, collection, and maintenance of all quality documents and records.

To satisfy this ISO guideline there are three requirements.

1. *Documentation of specific quality standards and procedures.* This requirement is perhaps the easiest to comply with, since the company defines how they do what they do. The intent here is to ensure that a firm's way of doing business can be evaluated and follows the ISO standard. The organization is expected to produce a true reflection of the way the firm does business and the way employees and suppliers perform their functions. This fundamental principle of standard compliance can be summarized as Say what you do, Do what you say you do. It can also be formalized in the quality manual, quality procedures, and instructions.

2. *Documentation of product development life cycle results.* This requirement consists of specifications, design documentation, test plans, and other descriptions of the product or the development and acceptance process. Its purpose is to establish continuity and control during product development.

3. *Documentation of the outcomes that are required under the standards.* This requirement represents the verification of outcomes from specific tasks, reviews, audits, inspections, etc. They are the quality records and produce an audit trail that is used to verify that the organization performs the functions described in its standards and procedures documentation. Quality records, in general, provide the basis for performance evaluation toward continuous process improvement. Appendix A provides a docu-

Say what you do,

Do what you say

you do.

mentation matrix that identifies some generic characteristics of documentation as defined in the ISO 9001 and the ISO 9004 as well as a summary of tools that facilitate the documentation process.

So far, we have addressed the issue of documentation from the standard's perspective. Let us now look at some of the specific benefits that the organization may gain. First, all documentation—regardless of source—should benefit the organization in some way, either directly (internally) or indirectly (externally). Second, all documentation should be as specific as possible in order to guide the organization's continual improvement. For specific benefits, we examine the following components of documentation.

• *Standards and procedures.* If they indeed represent reality (current practice) and are accurate, they will contribute to the firm so as to

Make the training of new staff easier.

Permit more objective evaluation of performance.

Provide continuity and consistency when there is staff turnover.

Facilitate training current employees for specific tasks.

Provide a benchmark for future improvement.

• *Quality records.* They document an activity and provide the evidence and documentation of compliance with preestablished standards and procedures. In addition, as records accumulate, they provide a database for performance analysis and performance improvement.

• *Life cycle documentation.* It provides continuity across the product development life cycle, which permits project control and product quality evaluation during the development process. It also helps product quality evaluation for future products.

• *Document control.* Document control is a requirement. The idea of document control is that documentation must be accessible to those who have need and authorization to use it and that it must be kept up to date. See Appendix A for generic control documents.

STRUCTURE OF THE DOCUMENTS

The structure of documentation is as important as its content. The structure is the way the information is organized. It enables readers to find information easily and to pinpoint what they need. Structure can be examined from the following points of view:

Level of detail within subject areas.

Parsing, based on content, into subject areas.

Both points of view are legitimate and appropriate. Their use depends upon the organization and the writer.

If the documentation is expected to be procedural or technical in nature, a hierarchical structure is effective and highly recommended. In a hierarchical structure the information is presented in levels of detail. It starts out with an overview and then branches into one or more levels. A typical hierarchical structure is shown in Figure 2–1.

The overview is the road map of the detailed information and should allow the reader to select the specific part of the topic that is of interest or to skip the topic entirely. An example of an overview in procedures is a process flow diagram. Overviews are encouraged, and their frequency or length depends on the complexity or levels of the specific documentation.

The first level of detail is usually the material that contains the main substance of the topic. In a procedure, it is the specific steps to be taken so that the procedure's objective is accomplished. When the levels of detail become cumbersome, they should be put in an appendix or some other reference area.

With the proliferation of computer technology, documentation structure can be fun and easy to design. With computer-generated documentation you can chain or cross-reference your documentation, depending on the software and the ability of the user. Some commercial software programs for writing documentation are Quark Xpress®, HyperText, PageMaker®, and WordPerfect®. Figure 2–2 shows a computer-generated hierarchical structure.

FIGURE 2–1

The Hierarchy Structure

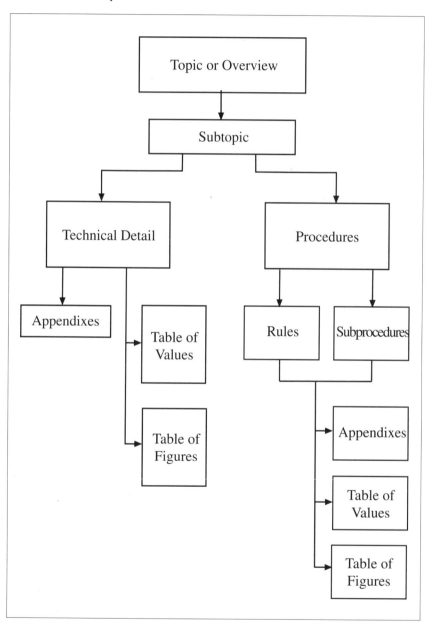

Definition of the Levels of Structure

While the hierarchical structure defines the level of complexity, parsing (content) is a way of separating things into logical groupings. It is a very subjective activity and care should be taken to make sure that the parsing really reflects common ground of the areas involved. An example of parsing is when information is grouped by volumes, chapters, sections, etc. In procedure writing, a given procedure may be parsed based on the type of work, the performer, the time in the process, or alphabetically by the title of the procedure. A pictorial view of parsing is shown in Figure 2–3. The following list explains each component in the figure.

- A volume is a bound document (paper document), and it is generally no more than 1 1/2 inches thick. It is defined by the user, time and frequency of use, and the level of detail. Whenever possible, use only one volume. Volumes may be collected and bound so that they are kept together.

- An appendix is stand-alone information that supplements but is not essential to the main information in the chapters, sections, or subsections.

- Chapters, sections, and subsections are based strictly on the logic of the material. The deciding factor should be the need and convenience of the reader. A chapter is a combination of sections.

- A section is a labeled set of paragraphs, graphics, or other elements that fully address a topic. A section is a combination of subsections.

- A subsection is one to three paragraphs on a specific topic.

- An informational element is the finest level of detail that expresses a complete piece of information relevant to the topic. Usually it is found as a definition, a step procedure, a description of a part or component, or sometimes as an overview of a topic. An informational element is a subsection at the lowest level of the hierarchy.

The discussion of hierarchical structures and parsing may be a bit frightening to a novice. However, there are some basic rules and guidelines that can help you get started.

FIGURE   2–2

A Computer-Generated Structure Design

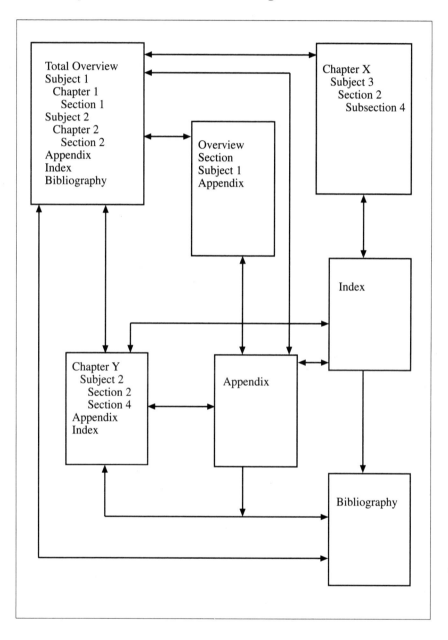

FIGURE   2–3

A Typical Content Hierarchy

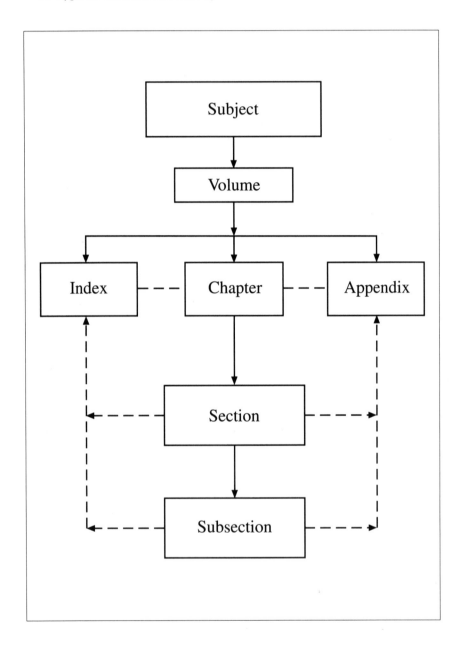

• There is no single correct approach for the documentation structure. Both the hierarchy and the parsing methods are acceptable. The selection process is highly subjective and a matter of preference. For example, for procedural documentation, the flow of the actual procedure is the most common basis of the breakdown.

• Hierarchy and parsing in documentation make writing easier because the writer can divide the document into small chunks and write each one independently. In fact, it is this attribute that allows several people to write parts of the same document. In addition, reading is easier because the information is presented in small chunks. Furthermore, the reader is advised of the content of a section before reading it, by the use of headings and subtitles, which facilitate comprehension.

• When you are ready to write any form of documentation, start with an outline that establishes the contents of the document. The outline (the content hierarchy) will keep you on track. It is always possible to change the outline during the writing process.

• The table of contents permits the reader to find topics and to get an overview of the document's contents. Sometimes the table of contents is divided into sections and subsections to facilitate finding a particular topic. Generally, the table of contents is written after the completion of the document.

• Indexing is essential in any form of documentation. Indexing is a cross-reference mechanism that locates subjects across the content hierarchy. The structure and the detail of the index is the writer's choice. However, the writer should keep in mind the reader's need of cross-references to find information. Generally, the index is written after the completion of the entire documentation.

SUMMARY

In this chapter we gave an overview of the documentation process and described the generic structure of the documentation. In the next chapter we will examine the details of documentation.

REFERENCES

"How to Prepare Your Documentation for ISO 9000 Registration." (February 1993). *Continuous Improvement Newsletter*. National ISO 9000 Support Group. Caledonia, MI. pp. 1–3.

Irwin Professional Publishing. (September 1993). "ISO 9000 Survey." *Quality Systems Update*. Burr Ridge, IL: Irwin Professional Publishing. pp. 1–8.

Quality System Documentation

This chapter provides a detailed discussion and analysis of the full set of documentation required to describe an organization's way of doing business. Chapter 3 goes beyond the overview of Chapter 2, and its focus is defining and implementing the documentation system.

OVERVIEW

A *quality system* is the set of policies and procedures that represent the way an organization performs its process. The quality system assures that a quality program exists and is followed so that the quality of the product or service is delivered to the customer without problems or nonconformances.

The content of the quality documentation is derived from an analysis of the quality system. Quality events are identified through procedures analysis, typically using a process flow diagram. To generate the content, one must go to the source of the task. The people doing the work know what they do, and they are indeed the best source of information. Therefore, allowing the workers to be active participants in the writing and validation of the quality documentation is a means of ensuring that the documentation accurately reflects the way the firm operates. In addition, it allows employees to have ownership of the documentation, which helps promote quality and increases the intrinsic motivation of the individuals involved.

The objective of all quality documentation is to reflect accurately the way the organization operates. It should describe the current baseline and not the way things ought to be. In addition, the documentation must always be up-to-date, even though things change. The ISO 9000:1994 edition includes 21 specific clues in the notes section of the standard (nonauditable and noncertifiable items) to help in the interpretation and the implementation of the standards.

THE STRUCTURE OF DOCUMENTATION

Figure 3–1 shows how a typical documentation of an organization may be structured to meet the requirements of the ISO 9001, ISO 9002, ISO 9003, and QS-9000. The records and forms on the base of the triangle are only representative departments of the organization. They can be arranged to suit to the organization. What is important here is the notion of the involvement of the whole organization.

Even though Figure 3–1 shows four layers of documentation, not all organizations require the same divisions. The actual layers will depend on the complexity of the organization and its products or services. However, these four layers are quite common in most organizations.

1. *Quality manual.* Sometimes called the *management manual, operations manual,* or *policy manual.* The quality manual is the highest level of documentation and represents the policy of the organization. It must cover all the elements of the ISO standard and the QS-9000 requirement.

2. *Procedures.* The procedures define the flow of the task or operation. They serve as an overview of the process, job, or task.

3. *Job/work instructions.* Sometimes these instructions are called *standard operating procedures* (SOPs). Job/work instructions define *how* the task or operation is done.

4. *Forms, records, documents, books, or files.* These are miscellaneous items that sometimes appear as single items and sometimes as part of other documentation.

Each organization defines the need for documentation, and these layers may indeed overlap from company to company. For these four levels of documentation to be fully effective, a cross-reference system must be developed to show the interrelationships between layers. These interrelationships within a total documentation system are shown in Figure 3–2.

The ISO/QS certifiable standards require approval for all classes of documentation. The approval should be at an appropriate and applicable

FIGURE   3–1

The Documentation Hierarchy

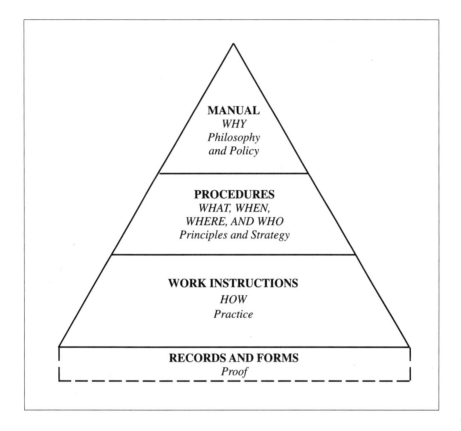

MANUAL
WHY
Philosophy
and Policy

PROCEDURES
WHAT, WHEN,
WHERE, AND WHO
Principles and Strategy

WORK INSTRUCTIONS
HOW
Practice

RECORDS AND FORMS
Proof

level within the organization. Generally, the higher the level of documentation, the higher the approval authority. A rule of thumb—from the author's experience—is that documentation approval should be from two levels higher than the level seeking the approval. When the complexity of organization or product/service is high, the approval process may be assigned to more than one person. Otherwise, one person should be responsible for granting approval.

Another requirement of the ISO/QS standard is a control mechanism to ensure that only pertinent documents are used. Pertinence in this case applies to both the relevance of the subject matter of the document to the work at hand and the currency of the contents. This control entails

FIGURE   3–2

The Quality Documentation System

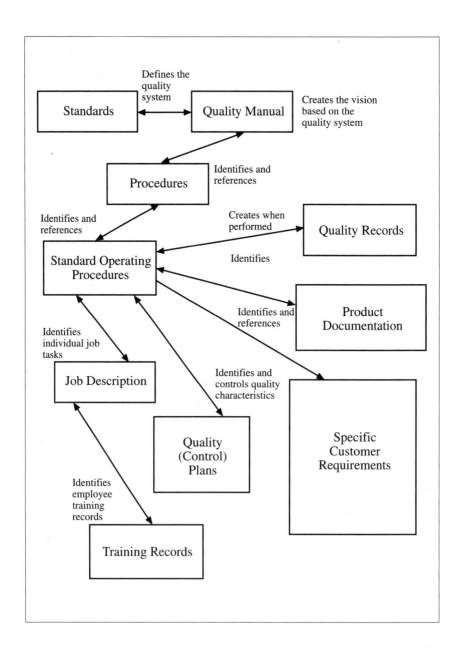

issuing the documents needed at the correct revision level wherever and whenever they are required and ensuring that they cannot be inadvertently replaced by documents relating to another subject or to the correct subject but at a different issue. Therefore, all unnecessary documentation must be removed from the workplace without delay, and all revisions must be correct and current.

When there is a need to copy documents—perhaps for marketing or public relations purposes—control of the copies must be proportional to the risk and their use. A unique document format, special paper color, or the incorporation of a colored mark in all legitimately issued documents all make satisfactory controls.

Alteration to documents must be controlled. To prevent irrelevant changes, the standard requires that the document *shall* be reviewed and approved by the original reviewers or by other authorized people thoroughly conversant with the background information on which the original documents were based. In order to ensure that the correct documents may be issued and withdrawn, a control mechanism must exist to identify documents, revision levels, and their holders. Figure 3–3 shows a typical document control form.

THE QUALITY SYSTEM MANUAL

The purpose of the quality manual is to describe at a high level of detail (30 to 60 pages in length) the organization's quality policy, vision, and quality system in order to

- Provide a reference point from which a reader can identify and locate specific procedures and operating instructions.
- Advise the organization's staff of the full range of standards and procedures and the interrelationships among them.
- Ensure common understanding of the way the firm does its business and how it regards quality.

The quality manual is not the full documentation of the quality system. The full documentation consists of the quality manual, procedures, work instructions, and records as shown in Figure 3–1. Because the quality manual is an overview and the first tier in the documentation, it is likely that individual task performers will not use it very frequently. In fact, the primary readership of the quality manual is the management and staff of the organization.

FIGURE 3–3

Master Document Distribution Control

Copy Number	Version Number	Version Date	Copy Holder

Contents of the Quality Manual

The quality manual should contain the following items:

- The organization's quality policy statement.
- Proper authorization.
- Issuing date.

- The organization's principles and objectives.
- A short description of the products/services.
- A short description of the customers and suppliers.
- Organizational structure.
- Overview of the functions of the organization's executives.
- Description (one to four pages) of each functional area and its relationship to quality.
- Cross-reference between functions, procedures, and work instructions.
- Cross-reference between the organization's functions and the ISO requirements and other standards or customer conditions.
- Distribution list.
- Document change and control procedures and responsibilities.
- Copyright statement (optional).

The scope of a manual should be site specific because certification is site specific. Therefore, a corporate quality manual may summarize the entire quality system, but when there are multiple divisions, each should have its own quality manual.

Sometimes, when there is a need for an abridged version to indoctrinate new employees or to brief management the quality manual is printed in a pamphlet format. When literacy is a problem in the organization, the pamphlet format allows employees to carry the document in a pocket and review it as needed.

When confidentiality is a concern, the quality manual may be published as a quality policy (same as the quality manual but with the sensitive data removed) and distributed to customers and suppliers without divulging confidential information. Such a manual may be defined as a noncontrolled document.

The overall structure and content of a typical format for the quality manual is presented in a series of figures. Figure 3–4 identifies the parts (components) of the QM. Figure 3–5 identifies the items on the cover (title) page. Figure 3–6 identifies the components of the table of contents. Figure 3–7 identifies the components of the QM body. Appendix C contains two full-length quality manuals (one based on the ISO and Good Manufacturing Processes [GMPs], and the other on the QS-9000). Both samples provide the reader with much more information than the average organization may need.

FIGURE   3–4

Components of the Quality Manual

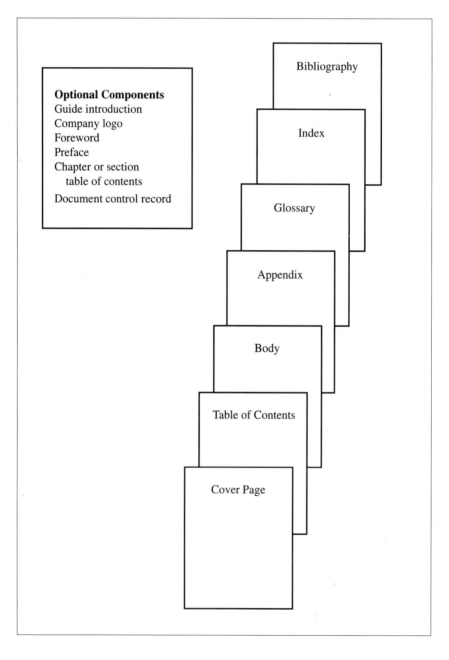

FIGURE 3–5

Quality Manual Cover Page

Document Reference:
Revision Number:
Date Issued:
Supersedes:
Section:

Company Name
Manual Title and ID

FIGURE   3–6

Quality Manual Table of Contents

Document Reference:
Revision Number:
Date Issued:
Section:
Page _____ of _____

Table of Contents

Section Number	Section Title	Revision Number	ISO Standard	Page

FIGURE 3–7

Quality Manual Body Components

Title:	Document Reference:
	Revision Number:
	Date Issued:
	Section:
	Page _____ of _____

Body

> **Section**
>> **Subsection**
>>> **Figure**
>>>> **Table**

An optional introduction summarizes the contents of the quality manual. It may cover special vocabulary and information to help the reader and the auditor understand the company and its products or services better. By understanding the organization better, the evaluation will be more meaningful.

Specific Requirements of a Typical Quality Manual

The importance and high visibility of the QM—both internally and externally—warrant a detailed discussion of each individual element. The discussion is based on ISO/DIS 10013, which is the official guide for writing a Quality Manual. Although the requirements that follow are very detailed, they are all generic in nature and they may not apply to all organizations. Some of the requirements discussed in this section may be adequate, where others are not even mentioned. What is important is the notion that the QM defines the vision of the organization, identifies the appropriate documentation, and references the appropriate tools for such documentation (all the key supporting documents shown in Figure 3–2). The proof, however, of their existence will be established during the actual audit.

Section 1.0 Introduction

The introduction shall include

- The name of the organization and its position in the corporate operational structure.
- A summary of the purpose of the organization, including a general description of its products and services.
- An indication of the organization's quality system conformance to the specific ISO standard (9001, 9002, or 9003). If there are other customer or regulatory requirements, they are applicable.
- A reference to other supporting documentation.
- An indication of intent to review and or revise the quality manual periodically.
- A simplified product flow diagram (optional).
- An indication of the organization's commitment to continuous quality improvement.

Section 2.0 Distribution List

The distribution list should indicate at least three items:

- Copy number.
- Name of the holder.
- Location of the holder.

Any special instructions regarding distribution should also be included here; for example QM distribution to customers, to suppliers, and for public relations purposes, as well as special reproduction instructions.

Section 3.0 Control of Manual—Procedure for Change

This section shows that the organization has a system that documents, implements, and maintains a control procedure and should include the following:

- The responsibility for approving changes to the QM.
- The responsibility for reviewing, maintaining and updating the QM.
- The process for making changes to the QM.

Section 4.0 Quality System Requirements

Section 4.1 Management Responsibility

Perhaps the most important issue in any QM is management responsibility. When the ISO addresses this concern, it focuses on the quality policy (4.1.1); quality objectives; and understanding, implementation, and maintenance. Specifically, the quality policy must be in a concise, exact, and easy to understand language. Furthermore, it is the responsibility of the QM to show the organization's quality policy and conformance to quality policies in the organization chain (4.1.2). An organizational chart is quite appropriate here. The authority for quality must be traceable to the top level of management with all the important supporting departments/positions clearly defined.

The quality objectives are the items that support the documentation and are an integral part of the QM. They identify improvement opportunities in the quality system and contain specific improvement programs. Appendix B contains examples of quality policies from various organizations.

This section also defines how management supports and ensures that all personnel understand and implement the stated quality policies and objectives of the organization. One way to show how management maintains the organization's policy and objectives is by defining the interval of the review (4.1.3).

Section 4.2 Quality System

The QM shall show that the organization has established and maintains a quality system in conformance with the appropriate ISO standard (4.2.1). Section 4.2.2 requires appropriate documentation consistent with the requirements. Section 4.2.3 requires appropriate definition and documentation for quality, including quality planning consistent with all other requirements. The following items fulfill the ISO 9001 section 4.2.3.

- The preparation of a quality manual.

- The identification and acquisition of any controls, processes, inspection equipment, fixtures, total production resources, and skills needed to achieve required quality.

- The updating as necessary of quality control, inspection, and testing techniques, including development of new instrumentation.

- The identification of any measurement requirement that exceeds state-of-the-art techniques in sufficient time for the needed measurement to be developed.

- The clarification of standards of acceptability for all features and requirements, including those that contain a subjective element.

- The compatibility of the production process, installation, inspection and test procedures, and the applicable documentation.

- The identification and preparation of quality records. For more details see section 4.16.

- The QM shall show that the organization has developed and maintains documentation for the quality system.

- The QM shall show that the organization's intent is to operate the quality system as documented.

Section 4.3 Contract Review

This section covers contracts with customers and suppliers. These may be formal contracts with customers and suppliers or agreements with suppliers and customers within the company. In essence, the QM shows that the organization has a documented system for contract review.

- Contract review responsibilities (4.3.2) may include
  - Responsibilities for assurance that a supplier has the ability to manufacture the product to designated specifications and to deliver in specified quantities and on schedule as required by the customer.
  - Responsibilities within the organization for agreements with suppliers and with customers with outside suppliers.
  - Responsibilities in purchasing, materials support, and organizing contracts with outside suppliers.
  - Responsibilities in distribution, marketing and organizing contracts with outside customers, which may include scheduling and production planning agreements.
- All individual contracts are reviewed to assure that
  - Requirements and specifications are adequately defined and documented.
  - Quantity and delivery schedules are documented.
  - Differences in requirements are resolved and documented.
- Amendment to contract (4.3.3). When changes, modifications, or amendments are needed, appropriate procedures and instructions will be in place.
- Records of reviews (4.3.4). Records dealing with a review of the quality system shall be maintained. See section 4.16.

Section 4.4 Design Control

Design control requires procedures for controlling and verifying product design to ensure that specified requirements are being met and to include procedures for design or development, planning, design input or output, design verification, and all design changes (4.4.1). The QM should include the following information:

- Design and development planning (4.4.2). Shows the organization's documentation, implementation, and maintenance for controlling and verifying product design in order to meet specified requirements.

- Organizational and technical interface (4.4.3). Organizational and technical interfaces between different groups shall be identified, and information shall be documented, transmitted, and regularly reviewed.
- Design input (4.4.4). Design input requirements relating to product shall be identified, documented, and their selection reviewed by the supplier for adequacy. All incomplete, ambiguous, or conflicting requirements must be resolved with the personnel responsible for drawing up these requirements.
- Design output (4.4.5). Design output must be documented and expressed in terms of requirements, calculations, analysis, or whatever the company defines as adequate and appropriate. Minimum considerations may be the following:

  Meet design input requirements.
  Contain or reference acceptance criteria.
  Conform to appropriate regulatory requirements even if these are not stated in the input information.
  Identify characteristics of the design that are crucial to the safety and proper functioning of the product.

- Design review (4.4.6). Shows that design and verification activities (reviews) are planned, conducted, and assigned to qualified personnel equipped with adequate resources.
- Design verification (4.4.7). The organization must plan, establish, document, and assign functions for verifying the design to competent personnel. Design verification shall establish that design output meets design input requirements by means of design control measures such as

  Holding and recording design reviews (see 4.16).
  Undertaking qualification tests and demonstrations.
  Carrying out alternative calculations.
  Comparing the new design with a similar proven design (if available).

- Design validation (4.4.8). The organization must have validation procedures to ensure that the product conforms to the requirements.

- Design changes (4.4.9). The organization must establish and maintain procedures for identification, documentation, and appropriate review and approval of all changes and modifications.

Section 4.5 Document and Data Control
The QM should include the following sections:

- General (4.5.1). The QM shall show the organization's documentation, implementation, and maintenance of the document control process with reference to supporting documents that provide further detail.
- Document and data approval and issue (4.5.2). Organization documentation, implementation, and maintenance of a document identification system shall be noted in the QM. This system includes a unique identification number for each document. All documents of the organization should have the date of issue or revision. All pages of the QM shall have the document identification number and date of issue or revision. The preferred dating method is year-month-date, which is found in the ISO 8601 standard "Data Elements and Interchange Formats—Information Interchange—Representation of Dates and Times."
- Master list (index). The QM shall identify a master list or equivalent means of accounting for all of the organization's controlled documents, including the latest revisions. The list shall include the QM, quality plans, and all procedures. It does not include quality records. Quality records are covered in section 4.16. If procedures are in groups or series, all documents in each series should be listed together. Documentation coordination shall also maintain a master copy of each document and its revision(s). Master lists should contain originals in loose form to allow duplication.
- Document and data changes (4.5.3). The QM shall reference the procedure detailing the process of review and authorization for new or revised documents.
- Distribution. The QM shall reference the procedure detailing the distribution process for new or revised documents. This procedure indicates how the organization assures availability of the latest revision of any document. At a minimum, the procedure should include records of distribution, identification, and

dating of all documents. Numbering of individual copies of
documents (copy numbers) may be appropriate when the
documents include critical information or are not for general
use.

Section 4.6 Purchasing

To write a proper policy for the purchasing function, one must define *purchased product.* A purchased product in the context of ISO 9001, section
4.6.1, is any material or component feeding into the process from sources
internal or external to the organization. Specifically, the QM should cover
the following items:

- Purchased products. The QM shall show that the organization
  has documented, implemented, and maintains a purchasing
  process to ensure that purchased product(s) conforms to specifications or requirements. The QM shall reference supporting
  documentation detailing the purchasing process.
- Evaluation of subcontractors (4.6.2). The QM shall show that
  the organization has documented, implemented, and maintains
  procedures for the selection of suppliers on the basis of their
  ability to meet quality, quantity, and delivery requirements. The
  organization or designated purchasing organization shall
  maintain records of acceptable suppliers. (If the organization
  depends on third-party certification, it should be stated. On the
  other hand, if the certification is based on a second party—
  certified, preferred, or approved—it should also be stated.)
- Supplier screening. The QM shall show that the organization
  has documented, implemented, and that it maintains a process
  of supplier review. This review should utilize a list of acceptable suppliers of similar products, as well as new suppliers even
  when background performance data may not be available.
- Supplier performance records. The QM and/or supporting
  documentation shall show that the organization maintains
  individual supplier performance records based on specifications
  and contract agreements.
- Purchasing data (4.6.3). The QM shall show that the organization documents and maintains procedures for preparing incoming material purchasing documents. These procedures should
  clearly describe, where applicable, the following information:

type, class, style, grade, positive identification of material, relevant technical data, and applicable international or national standards. (These standards should include the quality system model to be adhered to as well as any applicable standards covering a specific product.)

- Document review. The QM should show that the organization has documented and has a system that maintains procedures for review of purchasing documents.
- Customer product verification. If an agreement or contract gives a customer the right to verify product conformance at the organization or at the supplier level, the provision shall be noted in the QM. This verification shall not be used as evidence of effective control of quality by a supplier nor does it preclude later rejection of the product by the customer.

Section 4.7 Control of Customer-Supplied Product

This confusing section of the standard should cover materials supplied by the customer for inclusion in the manufacturing process. If the organization does not use customer-supplied products, the QM shall indicate that this section has been considered but does not apply. If this section is applicable, the QM shall show that the organization has established, documented, and maintains procedures and supporting documentation for customer-supplied product, which include the following:

- Verification. Procedures for verification shall show determination of suitability for use of customer-supplied product.
- Storage and maintenance. Procedures shall include any special handling, special storage and maintenance for customer-supplied product.
- Unsuitable product. Procedures shall state that receipt of unsuitable product is noted in records and that the supplier is notified promptly.

Section 4.8 Product Identification and Traceability

The QM should cover at least two issues.

- Identification. The QM shall show that the organization has documented, implemented, and maintains the procedures to identify materials and product through all stages of manufacturing and delivery of the finished product to the customer.

Reference shall be made in the quality manual to key supporting documentation.

- Traceability. The QM shall show that the organization provides traceability of a product through manufacture and distribution and maintains records of unique identification given to products. This traceability should consider the risk of nonconformance and allow for batching of product into lots small enough to discard reasonable quantities in event of a problem.

Section 4.9 Process Control

The QM shall show that the organization has identified, documented, and maintains procedures for production processes with reference to supporting documentation for the operation, monitoring, and control of the process. The organization's production process procedure may include facilities, equipment, environmental conditions, materials, and personnel to ensure that product is manufactured in conformance to requirements. Interfaces between groups or functions and required product installation that affects quality should be clearly identified and defined.

The QM shall show that the organization has documented, implemented, and maintains—in referenced supporting documentation—procedures to cover the following items:

- Process control documentation. To operate, monitor, control the process, maintaining process aims and product quality standards.

- Reference standards. Required for process control or product testing.

- Product standards. These standards are based on documented product specifications.

- Process and/or equipment changes. New equipment or process changes are tested for accreditation, the impact assessed, approval by appropriate personnel, and clearly documented.

- Process maintenance. To ensure that equipment is adequate to meet quality needs. This section should include some form of preventive maintenance to ensure continuing process capability.

- Processes to assure conformance with product requirements. Details of each special process are contained in supporting documentation.

- Records to document qualified processes, equipment, and personnel.

Section 4.10 Inspection and Testing

Section 4.10.1   This section identifies the required inspection, testing, and records to verify quality to the specified requirements.

Section 4.10.2 Receiving Inspection and Testing   This section considers incoming materials.
- Incoming materials and products. The QM shall show that the organization has documented and maintains procedures assuring fitness for use of incoming materials and products prior to their inclusion in the manufacturing process. This may be accomplished by acceptance testing or as the result of quality information supplied by the producer (4.10.2.1). Quality is verified according to the documented procedures. The QM shall reference key supporting documentation that provides details of receiving inspection and testing (4.10.2.2).
- Exceptions (4.10.2.3). The QM shall show any exceptions to documented procedures for receiving inspection and testing. If urgent production needs are encountered and the material or product is used before its quality is known, the organization has identified and documented a procedure that allows the finished product to be segregated or recalled. Product and material identification are carried out according to these procedures.

Section 4.10.3 In-Process Inspection and Testing   The QM shall show that the organization has established, documented, and maintains procedures for in-process inspection and testing. Supporting documentation provides details for the following events:
- Product testing and identification. All inspections, product tests, and identification are carried out as documented.
- Process monitoring. All critical process parameters are controlled throughout the various processes to assure that quality is maintained.
- Quality verification. Product is either held within your organization until completed tests show verified quality or conditionally released to subsequent operations.
- Nonconforming product identification. Nonconforming product is clearly identified to assure segregation from acceptable product.

Section 4.10.4 Final Inspection and Testing   Under this section the following items should be addressed:
- Final product verification. The QM shall show that the organization's procedures and supporting documentation detail how incoming material tests, in-process data, and final product testing are used to verify that the final product meets quality requirements.
- Authorized release. The QM shall show that the organization has clearly documented product-test information with proper authorization prior to product release.

Section 4.10.5 Inspection and Test Records   This section emphasizes the importance of quality records. The QM shall show that the organization maintains records to verify that released product has met documented acceptance criteria.

Section 4.11 Control of Inspection, Measuring, and Test Equipment   The QM shall show that inspection, measuring, and test equipment are controlled and calibrated to assure that product conforms to specified requirements. It shall also show that equipment is used in a manner that ensures measurement uncertainty is known and is consistent with required measurement capability. This proviso applies to test equipment within the organization as well as to test equipment within supporting organizations, whether on loan, owned, or provided.

Section 4.11.1 General   The QM shall provide key responsibility assignments for measurement assurance elements and reference supporting documentation. The organization management has assigned and documented responsibilities for each element of measurement assurance and control, including (1) test specification development, documentation, and maintenance; (2) equipment calibrations, maintenance, and adjustment; (3) assessment of out-of-calibration conditions and responsibility for notification to product staff; and (4) measurement-assurance audits.

The QM shall also show that the organization management has defined and documented specific purposes for conducting measurements. Each specific purpose should not be included in the quality manual, but shall be part of the product-test plan or supporting documentation.

Section 4.11.2 Control Procedures   The organization's policy of conformance to calibration reference standards shall be noted in the quality manual with details in supporting documentation. The QM shall show that equipment calibrations are conducted against certified reference standards or equipment that has a certified relationship to corporate or nationally recognized standards. Where no certified reference standards exist, the basis used for calibration shall be identified in supporting documentation.

The QM shall show that personnel performing calibration functions have appropriate training and experience. Supporting documentation shall detail required training.

The QM shall reference key supporting documents that show the organization's commitment to

• Equipment identification. Inspection, measurement, and test equipment affecting product quality is uniquely identified with a label or other marking referencing calibration status record.

• Equipment calibration and records. All pertinent records as to the calibration, traceability, and periodicity of the calibration cycle must be identified. Appropriate records must be established for proof of the existence of such documents.

• Preventive maintenance (PM) and records. All pertinent records with reference to PM must be identified.

• Equipment out of calibration. These procedures shall identify key personnel to be notified for validation of prior tests on that equipment. Validation assessments and corrective actions shall be recorded.

The QM shall reference key supporting documents for

• Environmental conditions. Control environmental conditions necessary for calibration and operation of test equipment.

• Handling and storage. Inspection, measuring, and test equipment are handled and stored in a manner that will protect measurement capability of that equipment.

• Unauthorized adjustments. Measurement equipment hardware and software must be protected from unauthorized adjustments, which could invalidate the measurement calibration and control.

Section 4.12 Inspection and Test Status

The QM shall show that the organization's documented procedures provide for the identification of releasing authority on inspection and test status records. In addition, the QM shall show that the organization has documented, implemented, and maintains procedures for recording inspection and test status. The QM shall reference key supporting documentation detailing this process. Supporting documentation in the manufacturing process shall include procedures for recording inspection and test status of incoming materials and product, in-process product, and finished product.

Section 4.13 Control of Nonconforming Product

The QM should account for two items in this section: (1) the establishment and maintenance of documented procedures to ensure that nonconformances are not used (4.13.1) and (2) the review and disposition of nonconforming product (4.13.2). The QM shall show that the organization has documented and maintains procedures to ensure that suspected nonconforming product and materials are not used inadvertently. The following topics shall be specifically noted in the QM with reference to key supporting documentation identifying the method of

• Identification. How suspected nonconforming material or product is identified.

• Record keeping. Records of nonconformities are maintained to provide assurance that the situation has been isolated and controlled, and that appropriate corrective action has been taken.

• Evaluation. Personnel have been designated as responsible for review and given proper authority to determine if nonconforming product should be

Reworked to meet specifications.

Released (accepted). This presupposes that a suspected product or material has been tested and found to be conforming.

Regraded to alternative applications.

Rejected.

• Segregation. Nonconforming materials and products are segregated by whatever means necessary to assure that they are not used. Segregation may require physical isolation, physical marking, or a fail-safe inventory management system. The key is that the organization must be able to show that the approach it uses for segregating nonconforming materials and products works effectively.

• Disposition. Disposal of nonconforming materials and product is carried out expeditiously. Decisions to accept (pass) nonconforming product for alternative applications or through special agreement with a customer or supplier are recorded with some form of waiver (Reviewed Release).

• Reporting. Instances of nonconforming material or product and resulting action are reported to all interested parties, especially to those responsible for the nonconformity.

• Reinspection. Reworked product is reinspected to ensure acceptability.

• Basis for corrective action. The organization uses nonconformance incidents as the basis for corrective action.

Section 4.14 Corrective and Preventive Action

The QM in this section shall show that the organization has documented and maintains procedures for investigating cause(s) of nonconforming product, material, or process and for taking corrective action as appropriate to eliminate the cause(s) (4.14.1). Requirements for corrective action (4.14.2) for each of the following should be specifically noted in the QM and reference made as needed to key supporting documentation.

• Customer complaints
• Nonconformance of materials
• Nonconformance of process
• Nonconformance of product

The QM shall further show that the organization has documented and maintains procedures to

• Identify nonconformities.

• Record and analyze nonconformance. Maintenance of records of nonconformance, the analysis process, and corrective action.

• Analyze potential cause(s) of nonconformance. A program for analysis of process, quality records, maintenance records, production records (including waste), and customer reactions to detect and eliminate potential causes of nonconformance.

• Monitor corrective actions. Corrective actions are reviewed and approved by appropriate authority before being implemented, and they are properly monitored to assure that the desired effect is obtained.

• Use appropriate preventive action and application controls to eliminate nonconformities (4.14.3).

• Establish policies that confirm management review.

• Change procedures because of corrective action. When corrective actions are necessary, appropriate documentation changes reflect the changes.

Section 4.15 Handling, Storage, Packaging, Preservation, and Delivery

This section of the QM and its supporting documentation should show that the organization has defined, documented, and maintains procedures for handling, storage, packaging, preservation, and delivery of products and services. These procedures may exist as process procedures for each activity or may be defined in individual product specifications.

• Handling. Product handling procedures are defined in order to assure quality, prevent damage, and minimize deterioration of product.

• Storage. Specific products are stored as documented in process and product specifications. Storage areas and stock rooms are provided with security levels and inventory procedures to ensure product quality and integrity. Documentation shall include procedures for product condition assessment after extended storage.

• Packaging. The procedures for packaging, marking, and preserving product are documented in product and/or process specifications. These procedures shall assure product integrity and quantity while the product is the organization's responsibility.

• Preservation. Policies and procedures for preservation and segregation of product when the product is in supplier's control.

• Delivery. As covered by internal agreements or formal external contracts, product quality will be protected during delivery.

Section 4.16 Control of Quality Records

The QM should address the following minimum requirements:

• Procedures. The QM shall show that the organization has documented and maintains procedures for identifying, collecting, filing, storing, maintaining, and disposing of quality records. The QM shall reference key supporting documentation for quality record management.

• Data (quality records). The QM and supporting documentation shall show how quality records are identified, collected, and retained by the organization and demonstrate an effective quality system operation. The QM may, and supporting documentation shall, require that quality records be dated and legible and clearly identify product(s) involved.

• Data (storage). The QM shall show organization has documented and maintains procedures outlining responsibility for record retention, storage of records to provide ready retrieval, and storage facilities designed to minimize deterioration. The QM shall reference key supporting documentation for storage and records management. The QM may, and supporting documentation shall, include record retention times, scheduled reviews of stored data, and methods of disposition of outdated records.

• Availability to customer. The QM shall show, where agreed to in the contract, that quality records are available to the customer.

Section 4.17 Internal Quality Audits

The QM shall show that the organization has documented and maintains procedures for internal auditing of the quality system by qualified personnel. These audits measure both conformance and effectiveness of the quality system to requirements as outlined in the QM and supporting documentation. Specifically, the QM shall show

• Frequency of internal audits. How often they are performed.

• Requirements for audit report. Who determines the report, what is being reported, to whom it is being reported, and why?

• Corrective action responsibilities. How are the corrective actions being handled?

The supporting documentation shall show the following:

• Audit plan. Audit method and specific quality system parts to be audited.

• Audit report. Method of reporting and distribution of reports.

• Records. Which audit records are to be maintained, including at least the following items:

Audit results.

Audit report to management.

Auditor qualifications.

Corrective actions.

In addition, the QM shall show that internal auditors are qualified and have no direct responsibility for the functions being audited. The QM shall also show the organization's commitment to conform to any external requirements, such as a registration agency or a national regulatory agency. The quality manual shall reference any key supporting procedures for such conformance and auditing.

Section 4.18 Training

The QM should be able to reference the organization's procedures and supporting documents for training personnel. Specifically the QM should focus on

• Identification of needs. Training needs are determined by analysis of job requirements. Organization management has established and maintains documented procedures for identifying training needs of personnel. This training shall include the understanding and operation of the organization's quality system.

• Training program. The organization has established and maintains documented procedures for training personnel who affect quality during production. A comparison of training needs and individual skills determines the training program and brings skills up to desired levels. As appropriate, certification and recertification procedures shall also be documented, monitored, and maintained.

• Records. Completion of training will be documented, recorded, and maintained by the organization. These records should contain documentation that reflects appropriate education, training, and experience of each employee who performs activities that affect product or service quality.

Section 4.19 Servicing Specified in Contract
The QM shall show that the organization has documented servicing requirements as specified by contract. In addition, the QM shall show that the organization has established and maintains procedures for performing and verifying servicing activities in meeting servicing requirements.

Section 4.20 Statistical Techniques
This section is perhaps one of the most misunderstood sections of the standard. It focuses on the application of statistical techniques (4.20.1). In the QM the organization must define these techniques and describe when they are used (4.20.2). The QM shall show that the organization has documented a program for the application and measurement of appropriate and adequate statistical techniques in its process(es). The idea of section 4.20 is to establish, control, and verify process capability and product characteristics. An example might be using statistical process control (SPC) to monitor key process characteristics of a particular operation or equipment. However, SPC is not a required item. Other tools might be just as good or efficient for the particular process. The organization's management or customer's requirements define these tools, and once the requirements are defined, then the standard requires documentation and proof of their existence.

SUMMARY

In this chapter we have discussed the structure of a typical quality system documentation, the quality manual, the contents of the quality manual, and the specific requirements of each clause of the quality manual. In the next chapter, we will discuss the mechanics of how to write procedures.

REFERENCES

ISO 9001: 1994 Quality Systems—Model for Quality Assurance in Design, Development, Production, Installation and Servicing. Milwaukee, WI: ASQC.

ISO 9004:1994 Quality Management and Quality System Elements—Guidelines. Milwaukee, WI: ASQC.

ISO/DIS 10013 Guidelines for Developing Quality Manuals. Milwaukee, WI: ASQC.

Chrysler, Ford, GM (1994). *Quality System Requirements: QS-9000.* Southfield, MI: Chrysler, Ford, GM through AIAG.

CHAPTER 4

How to Write Procedures and Instructions

This chapter provides the rationale and some guidelines for the content and format of procedures and instructions. In addition, it explains the mechanics and requirements of design control, control documentation, and the communication of the documentation in the organization.

Procedures are specific to a particular function and are identified and or referenced in the quality manual. Instructions, on the other hand, may be parts of the procedures or separate documents. In either case, they represent detailed instructions for the performance of a particular task within a procedure. For more information on instructions see Wilson (1996), Brumm (1995), and Clements et al. (1995).

PROCEDURES

A pictorial overview of the ISO documentation can be seen in Figures 3–2 and 4–1.

The quality manual—as already discussed—identifies the organization's policies and functions and places them in a context that describes the relationships between them. A procedure identifies the procedural steps for a function. Depending on the scope and complexity of the function(s), there may be one or more procedure manual(s). Some examples of procedure manuals are procurement manuals, operations manuals, manufacturing manuals, and engineering manuals. Each of these manuals relates to the procedures of a particular department.

FIGURE   4–1

The Four Tiers of Documentation

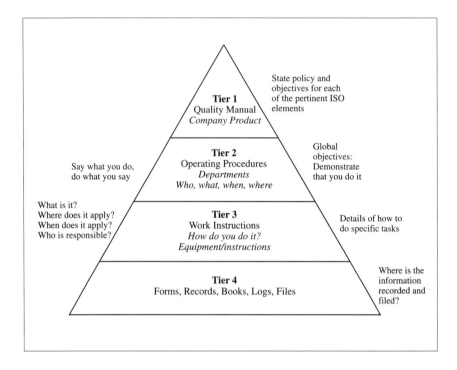

If the documentation is in an electronic form rather than on paper, it may not be necessary to divide it into separate manuals (see Figure 2–2). However, access to the procedures may be restricted on a need-to-know basis.

INSTRUCTIONS

The terms *operating instructions*, *instructions*, and *standard operating procedures* are used interchangeably. They all describe details of specific steps of higher-order (less detailed) procedures. For example, a machine setup may be a step in the total calibration procedure. The SOP for the setup is the specific description (the process, the method) for this particular kind of setup.

As a general rule, instructions are at a lower level of detail than both the Quality Manual and the procedures. Instructions describe a step-by step approach to guide an operator through a task.

If the overall procedure is short and simple, the operating instructions may be part of the procedure manual or they may be bound separately. Because instructions are detailed and specific, they may be posted in the work station, provided to the operators as job aids, or made available on demand through electronic devices. No matter how the instructions are distributed **all instructions must be available to the operators performing the task or the process and they all must be current**.

CONTENTS OF A PROCEDURE

Although there is no definite way to identify specific content, there are some generic ways to build a procedure. The following questions may help in structuring a procedure.

Purpose, objective	Why is this procedure performed?
Inputs	What materials come into this process?
	Which inputs need to be measured or evaluated?
Outputs	What specific outcomes are expected?
	Are there any interim or end product measurements?
Acceptance criteria	How are the tests, standards, or tolerance limits selected?
Procedure steps	How is the process performed?
Responsibility	Who is responsible for initiating, performing, and monitoring the process?
Audit requirements	How is the frequency of the audit determined?
	Who performs the audit? What happens to the results?
Resources	What resources (machine, method, material, manpower, measurement, environment) are required to perform the procedure?
Training requirements	What training courses, seminars, workshops, etc. are required for the operators of the particular task?
Approval authority	Who approves and authorizes the procedure?

Although all of the preceding elements are not mandatory in every procedure, the organization must define the applicability of the content and as a consequence incorporate the appropriate material. The level of detail for each procedure is unique to itself and the organization, and there is no specified length for a procedure. However, to ensure maximum applicability and appropriateness of the individual task, the operator must be included in defining the task. The following guidelines may help in procedure writing.

- Provide an overview that includes the procedure's purpose.
- Identify all materials, tools, and ingredients for the procedure.
- Identify both prerequisite and requisite skills.
- Provide an estimated time to complete the procedure.
- Do not assume. Do not skip obvious steps.
- Follow the correct order (logical, hierarchical, procedural, etc.). If order is not important, say so.
- Each step should be simple and self-contained.
- Use a hierarchical structure whenever possible. It is very easy to develop.
- Start with the most important step and keep developing them until the size and complexity of the steps give you the desired results.
- Try to start each instruction with an active (direct) verb (e.g., place, drill, position) or with the prerequisite, if there is one.
- Number each of the steps and use the numbering system consistently throughout the documentation (e.g., the numerical system of the standard itself or numerical [#.#.#]; roman [I., II.]; alphabetical [A., B.]; combination [I. A. 1.a.i.]).
- Always verify the procedure. Test it against current knowledge. Do not assume the procedure is correct because you just finished writing it.

FORMATS FOR PROCEDURE WRITING

Several formats are used in procedure writing.

Paragraph form (not recommended).	Hard to write, hard to maintain, hard to read and use.
Numbered instructions	Used when the sequence or hierarchy is important and must be identified.
Playscript	Used with low-literacy employees. Performers are identified with the steps in the procedure they perform.
Bullets and hyphens	Similar to numbered instructions but the sequence is not important.

Process flow chart	Used with long and semicomplex processes. Traditional symbols identify each task.
Parallel form	An annotated process flow chart. Highly recommended for all processes. Instructions are keyed to the process chart.
Interactive dialogue	Similar to the numbered instruction format but with the addition of responses from a machine, usually a computer. Expensive to maintain.

In addition to the specific content, each page of the procedure should have the following information:

The name of the procedure.

The name of the organization.

The authorizer.

The page within the procedure.

The effective date.

The revision date.

This information may be split between a header and or a footer within the page as in Figure 4–2. However, it is recommended that all the information appear as a header on all pages. Consistency is important. Appendix D contains six written procedures.

Job aids are specific cards that usually contain excerpts from the quality manual. They give operators easy access to specific instructions, overviews, and reminders. Typically, the cards include highlights or outlines of procedures or guidelines such as tolerance limits for specific tests. The nature of the work process dictates the content and function of job aids.

THE PROCEDURE AND INSTRUCTION DEVELOPMENT PROCESS

As we already have discussed, the focus of documentation is to describe accurately the current state of the organization and to demonstrate compliance to the appropriate standard. The documentation—quality manual, procedures, and instructions—must demonstrate this compliance through an objective approach. This approach can be summarized in a five-step procedure development process.

1. Determine requirements. What does the standard require? Is the standard appropriate? What do we have to do as an organization to meet the requirement?

FIGURE 4–2

Procedure Header and Footer Example

Title of Procedure:	Effective Date:
Authorized By:	Revision:
Contents:	

Date Printed:	Page _____ of _____
Company Name:	Reference No.:

2. Perform a need (gap) analysis. What is the gap between the existing documentation and the requirements of the standards?

3. Define the documentation effort. What tasks must be performed to add new documentation and revise existing documentation to comply with the standard? Who will perform them? When? How?

4. Develop and refine the documentation. Define and document the roles and responsibility of the appropriate people, organizational structure, appropriate standards, and procedures. Write the documentation and verify that it is accurate and usable. Publish the documentation. Distribute the documentation to the people who will use it.

5. Control the documentation throughout its life in accordance with the procedures established for document control in the quality manual.

EFFORT AND COST

The level of effort required to develop quality documentation depends on the current state of the organization's quality standards and procedures. A given organization may have adequate and documented standards or have inadequate standards.

Standardization of the formats as much as possible throughout the writing and editing process will make the job much easier. Other ways to develop documentation are through teams or through the business structure of the organization.

If the team approach for documentation development is used, the team should be made up of people who

- Are knowledgeable about the process.
- Have been trained appropriately in the areas of the standards, group dynamics, and problem-solving techniques.
- Are considered leaders by their co-workers.
- Have the authority and the time to do the work.

Once the team is in place the development of the quality system can begin. At least three areas of investigation and analysis are important.

1. Where are the quality events performed? (Quality events can be defined as reviews, inspections, tests and audits. These events may be internal or external to the organization.)
2. What standards will be applied?
3. What specific procedure steps will be performed throughout the process and at the quality events?

The authority to investigate and or analyze these areas must be defined early on and must be visible to everyone. A good general rule to follow for appropriate approval in any documentation situation is the two to three levels above the level at which the documentation is used. If multiple utilization is expected, multiple approvals may be required.

Having visible authority is not the only parameter that will define the success of the documentation. In fact, visible authority may sometimes inhibit success. What is really necessary is appropriate knowledge of the quality events. In a typical internal manufacturing setting, quality events occur

- Upon receipt of material
- At key points in the manufacturing process at which the identification of a discrepancy can avoid unnecessary expense or effort farther down the line.
- At the completion of the manufacturing process.
- At the time of shipment.

In a typical external manufacturing setting (with a supplier certification program), inspections, and product verification to a set standard can be performed by the supplier. The purpose of reviews, inspections and tests is to identify deficiencies in the process or the product in order to avoid unnecessary effort and to ensure that the end product is acceptable. Furthermore, they provide one more input for continual improvement.

Audits of quality events monitor compliance with standards and procedures. A quality event is the quality attained for a specific task as defined by the requirement(s). Audits on quality events may be conducted at regular intervals or be completely unannounced.

While reviews, inspections, tests, and audits are very easy to develop and document, establishing design standards is a complex effort, often performed over many years as the product(s) evolve. In any case design standards are usually identified through customer requisition, product planning, or as a result of product evaluation and improvement.

Finally, the contribution of the team may be affected by the administration procedures that quite often define the following:

1. How the organization documents standards, procedures, and quality events.
2. How the organization addresses the verification of compliance.
3. How the organization handles the variance process. (Variance here is any deviation from a standard.)

The second approach to documentation is the approach of the business structure. Because different organizations have different ways of handling organizational objectives, the ISO standards deal with the functions that are critical to product and service quality. As a consequence, the standards exclude the executive, sales and marketing, and accounting functions from specific responsibility. However, these functions make a major contribution to an organization, and without their support the certification will not take place. For example, without executive commitment, how can the organization fulfill the ISO 9001 clause 4.1? Without the contribution of sales and marketing, how can the organization define customer requirements and corrective action? Without the active participation of accounting, how can the organization calculate the figures for nonconformance?

The business structure in some organizations may dictate that the documentation be based on departmental control, central control, or a business unit. In any case, what is important is the participation of the entire organization, and everyone will contribute if success is to be the end result.

The cost for such an undertaking depends upon whether the organization has a quality system in place. The cost is minimal if the organization already has a workable quality system. On the other hand, the cost can be very high if the organization starts without a quality system. In the author's experience the average cost for documenting an organization of up to 200 employees is about $150,000.

QUALITY PLANS

Standard 8402(A3), clause 2.5.3, page 4 defines a quality plan as a document setting out the specific quality practices, resources and activities relevant to a particular product process, service, contract or project (ANSI/ ISO/ASQC A8402–1994). Another way of describing the quality plan is to define it as the entity that contains the standards and procedures for special situations. More often than not, these standards and procedures supersede the normal ones for the specific situation.

Sometimes the term *quality plan* is used interchangeably with the terms *project plan* and *control plan*. Because of its special orientation, the quality plan more often than not is required to cover instructions that are unique to a process, product, or customer. If the uniqueness is of contractual nature, then the quality plan may be a separate document. However, in most organizations the quality plan may be part of the work order or blueprint or an addendum to the specific job.

One of the most often asked questions in reference to quality plans is, What situation warrants a quality plan? To answer this question we must first look at the customer requirement and accordingly provide for the specificity to the standards and procedures. Second, care should be taken to correlate the quality plan clearly with the specific situation to which it applies and to provide a means for signaling the situation to the task performers.

This second requirement is very powerful, for it allows the task performer to demonstrate empowerment at the job location as well as demonstrate the quality commitment to prevention as defined by the organization. For this demonstration to take place, the performers must come in direct contact with the project, product, client, etc. so that they can identify as closely as possible the work being performed and then choose the appropriate quality procedure. To facilitate this process, posters and job aids may be used to remind the performers of the special handling procedures.

If the quality plans are extensive, some organizations may use a master index to assure consistency and properly identify all special procedures with the appropriate jobs on the work orders. To ensure consistency in even the most complex procedures, it is not uncommon to establish the basic (generic) procedure for the plan and then add each requirement as needed.

To demonstrate this generic procedure, let us look at a chemical organization. The organization has many processes with many individual (unique) products. One way to address the quality plan is to identify each product with its own idiosyncrasies. Another and more efficient way is to define the generic process and then refer to the products as they are produced. The generic procedure follows.

Procedure for Process Y

1. Get or receive materials.
2. Place material in ladle.
    See Table Y.1 for specific measurements.
3. Mix well until predetermined viscosity is reached.

Table Y.1 Measurements

Standard measurements
     X lbs of A
     Y lbs of B
     Z lbs of C

Measurements for client CC; Contract 1299

>   S lbs of A
>   T lbs of B

Measurement for client SP; Contract 15668

>   U lbs of B
>   etc.

The typical information included in a quality plan per ISO 9004 clause 5.3.3 follows:

The quality policy statement.

Description of the particular situation.

The objectives to be attained.

Acknowledgment and approval from the responsible authority(ies).

Description of the products, services, customers, and suppliers.

Organizational structure unique to the situation.

Overview of the procedure or process.

Roles and responsibilities unique to the situation.

If testing or inspection is performed, the criteria and testing, review, or auditing should be identified.

Description of each functional area's procedure.

Cross-reference matrix between functions, procedures, and operating procedures.

Distribution list.

Document change and control procedures and responsibilities.

Even though the list seems to be quite extensive and inclusive for specific requirements, it must be emphasized that these are only guidelines. The specific quality plan may not include every item, but in some cases it may have more items, depending on the requirements of a particular customer.

QUALITY RECORDS

ISO 9001 clause 4.16 addresses the issue of quality records by stating:

> The supplier shall establish and maintain documented procedures for identification, collection, indexing, access, filing, storage, maintenance, and disposition of quality records.

How does one really define a quality record? A quality record is the result of the performance of a task, audit, inspection, test, and/or review. Generally, a quality record provides the basis for analysis of the work in process and is used to determine corrective action and improvement to the process and to provide the basis for comparison (compliance) to standards or auditing certification.

Quality records may be generic or very specific to a given organization. However, all quality records fall into the following categories:

1. Process control results. They measure various aspects of both the products produced and the process itself. Based on these records, adjustments, improvements, and automation are introduced wherever applicable and appropriate. Important characteristics of all process control results are the issues of

- Retention of records. How long do we keep the records?
- Sampling size. How much of a sample is adequate?
- Frequency. How often do we sample?
- Appropriate statistical analysis? What statistical analysis do we use? Why?

2. Inspection and test results. Both are means by which humans or automated equipment use preestablished acceptance criteria to evaluate in-process products, end products, components, materials, processes, or services. Generally, the data provide a means to prove that tests were performed, to evaluate the effectiveness of the process, and to identify problems. Inspections results, on the other hand, verify of a set quality expectation. Important characteristics of all inspections and tests are

- Date and time of test or inspection. When was the test or inspection performed?
- Test or inspection identification. What is the specific name of the test? What is the specific approach of inspection (e.g., stratified, sequential, or sampled)?
- Test criteria. What is or is not acceptable? How are they determined?
- Inspector or tester. Who performed the test or inspection?
- Results. What are the results? How do the results compare with the test criteria?

- Follow-up. Is a follow-up required? Who is responsible for the follow-up? How much time is available for the follow-up? Is corrective action required? Is improvement required? Does a deficiency need to be tracked and fixed?

3. Audit results. They are the documentation (records) of the audit itself. They may be formal (form) or informal (memo). Specifically, they should include the initial response, the findings, the resolution, and the expected action based on the findings (follow-up). Important characteristics of all audit results are

- Date and time of audit. When was the audit performed?
- Process audited. What was audited?
- Auditor's name and organization. Who is the organization being audited? Who performed the audit?
- Responsible management organization. Who authorized this audit? Who is receiving the results?
- Discrepancies and outstanding findings. What discrepancies (noncompliances) were found? What outstanding items were found? Each finding should have the following information:

  > Identification item.
  > Standard associated with the particular finding.
  > Time frame to correct.
  > Criticality of noncompliance.

- Overall result. Did the organization pass the audit? The result is always pass/fail and never a numerical score.
- Audit report distribution. Who receives a copy of the audit?
- Checklist. Audit checklists are part of the audit documentation. They show the audit criteria or the subject areas of the audit. Has a checklist been developed? Are all areas represented in the checklist? For checklist guidelines, see Appendix E. For actual checklist questions, see Appendix F.

An audit response is part of the quality record, and its content should include the following:

- Reference to the audit report.
- Acknowledgment of deficiencies reported and acceptance.

- All issues not acknowledged and accepted.
- Time table for removing deficiencies.
- All responsible parties.

The corrective action report is sometimes included as part of the audit results, although it can be an independent document. When it is part of the audit results, the following content is suggested as a very minimum:

- Reference to the original discrepancy.
- Description of corrective action.
- Request for re-audit or review.
- Date of corrective action.

4. Training records. They are all the records associated with the employee's training. They may be found either in each employee's department or the human resources department.

5. Product and process reviews. Product reviews ensure that interim and end products comply with the standards and customer requirements. Process reviews ensure that ongoing performance evaluation is effective. Process reviews are performed by the performers of the task on a continual basis, and they generally follow the audit format. Their focus is process improvement rather that deficiency identification.

6. Logs and service calls. Logs are usually informal documents listing particular discrepancies, review results, and events. Service calls, on the other hand, are documents relating to customer (internal or external) communication in reference to a particular complaint, discrepancy, etc.

To identify the quality records in a given organization, one must keep thinking of the appropriateness and applicability of the record to the organization. The ISO 9004 clause 17.3 states: "The system should require sufficient records be maintained to demonstrate achievement of the required quality and verify effective operation of the quality management system."

The following items are some of the types of quality records that require control.

- Inspection reports.
- Test data, plans, acceptance criteria.
- Qualification reports.
- Validation reports.

- Audit reports.
- Material review reports.
- Calibration data.
- Quality cost reports.

It is important to recognize that these records mentioned in the ISO 9004 are minimum events that occur across the organization's process. As a consequence, additional reports may be required to satisfy the overall quality management system.

Two other aspects of the control of quality records are the issues of retrieval and retention. First, the issue of retrieval. ISO 9001 clause 4.16 states: "Where agreed contractually, quality records shall be made available for evaluation by the customer or the customer's representative for an agreed period." In essence, the standard requires that quality records should be retrievable by some criteria. On the issue of retention, ISO 9004 clause 17.3 states: "the quality system should provide a method for defining retention times, removing and/or disposing of documentation when that documentation has become outdated." In addition, clause 17.3 also mentions that "all documentation should be legible, dated, clean, readily identifiable, retrievable and maintained in facilities that provide a suitable environment to minimize deterioration or damage and to prevent loss."

One can see quite clearly that the standard is explicit as to the need for retention; however, it does not provide specifics. The specifics of document retention need to be defined by the organization and the customer. Generally, for most companies the retention period is between five and seven years. It is the organization's responsibility to retain the quality records intact and away from all hazards.

DOCUMENTS FOR DESIGN CONTROL

In some organizations, design is an integral part of the business. As such, specific documentation must exist to satisfy the ISO 9001 clause 4.4.1, which states that "the supplier shall establish and maintain documented procedures to control and verify the design of the product in order to ensure that the specified requirements are met." The procedures to ensure that requirements are met are essentially the project planning and control process procedures.

Projects are efforts to achieve an objective in a finite time and within a finite budget. When the objective is achieved, the project is over. With an ongoing activity the process is perpetuated. In projects, one must always be cognizant that the quality assurance events are checkpoint reviews, which are mapped to the major phases of the project.

The objective of the reviews is to validate that the work performed to date is acceptable. The reviews are performed throughout the project. On the other hand, the objective of the checkpoint review is to validate the entire results of the project phase and to re-evaluate the go/no go decision. Checkpoint reviews are special reviews. The focus of both reviews and checkpoint reviews is to minimize the impact of errors by uncovering them early in the process, to avoid unnecessary effort by readdressing the go/no go decisions, and to uncover opportunities for process improvement.

Each project may be totally unique and unrelated to anything else. Therefore, is it possible to really focus on a standard documentation? The answer is a definite yes. The reason for such a positive response is that in all projects, the project life cycle is a standard set of steps that can be applied to any kind of project. In fact, the following characteristics—also shown in Figure 4–3—are major tasks that should be the focus in any documentation endeavor.

> *Project initiation or feasibility study.* Typical documentation may be input requirements, cost-benefit analysis, design, estimates, tasks, roles and responsibilities, and statement of feasibility.
>
> *Requirements definition.* Typical documentation may be review of requirements, analysis, resolution, regulatory requirements, fitness for purpose, and safety requirements.
>
> *Product design.* Typical documentation may be detailed specifications, design reviews, and reliability.
>
> *Prototype development.* Typical documentation may be request for changes, design results, design reviews, follow-up requests, and checkpoint reviews. In the prototype development stage, we are concerned with detailed design, development, and integration and testing.
>
> *Implementation.* Typical documentation may be tests, validation, reliability, evaluations, acceptance criteria, and cause identification.
>
> *Postproject evaluation.* Typical documentation may be specific verification techniques, formal reports of deficiencies identified during implementation, and corrective action reports.

FIGURE   4–3

Project Life Cycle

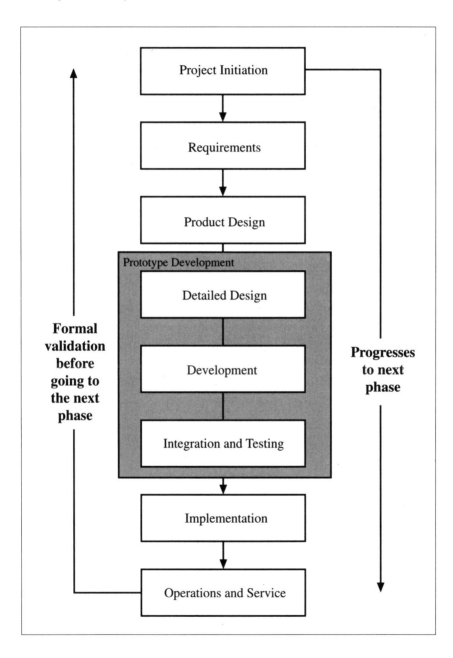

To guide us in the documentation process of a design with some specificity, the ISO 9001 clause 4.4 identifies some requirements. They are not exhaustive nor are they intended to fulfill every requirement of a design situation. A selected summary of the requirements follows:

• 4.4.2 Design and development planning. Create a project plan that identifies the activities (tasks) to be performed, the responsible performers, and their organizational and technical interfaces.

• 4.4.4 Design Input. Identify, clarify, accept, and document the business requirements that are the inputs to the design process and the ultimate criteria for success of the project.

• 4.4.5 Design Output. Document the detailed specifications, calculations, etc., that represent the design, and:

Satisfy input requirements.

Identify acceptance criteria (for the product).

Conform to regulatory requirements.

Identify safety characteristics of the design.

• 4.4.6 Design Review. Records for the documented reviews of the design, which will include all planned activities and representation involved during the design and development, as well as design input stages.

• 4.4.7 Design Verification. Plan, staff, and document the procedure for verifying that the design output meets the design input requirements by means of control measures such as

Design reviews.

Tests and demonstrations.

Alternative calculations.

Comparing the new design with similar proven designs.

• 4.4.8 Design Validation. Design appropriate validation procedures so that the product conforms to defined requirements.

• 4.4.9 Design Changes. Identify, document, review, and approve all changes/modifications to requirements and design.

DOCUMENT AND DATA CONTROL

One of the most vulnerable areas in the ISO certification process is the area of document control. The ISO 9001 clause 4.5 identifies the following requirements:

- 4.5.2 Document approval and issue.
  - Establish and maintain procedures to control all quality documentation.
  - Ensure that documentation is reviewed and approved by authorized personnel prior to issue.
  - Ensure that only the current version of a document is available where and when needed.
- 4.5.3 Document changes/modifications.
  - Review and approve changes.
  - Identify the nature of the change.
  - Maintain a control procedure to identify the current revision of a document and its location and ownership to preclude the use of nonapplicable or outdated documents.
  - Reissue documents after a "practical" number of changes have been made or when documents are illegible, messy, etc.

ISO 9004 clause 17.2 goes even further in addressing the subject of document control: "Pertinent sub-contractor documentation should be included. All documentation should be legible, dated, clean, readily identifiable, retrievable and maintained in facilities that provide a suitable environment . . . Data may be hard copy or stored in a computer."

Often the question arises as to what constitutes document control. The answer is not an easy one. It depends on the organization and the documents needed for verification of a particular task. To help define document control, we will consult the ISO 9004 clause 17.2, which provides the following guidelines:

Product documentation (drawings, specifications, blueprints).

Inspection instructions.

Procedures (tests, work, operational, quality assurance).

Operations sheets (process documents).

Quality manual.

Although these are very general guidelines, document control fundamentally addresses two issues: document administration and the document change process.

On the first issue, document administration, document control consists of the following:

Obtaining original content or changes.

Technical editing.

Ensuring that content is reviewed and approved.

Publishing the documented material.

Keeping track of the location and ownership of the documents.

Ensuring the security of the document.

Distributing the changes promptly and with appropriate removal instructions.

Denoting changes according to the documentation standard.

Replacing documents after a practical number or changes have been made.

The responsibility for the review and approval of the contents should be with the people who will have to comply with the contents. After all, what is being documented is the way work is being performed, not the work that is going to be performed.

On the second issue, document change process, document control consists of the following:

Identifying of the required change(s).

Writing the change(s).

Approving the change(s).

Distributing of the change.

Including the "new" documentation.

Removing the "old" documentation.

Distribution control is one of the most critical functions of document control. It is necessary to ensure that documents are distributed to the appropriate people or locations and that changes to the documents are distributed so that the documents can be kept up-to-date. Anyone with knowledge of the performance, task, process, etc. may propose the changes. On the other hand, only with the person—or the equivalent of his or her position—who authorized the original can approve the change. As a general rule, approvals are performed by a person who is at least two levels higher than the seeker of the approval.

When documents are distributed in a hard copy form, the document must be maintained in a master file by the document administrator (see Figure 3–3). Typical contents of the master list are:

Title.

Copy number.

Version number.

Version date.

Holder of the copy.

Date of last revision (optional).

Not all documents are controlled documents. Some documents are uncontrolled because they are not used in the actual work process. When that is the case, the copies must be clearly labeled to avoid inadvertent use. A common identification is a stamp notifying the reader of the status of the document. The stamp may read *controlled* or *uncontrolled document; classified or unclassified document;* or any other statement. Sometimes the differentiation may be through the use of a different color ink or a completely separate stamp.

Document administration is an ongoing process in the organization and is clearly stated in the quality manual. The document change process, on the other hand, is a process that is defined in the quality manual and that actuates itself when needed. The frequency of change, for example, may be defined as a result of a change in the process due to improvements or to changes in standards, policies, roles, or responsibilities.

Very frequent changes in procedures will cause a great deal of administrative and control work for those responsible for documentation control. Because of this lengthy work effort, it is recommended that procedures be constructed in generic terms and that the individual quality plans or instructions be constructed in very detailed terms. Frequent changes may be the result of performing custom work for individual customers; the changes are unavoidable, however welcome the work.

When frequent changes are common, and not profitable to the organization at large, a review of the structure and objective(s) of the documentation may correct the situation. It turns out that the most frequent causes for such changes are lack of procedure analysis and development. A good tool for this analysis is the process flow chart.

A document should be reissued when a number of changes have been made, either over a period of time or at one time, that could be misinterpreted or confuse the reader. Another reason to reissue a document is the physical condition of the document itself.

In the case of electronic distribution, security is also an issue. The document control administrator is responsible for updating and maintaining the functionality of the documents. Restrictions should be placed on printing and modifying all the documents in the electronic distribution system. Even though the electronic system provides an easier and more effective system for changes and control, it should be remembered that once a quality document has been printed, hard copy controls must apply.

In the electronic system document control usually consists of the availability of access at the work stations where the documents are used and of security features that are part of the electronic distribution system such as passwords or special access codes.

PRODUCTION ISSUES IN THE DOCUMENTATION PROCESS

The appearance of the quality documentation is an important aspect of the documentation effort. Although the ISO/QS standards do not require any particular level of aesthetic presentation, attractive presentations enhance both the readability and usefulness of the documentation. Production issues include layout, fonts, position, spacing, underlining, bolding, use of footers and headers, references, indexing, related documentation, tables, figures, and other pertinent information. The specific use and appearance of any of these items depend on the organization and the requirements of the ISO/QS standards and/or the customer.

A word processor and desktop publishing and graphic software should be used to facilitate production of documentation. The use of good software will save a tremendous amount of time in revising and updating the information.

The usual presentation for paper documents is on 8 ½" by 11" paper; online documents may be distributed via a network, on disks for stand-alone PCs, or via a mainframe computer. The distribution is a matter of personal preference. Both methods require maintenance of the documentation, and the specificity of the maintenance should be discussed under document control.

The components of the documentation follow a standard sequence.

Cover page.

Table of contents.

Foreword (optional).

Preface (optional).

Index or matrix.

Body (may be divided into chapters, sections, and table of contents).

Glossary (optional).

Appendixes (optional).

Bibliography (optional).

A typical cover sheet will include the following items:

Company name
Manual title
Identification signature
   Prepared by
   Revision date
   Copy number
   Authorization signature

Figure 3–5 shows a sample cover page.

A typical table of contents sheet will include the following items, but not necessarily in this same order.

Title
Table of contents
Section title
Section number
Page
Authorization
Last revision (optional)

The body of the documentation should contain the following items.

Document title.

Section explanation. The appropriate detail of this section is of importance so that the reader gains the information without turning the page or the screen. The explanation is usually given in a form of a flow chart; however, in some cases the prose form is used. In the case of the computer scrolling, it can be used; however, limit its usage to only when it's absolutely necessary. Its usage disrupts the reader's concentration and therefore is not recommended. Typical items are:

Date.

Revision date.

Page number.

Company logo.

Figures, tables, and forms (optional). If figures, tables, or forms are used, whether in a hard copy or electronic media, special care should be taken not to split these elements between pages or screens.

Basic Issues of Technical Writing

A final consideration in writing quality documentation is good technical writing. It is imperative to write the documentation with some form of standardization and some consistency. The issue of consistency is very important, since the documentation will undoubtedly have more than one author.

To focus on the mechanics of writing, we recommend a writer's guide, or perhaps fill-in-the-blanks outlines or word processor documents to reduce the writing effort and to maintain maximum consistency and standardization.

To write the actual documentation, we recommend the following:

Write short and simple sentences; try to follow the rule of one sentence, one thought.

Use the right words—avoid jargon as much as possible.

Use the ISO 8402—A3 as a guide to special words.

Use active or direct verbs.

Write short paragraphs.

Use lists as much as possible.

   words

   phrases

   sentences

   pictograms

   flow diagrams

Use the right tone. Write to the reader's level of language and technical knowledge.

Edit, review, examine the readability, and proofread the material. Editing, reviewing, examining, and proofreading may occur at any stage of the writing and should consider the following concerns.

Content	Is the content accurate and complete? Is it usable? Does the content reflect the present system as opposed to what should be? The reviewer must be familiar with the content; appropriate reviewers are the operators, supervisors, or managers.
Usability	Is the document written for the intended audience? Is the vocabulary appropriate for the audience? Is the structure of the document appropriate for its intended purpose? Are the size, volume, graphics, and flow of the documentation suitable, and useful? Because usability is of utmost importance, the reviewer should be the actual user of the document. In some cases, in fact, pilot tests are recommended to check the authenticity.
Compliance with conventions	Are the headers, footers, font sizes, styles, etc., consistent with the requirements of the standards and the organization's conventions? Because this sort of editing requires special knowledge of standards and cultural conventions, we recommend that either a professional proofreader or a technical writer perform this task.
Grammar and spelling	Is the spelling correct? Is the structure of the writing correct? A word processor with a spelling checker and grammar checker is a very useful tool.
Production	Are the documents accurate, attractive, complete, etc.? This task should be performed by a technical writer or an editor.

A typical checklist for editing documentation may include the following areas:

Purpose of the document	Is the purpose of the documentation clearly defined? Is this purpose constant throughout the chapter or section? Can this purpose be reasonably met by this document?
Audience	Is the audience for the document clearly indicated? Is the document clearly oriented to this audience? Is the information organized appropriately for this audience? For this audience, does the document have the right level of technical information? An appropriate language level? An appropriate level of detail?
Content	Is the information complete? Has any irrelevant material been included by mistake? Are the concepts explained clearly? Is all information technically accurate? Have all procedures and operating instructions been tested? Are all terms defined clearly? Have all topics been given the appropriate emphasis?

Graphics and layout	Are all necessary graphics included in the document? Is every graphic discussed or referred to in the text? Are the graphics reproduction quality? Is the document in standard format? Is there enough white space? Is the page layout user friendly?
Writing and formatting	Have over-long sentences been shortened? Is the one sentence, one thought rule followed? Are sentences all the same structure? Should sentence length and grammar be more varied? Has the text been checked for errors in grammar, punctuation, and spelling? Can complex or fancy words be replaced by simpler words? Do transition words achieve flow? Are there helpful transitions from section to section? Are there hedging or passive sentences that should be stronger? Is the style sincere, polite, and courteous? Has the reader's point of view been taken into consideration? Have others reviewed the document and provided feedback regarding its appropriateness, applicability, and usability? Does the reader understand each step? Does the reader know the best way to use the material, especially if the document pertains to SOPs or the operating instructions? Has the Fog index been used to measure readability? (The Fog index is one of the simplest ways to determine the readability level of any document.) Table 4–1 shows the steps to take to calculate the readability level.

TABLE 4-1

The Fog Index Calculation Steps

Step 1

Count the number of sentences_____.

Count the number of words _____.

Calculate average sentence length (words/sentences) ____ = ____ (rounded).

Step 2

Count the words with three or more syllables (hard words) _____.

(Leave out the capitalized words, combinations of short and easy words [e.g., grasshopper, bookkeeper, verbs ending in *ed* or *es*].)

Count the hard words ____.

Calculate the percentage of hard words [(Hard words/total words) x 100] = _____.

(continued)

The Fog Index Calculation Steps *(concluded)*

Step 3

Add average sentence length _____ + percentage of hard words _____.
Total   _____.

Step 4

Multiply the total by **0.4** to get the readability level.

Note: A number equal to 9.0 indicates the material is for a ninth grade level reader. A number of 14.2 indicates the material is for two plus years of college. The lower the number, the easier the reading.

Production Concerns

Production and binding	Is the production style easy to use and update? Will the user be able to store and access the documentation easily? Is the cost acceptable? Will physical deterioration be an issue? Binding, reproduction, and distribution of the documentation are the final stages. In the case of binding, the following options are available:
Three-ring binding	Moderately expensive. Easy to add and remove pages, but the user might incorrectly arrange the pages. Highly recommended.
Stapled binding	Inexpensive. Looks very unprofessional. Difficult to add or remove pages.
Spiral binding	Fairly expensive. The document looks neat and lays flat, but material cannot be added or removed with ease.
Folders or portfolios	Inexpensive. Very unprofessional.
Laminated pages	Very expensive. Protects documentation in heavy-use environments. New material cannot be removed or added unless the full page is replaced.
Perfect binding	The most expensive. Very professional, magazine quality. Material cannot be adjusted without reprinting entire documentation manual.

In the case of reproduction the following choices are available:

Copying	Inexpensive and fast for most of the applications of documentation.
Offset printing	Somewhat expensive, but if slick graphics and color are needed, this type of reproduction is recommended. Requires a commercial printer.

Finally, the document distribution will be based on the document control procedures of the quality manual.

SUMMARY

In this chapter we have addressed how to write documentation. In addition, we have provided detailed explanations for a variety of formats. In the next chapter we will address the issue of auditing.

REFERENCES

ANSI/ISO/ASQC A8402–1994. *Quality Vocabulary.* Milwaukee, WI: ASQC.

Brumm, E. K. (1995). *Managing Records for ISO 9000 Compliance.* Milwaukee, WI: Quality Press.

Clements, R.; Sidor, S. S.; and R. E. Winters. (1995). *Preparing Your Company for QS-9000: A Guide for the Automotive Industry.* Milwaukee, WI: Quality Press.

Wilson, L. A. (1996). *Eight Step Process to Successful ISO 9000 Implementation: A Quality Management System Approach.* Milwaukee, WI: Quality Press.

CHAPTER 5

Audits

This chapter focuses on the issue of audits as they relate to documentation. Our objective is to present the rationale, the objective, the execution, the benefits, and the ethics of both planning and conducting the audit. For more details on the audits, the reader is encouraged to see Keeney (1995, 1995a) and Parsowith (1995).

OVERVIEW

ISO 8402 defines a quality audit as "a systematic and independent examination to determine whether quality activities and related results comply with planned arrangements and whether these arrangements are implemented effectively and are suitable to achieve objectives." (ANSI/ISO/ASQC A8402–1994). Thus, an audit is a human evaluation process to determine the degree of adherence to prescribed norms and results in a judgment. The norms, of course, are always predefined in terms of criteria, standards, or both.

To avoid confusion and misunderstandings, it must be understood from the very beginning of the audit that the norms are defined by the management of the organization and the auditor has nothing to do with evaluating the suitability of such norms. However, it is the responsibility of the auditor to evaluate the compliance of the organization to those norms. For this reason the audit is usually performed as a pass/fail evaluation rather than a point-system evaluation.

As defined then, an audit is an information gathering activity with the purpose of identifying noncompliances in the system so that improvement, corrective action, or both may be evaluated and implemented. It should be understood by all auditors and lead auditors that in a given audit there is neither a preestablished number of noncompliances nor a fair ratio of major and minor noncompliances. This is true for the first audit as well as for subsequent audits. Furthermore, audits are not public hangings.

Quality audits are neither inspection tools nor verification tools for actual acceptance or rejection of the product or service. The orientation of the quality audit is fact finding; its focus is the evaluation of the system or process. The focus of an audit is always prevention and planning, as opposed to inspections where the focus is appraising product quality after the fact.

Quality audits may be internal or external and take one of three forms:

First-party audit	This audit is conducted by an organization on itself and may be done on the entire organization or part of the organization. It is usually called an internal audit.
Second-party audit	This audit is conducted by one organization on another. It is usually an audit on a supplier by a customer, and it is considered an external audit.
Third-party audit	This audit is conducted by an independent organization (the third party) on a supplier. It can be conducted at the request of a customer or on the initiative of a supplier to gain certification. It is always an external audit.

A comparison of the three audits is shown in Table G–1. Regardless of the kind of audit, it is imperative that auditors and the lead auditor have no direct or indirect responsibility in the audited area or with the involved personnel.

The most common types of audits in reference to ISO are described next.

• *Conformity assessment.* They are developed for each *new approach* directive as they are being developed. In general a conformity assessment examines all activities that assure the conformity of products to a set of standards, including testing, inspection, certification, and quality system assessment. Depending on the products and health and safety risks they present, the conformity assessment can range from a full-quality assurance system guided by special requirements to manufacturer self-certification. Because there is a choice, the EU considers conformity

assessment a voluntary rather than mandatory process, that is, the manufacturer chooses the option.

• *Eco-management and audit scheme (EMAS)*. This audit system
was developed to prevent, reduce, and as far as possible eliminate pollution, particularly at its sources. It uses a polluter-pays principle that is
similar to the Environmental Protection Agency program that permits companies to trade emissions allowances. The binding part of the regulations
is that nations must establish methods for companies to validate the conformity and effectiveness of their environmental management systems.
Participation by companies is voluntary. The eco-audit program sets forth
requirements that EU member states participate in an international system
of conformity assessment for environmental management. This system in
all likelihood will be similar to the worldwide traceability system now
falling into place for ISO 9000.

• *Adequacy audit*. This audit is usually an internal audit known as a
system or management audit. Its function is to determine the extent to
which the documentation meets the applicable standard.

• *Compliance audit:*. This audit is performed by a company that
seeks to establish the extent to which its documentation system is implemented and followed by the workforce. The focus is the system or process, not the product.

• *External audit*. This audit may be an adequacy or a compliance
audit and is usually performed by a company on its own suppliers.

• *Extrinsic audit*. This audit may be an adequacy or a compliance
audit and is usually performed by an independent third party or a customer coming to look at a supplier or a supplier's supplier.

• *Internal audit*. This is perhaps the most common and most important of all audits. ISO 9001 clause 4.17 requires a company to audit its
own quality system, procedures, and activities in order to establish whether
they are adequate and being followed by the workforce. Furthermore, the
ISO standard calls for communicating the results to management as well
as for planning corrective action, if necessary. This type of audit provides
excellent communication in the organization and provides management
with appropriate and timely information about the quality system and its
effectiveness.

• *Product/process audit*. This specialized audit examines all the
systems that go into the production of a specific end product or service. It
is usually called a vertical audit and should not be confused with an inspection program of an item. Product audits are applicable to auditing

specific projects or contracts, especially in the software and electrical industries. A trained professional auditor should undertake the product/process audit. The auditor may be on company staff, a hired professional, or a third party. What is of paramount importance is that the auditor must be independent and not have direct or indirect responsibility for the audit area or its personnel. Whether the auditor has knowledge in the specific area or activity is not relevant because the auditor's responsibility is to look for objective evidence of conformity based on the requirements of the standard and provided by the documented system.

If the audits are done appropriately, they provide the following benefits to the organization:

- *Management orientation.* An audit will provide information on the current quality system to the management team so that appropriate evaluation can take place. The impetus for this evaluation may be the management team itself, the customer, or the competition.

- *Internal assessment.* An audit conducted as an internal assessment will provide a very good measurement of the effectiveness of the system and a strong benchmark for continuous improvement in the future.

- *External assessment.* An audit conducted as an external assessment will establish the credentials of procurement quality standard(s), that is, suitability, conformity, and effectiveness, and in addition will provide supplier certification.

WHO IS INVOLVED IN AN AUDIT?

A typical ISO 9000 or QS-9000 audit requires the following participants:

Lead Auditor. Usually the lead auditor is the person who plans the audit and does the preliminary as well as the closing paper work. He or she is a certified auditor and may be called the team leader.

Auditor. A person who is qualified to conduct the audit in accordance with the ISO standard.

Client. The organization that requests the auditing organization to conduct the audit.

Auditee. The organization to be audited. The entity on the receiving end of the audit activity.

Registrar. The body that issues the certification to the auditee.

The requirements and qualifications for the auditor and lead auditor are lengthy and numerous and beyond the scope of this book. However, the reader can find them in the ASQC (American Society for Quality Control) document *Certification Program for Auditors of Quality Systems* (1993). We summarize some of the requirements and qualifications in the following section.

Auditors

In addition to specific experiential background and educational requirements, the following aptitudes and attributes are necessary.

General Aptitude	Technical Aptitude	Personal Attributes
Qualifications	Knowledge of technical standards	Leadership
Certification CQE, CQA	Knowledge of cost accounting	Interfacing abilities
		Confidence
		Composure
		Independence
Knowledge of standards	Knowledge of quality cost systems	Planning abilities
		Understanding (industry, process, product, quality system)
		Investigative techniques
Knowledge of management systems and styles	Knowledge of statistical techniques Sampling Analysis Inferences	Communication abilities Oral Written
Ethics	Knowledge of diagnostic techniques	Critiquing ability
	Problem solving	Decisiveness
Integrity	Technical troubleshooting	

The term *external quality auditor* refers to auditors who are not members of the organization being audited. They may be

- A third-party organization or individual hired by the client to conduct the audit on its behalf.
- A third-party organization or individuals hired by an approval agency to conduct the audit, initiated at the request of the client.
- Second-party auditors, employed by the customer, potential customer, or other independent organization requesting the audit of the auditee.
- Second-party auditors, employed by an approval agency, carrying out an audit to determine the ability of the auditee to provide the desired quality system, product, service, or process.
- Auditors, employed by a corporate headquarters, carrying out an audit to determine whether a division or other element of that corporation complies with corporate policies and desires.

On the other hand, the term *internal quality auditor* refers to auditors who are employees of the organization being audited.

Lead Auditor

The basic requirements for a lead auditor are the same as for the auditor, but there are additional experience and training requirements for the lead auditor. The lead auditor must have at least 25 additional total audit days than the auditor and complete a 36-hour training program sanctioned by a certifying body.

Client and Auditee

No specific requirements except the desire to participate.

Registrar

Extensive requirements by the ISO Central Committee and the individual country of participation. In the United States contact the Registrar Accreditation Board (RAB) maintains the latest requirements.

PROCESS FOR DEVELOPING COMPLIANCE

The minimum requirements to start any audit fall into three categories. They are

Starting—knowing what to do.

Documenting—Writing it down.

Evaluating—self versus independent.

1. Starting   *Knowing what to do.* An auditor must gain some knowledge about the organization and the audit environment before starting the physical audit. The following recommendations will help in the preparation phase:

- Gathering and collating information, policies, procedures, and standard operating procedures.
- Developing additional documents to facilitate the audit. Checklists and work notes may prove worthwhile. Work teams and other resources may be applicable.
- Defining and recognizing the responsibilities and authorities, particularly those stated in ISO 9001, 9002, and 9003, for the specific organization.
- Communicating with all workers and certainly the worker(s) responsible for the audit. Audits should not be planned as surprises (with an attitude of "I'll get you"). Assumptions should not be made. Communication lines can be kept open with telephone calls, questionnaires, reconnaissance visits, or any other means that are applicable and appropriate for the situation.

2. Documenting   *Writing it down.* An auditor has the responsibility to be prepared, fair, impartial, inquisitive, honest, and observant. To do all that, some of the following recommendations may help.

- Writing down everything seen at the time of the audit and having the supervisor or operator sign the notes. This practice will eliminate confrontational statements later on during the reporting of the audit.
- Developing process flow diagrams with parallel information dealing with responsibilities, authorities, and special instructions. This information will help an auditor to prepare for the audit and to understand the process. Although a process flow diagram is not essential to conduct the audit, it does help the auditor conduct a cursory comparative analysis of the process at

hand and the organization. When used in conjunction with the checklist, the process flow diagram becomes a very powerful tool indeed.

- Communicate with all workers and certainly the workers affected by the outcome of the audit. Do not plan for any surprises. Be open, concise and easy to understand. Avoid jargon and traps of any kind.

3. Evaluating   *Self versus independent.* An auditor's ultimate responsibility is to evaluate the quality system of a given organization based on the organization's appropriate standards and follow-up—if this is a surveillance audit. The following suggestions may help in the evaluation process:

- Knowledge of applicable standards. If the auditor is not familiar with the organization and the audit standards, the evaluation may suffer.
- Independence of unit(s) assessed. As we have already discussed, the independence of the auditor is of paramount importance. Without this independence, bias and doubt enter into the evaluation.
- Experience in assessment(s). We addressed the issue of area-specific knowledge versus auditing knowledge earlier in this section. However, we must emphasize the importance of *auditing knowledge.* Unless the auditor is experienced in internal and external audits, the evaluation may omit essential issues and concerns. The following factors require experience and audit knowledge:
  - Recognition of a contractual requirement to audit.
  - Investigative procedures for actual or potential problems.
  - The appropriate audit for the appropriate standard.
  - Auditing a shut-down department or the records of a discontinued supplier.
  - Recognition of the life cycle of the contract or project.

Consideration and evaluation of these factors will indicate to the auditor whether or not an audit of the specific activity is required or whether that activity is worth pursuing. Depending on the evaluation, the auditor may select the appropriate type of audit, and may define or redefine the schedule of the audit.

Based on this evaluation, the auditor may define the type of audit (system, compliance, product, etc.) redefine the schedule of the audit, or change the sequence of the audit. What is more important is that the auditor will plan for the best—and most appropriate—audit and identify the scope of the audit, dates and schedule of the audit, and who will perform the audit.

In summary, an audit is a documented activity performed in accordance with written procedures or checklists to verify, by evaluation of objective evidence, that applicable elements of a quality assurance program have been developed, documented, and effectively implemented in accordance with specified requirements. It must always be remembered that the documented and written definitions of activities are in the domain of the management and that the auditor is looking for objective (replicated) evidence that quality assurance (quality planning) has been developed and implemented. Appendixes F, G, and H provide additional information for generating checklists and miscellaneous information about audits.

AUDIT PROCESS

All audits follow a sequential path that has four basic phases.

> **Phase 1** Preparation (preaudit). This phase includes selecting the team, planning the audit, and gathering the information.
>
> **Phase 2** Performance (on-site visit). This phase begins with the opening meeting and finishes with the actual audit.
>
> **Phase 3** Reporting (postaudit). This phase includes the exit meeting and the audit report.
>
> **Phase 4** Closure. This phase includes the actions resulting from the report and the documentation package.

Phase 1 Preparation

The planning activities depend on the organization and the certification it seeks. They are usually quite extensive and beyond the scope of this book. Some good sources for further information on the topic of planning for audits are Arter (1994), Hutchins (1992), Robinson (1992), Mills (1989), Sayle (1988), Duhan (1979), and Emmons (1977). Here we are identifying only the most typical planning activities.

The first planning activity is determining the implications of the quality audit.

1. Identifying the purpose of the audit. What do the customers want? Is the control system adequate? Is the control system working? Is the control system used by management?

2. Identifying the scope of the audit. What are the boundaries? Are they determined by product line? by process area? by customer? by systems? by organization? For ISO certification the boundaries are generally set by the facility.

3. Identifying the resources and defining the audit team requirements. How many members will the team have? One person will invite bias, and more than seven will create a mob. From the experience of this author, the optimum number of team members is four or five. Another consideration in the selection of the team is the composition. Care should be taken to have trained and qualified auditors who have both auditing experience and knowledge of the process to be audited.

4. Identifying the authority and defining the authority so that the auditor can establish legitimacy in the course of the audit, defuse hostility, avoid argumentation, and minimize—if not completely avoid—wasting time.

5. Identifying the initial contacts. When meeting with the auditee make sure some of the following items are under consideration. Set the date (be firm but remain flexible). Review both the purpose and scope. Make sure you know the names and the titles of the people you are to meet with. In case of formal contact by letter, that contact ought to be through the auditee's purchasing department or the executive department. The introductory letter should contain the following information:

Auditee name

Purpose

Scope

Appropriate standard

Activities to be audited

Applicable background documents

Identification of team members

Preliminary schedule

6. Determining the use of checklists. The auditor is responsible for ensuring that the audit flows smoothly and makes sense. A checklist

- provides structure in the audit.
- assures that the audit will cover the required areas.
- provides communication.
- provides a place to record findings (good and bad).
- helps in time management.

The checklist should not stifle the creativity of the auditor, limit the flexibility of the audit, or confuse the applicability of the audit.

7. Checking different sources for clues. The more information the auditor has, the better the chances of successfully evaluating the quality system. The scope of evidence includes the following:

- Physical evidence (current and historical).
  - Reinspect, retest, recheck.
  - Laboratory results, calibrations.
  - Any recorded documentation.
- Sensory observations (understand activity).
  - Observe tasks being performed (on-line).
  - Visual checks of products.
  - Storage of parts.
- Documents and records.
- Interviews and questions of personnel performing, storing, analyzing, and evaluating data. Because of the nature of interviewing, the responses should be corroborated by either another person, document, or direct observation.

The following activities are also part of the preparation phase.

- Understanding the resources needed for the audit. In every audit there are several items that require appropriate planning to ensure success. Some critical elements are personnel, office facilities, plant facilities, sequencing, scheduling, and working papers. Some of the background knowledge that will help ensure success is as follows:

  - Memory prompters for the auditor.
  - A comprehensive list to allow for grading of the effectiveness on specific element rather than a check-off sheet.
  - Detailed records of what was audited and where the activities of the audit were carried out, plus the findings.

- Applicable statistical techniques.
- Sampling and appropriate evaluation techniques.

• Scheduling the audit. How and when is the scheduling to be done?

• Sequencing the quality audit functions. Is the sequence of the operations important? Will the results be different if the sequence is not followed?

• Preparing or gathering working papers for the audit. These are all the documents required for an effective and orderly execution of the audit plan. By format and content they describe the scope and approach of the audit assignment and its operational elements. Specifically, they define the tools that are appropriate for use during the audit and applicable to the organization. Some of the tools and documents that the auditor may use or find during the audit are

• Process flow chart.
• Failure mode and effect analysis.
• Control plan.
• Critical path network.
• Matrix responsibility chart.
• Cause-and-effect diagrams.
• Appropriate statistics.
• Planning documents.
• Checklists.
• Reporting documents.
• Procedures.

• Determining the sampling procedures to be used in the audit. What is appropriate sampling for the processes audited?

• Deciding how the audit observations are going to be interpreted.

• Deciding how to report the results of the audit.

• Preparing procedures for requesting and following up on corrective action.

What are the results (product) of the preparation phase? There are at least four specific outcomes at the end of the preparation phase.

Creation of the audit plan.

Creation of the specific checklist questions.

Creation of an action plan for the specifics of the audit.

Some idea of a preliminary evaluation.

Phase 2 Performance

After all the background information has been completed, the audit team is ready to conduct the audit. There are two stages in the audit evaluation.

The manual versus the requirements audit.
The physical audit versus the organization's documentation.

In the manual versus the requirements audit (called a desk audit), the auditor thoroughly compares the documentation (generally the quality manual; sometimes the procedures as well) with the standard of choice (the seeking ISO 9001, 9002, or 9003 certification). If everything is in proper order, the audit will proceed to the second stage. If the review finds deficiencies in the documentation, appropriate corrections must be made before the second stage can take place. The desk audit usually is performed away from the site, quite often in the auditor's or registrar's office. The desk audit may be included in the preparation phase.

In the physical audit versus the documentation (called the site visit or site audit), the auditor thoroughly compares what actually occurs to what the documentation says will occur. Even though the physical audit is quite detailed, it is only a random snapshot, or sample of the system, in relationship to the entire organization.

A typical performance phase is made up of four stages. They are

Opening meeting
Understanding the controls
Verifying the system
Sharing information

1. Opening meeting. The opening meeting in any audit sequence is generally viewed as an introduction of all parties involved. It is mandatory, and all appropriate individuals must be present. The meeting should not last more than one hour. The typical events of an opening meeting are

Introduction of the lead auditor and the individuals present.
Company presentation (a short overview of the company).
Confirmation of the standard to be used.
Confirmation of all previous agreements as to scope and objective of the audit.
Confirmation and distribution of schedule and sequence of audit.

Confirmation of guide and arrangements such as phone, office, computer, logistical support, and meals.

Confirmation of the documentation system that will be used during the audit.

Confirmation that the organization is ready for the audit and that all staff and employees have been notified.

Distribution of the checklist (optional).

Explanation of the timing and purpose of the closing meeting.

Invitation of any questions regarding the audit.

At the end of the opening meeting the audit team goes forth with the site audit or adjourns to its designated office for a last minute briefing and to arrange times to reassemble for reviews, a meeting with the organization's representative, or both.

2. Understanding the controls. In most—if not all—organizations there are two levels of systems: the formal control system, which is documented, and the informal, which is not documented. The auditor must audit both systems and make sure both systems are followed appropriately and completely.

It is important to remember that the ISO 9001 clause 4.16 emphatically establishes that all quality records must be documented. However, the ISO 9004 clause 5.3.1 suggests that in some cases the documentation may be informal. The actual verbiage is ". . . care should be taken to limit documentation to the extent pertinent to the application." Therefore, even though we strongly recommend that the quality system (all documentation) be formal, we recognize and the standard recognizes the possibility that informal controls do exist and are legitimate under ISO. Conducting an audit of an informal system is very demanding, time consuming, and costly. An informal audit gives heavy emphasis to corroboration, personal interviews, and observations.

3. Verifying the system. There are as many verification systems as there are auditors. However, all of them present themselves in a general methodology.

Step 1. Putting the auditee at ease. Your presence is threatening. You are the outsider. Make sure you as an auditor defuse a possible difficult situation. You are looked upon as a spy and a person not to be trusted. Be prepared to answer questions that directly or indirectly ask, How dare you question my process? What do you know of me or my process? What are you going to do with this information?

As an auditor, you are looking for information that is controlled by someone who may or may not be friendly to the audit process. What do you do? Some of the following hints may help.

Dress for the occasion.

Talk in an appropriate manner.

Ask nonthreatening questions.

Be firm but informal.

Demonstrate professionalism.

Make the person comfortable.

Step 2. Explaining the purpose of the audit. This second step is perhaps the foundation of building good rapport with the operator. Typical actions are

Introduce yourself.

Demonstrate competence.

Explain why you are here.

Explain what you are going to do with the information.

Emphasize the process not the person.

Show that you are aware of the system, but don't show off your expertise.

Show your appreciation of the operator.

Step 3. Asking the workers what they do. An auditor obtains information during an audit by reading, observing, and listening. The auditor also needs to ask questions. To gather as much information as possible, the following suggestions may help.

Ask questions that are open ended and never personal.

Avoid leading questions.

Avoid questions that start with Why. They may imply criticism or disapproval.

Avoid questions that start with "I understand that you . . ."

Avoid tape recorders.

Focus all your questions.

Avoid questions with long introductions.

Avoid apologizing for your questions.

Ask for forms, records, procedures.

Wait for the response when you ask the question.

Control your idle talking; listen twice as much as you talk.

It is quite possible that workers may withhold, distort, or give incomplete information, either by accident or deliberate action. Being aware of this, the auditor needs to use excellent communication skills to ensure that all information received is valid and can be substantiated.

One of the many things that an auditor cannot dismiss when asking questions is the body language of the auditee. Body language is the name given to all those unconscious gestures, facial expressions, or body movements that are part of every personality. The study of body language is the new science of kinetics. Warning!!! When trying to interpret body language, remember that different nationalities, racial groups, etc. have different codes in this unwritten language. A good auditor is aware of this diversity and will limit body-language interpretation to the environment he or she knows.

Step 4. Analyzing what the workers said. In this step, the auditor analyzes all the information from the audit and writes the information in a notebook. The auditor must make sure to write only objective observations and data from the audit, not interpretations of suspicions or innuendoes. To maintain the integrity of the analysis, it is strongly recommended that the auditor ask either the operator or the department supervisor to initial the notes.

To make sure that the analysis is *fair* and *appropriate*, the auditor must address two fundamental questions.

Is the control system implemented?

Is the control system working?

To answer these questions the auditor (quite often) must look beyond the responses of the eye-to-eye questions of step 3. There are at least three primary methods used for verification: tracing, sampling, and corroboration.

• Tracing is an approach to auditing that traces something through all of the process steps. In the forward mode tracing starts at the beginning (order receipt) and works forward until the needed information is found. In the backward mode tracing begins at the end (order completion) and works backward until the needed information is found. The middle mode works both backward and forward from some critical point in the process. In most cases tracing is constantly utilized throughout the audit by all auditors.

• Sampling is trying to find the truth in a limited amount of time. Therefore, the more an auditor knows about sampling techniques, the better the audit will go. Some of the basic questions and concerns in regard to sampling techniques in auditing follow.

  • What to sample? The answer will depend upon the critical items or the area under consideration. Specific items that indicate the *what* are

    Important to the auditor.

    Important to the auditee.

    Overloaded areas.

    Areas with historical problems.

  • What will the results mean? Is the answer significant for final disposition? Is the information incomplete? Are the results acceptable? Why or why not?

  • How to sample? All sampling for any audit must be done on a random basis. Unless the sample is random, the results are meaningless because of bias or some other compromise in data selection.

  • How much to sample? Again, some knowledge of basic statistics and sampling may help the auditor define the sample. A general rule is that as the number of discrepancies in a population becomes small, the sample size must get bigger to have the same degree of confidence.

• Corroboration ensures data integrity. We know that people draw different conclusions from the same facts. We also know that every individual ranks important issues differently. As we mentioned, earlier some operators willfully or accidentally recollect events differently. The job of the auditor is to maintain the integrity of the audit so that the results will be useful to everyone concerned. Therefore, the auditor must

  • Persuade the auditee that the auditor's perception of the facts is better or more useful than the operator's perception of the facts.

  • Demonstrate to the auditee the benefits of sharing the facts accurately.

If the facts are so important and at times so elusive, how can an auditor establish the truth? It is the responsibility of the auditor to check and recheck the facts with whatever means are applicable and appropriate under the situation. Typically, the auditor will resort to corroboration when the facts don't agree or something is just not right. Corroboration may be obtained from

> Two different auditors.
>
> Two different records.
>
> Two different interviews.
>
> Any combination of the above.

As an auditor should remember that a statement made during an interview is not a fact until it is corroborated by someone else or verified by a document.

If the intent of the audit is to see how many noncompliances one can find in the quality system, then identify everything. Remember, however, that nothing is perfect. On the other hand, if the intent of the audit is to help the organization improve and establish a good benchmark of their quality system, then follow the Pareto (80:20) principle and *do not nitpick*. The idea is to focus on chronic or persistent problems or specific trends.

4. Sharing Information. At the end of the physical audit, the auditors meet and review the events of the audit. They discuss problems, concerns, and specific questions so that everyone on the audit team has a good idea of what went on in all the areas. Another reason for this meeting is to reach a consensus about the disposition of certain noncompliances. Quite often, the auditee makes minor adjustments based on the audit information. Sometimes the auditee will be briefed as to the status of the audit, pending final results and the resolution of special concerns and problems.

What is the result (product) of phase 2? In this phase the audit team collects data about the quality system and relates them to actual events. Phase 2 generates the objective evidence by which the ultimate decision of the audit is going to be made. Objective evidence may be qualitative or quantitative information, records, or statements of fact (corroborated) pertaining to the quality of an item or service or to the existence and implementations of a quality system element or documented requirement that is based on observation, measurement, or testing and that can be verified.

Phase 3 Reporting

The saying "I know that you believe you understand what you think I said, but I am not sure that what you heard is not what I meant" is precisely why the reporting phase is necessary. An auditor wants to pass on honest and accurate information. After all, the man purpose of the audit is to collect information in factual form and to pass it on as objectively without any bias. In this phase we are focusing on the passing on of that information. The two issues of concern are the reporting and the closing meeting.

1. The Reporting. The reports are short and contain the findings of the audit. A third-party audit usually states the findings as nonconformances to specific clauses of the certifiable standard. On the other hand, a first- or second-party audit, in addition to stating the nonconformances or noncompliances to the standard, may add recommendations to fix the noncompliances or to improve the quality system. The noncompliances are based on knowledge and objective evidence from the audit and hardly ever number more than 10. The reason for this low number is twofold. (1) The auditee has gone through at least one preassessment and very detailed preparation. The probability of having more than 10 noncompliances is indeed very small. An auditor who issues more than 10 noncompliances may be nit-picking. (2) More than 10 deficiencies can create management overload.

Unless the audit is internal, the auditor's findings and recommendations should not require specific problem solving actions. In addition, the auditor's findings and recommendations should not be based on perceived bias or gut feelings. Such findings are likely to lack legitimacy and credibility.

When ready to write the report, the auditor must keep in mind some very common definitions.

• *The audit corrective action report (ACAR)* is the report that the auditor uses to document the findings during the audit. Two generic ACAR forms are shown in Figures 5–1 and 5–2. The report form in Figure 5–1 is used on an internal audit; the report form in Figure 5–2 is used in an external audit. The difference between the two is that the internal report form has room for recommendations. Sometimes these reports are called nonconformance or noncompliance reports. If an ACAR is issued, the auditor has to evaluate the effectiveness of the corrective action before the audit is closed.

• A *major noncompliance item* is a significant nonconformity or deficiency in the quality system that affects or has the potential to affect the quality of the product. A typical major noncompliance is the exclusion of 1 of the 20 ISO clauses. One major noncompliance is enough to withhold the certification.

• A *minor noncompliance item* is an isolated nonconformity that does not represent a system deficiency. However, a series of minor noncompliances may constitute a major deficiency.

FIGURE   5–1

Audit Corrective Action Report (ACAR) for Internal Audit

Facility	ACAR No.	Date Audited
Lead Auditor	Document No.	
Auditor	Guide	
Discussed with	Verified with	

Statement of the Standard

Observation

Additional Comments

Recommendations

FIGURE   5–2

Audit Corrective Action Report (ACAR) for External Audit

Facility	ACAR No.	Date Audited
Lead Auditor	Document No.	
Auditor	Guide	
Discussed with	Verified with	

Statement of the Standard

Observation

Additional Comments

An earlier example may again clarify this point. As an auditor, early in the audit you observe a handwritten change in a document control record without the specified signature for authorization. You make a note of it and report the nonconformity to the area supervisor who assures you that this event must be an oversight. You proceed with the audit and find no more problems with missing signatures or anything else. The lack of signature is indeed a minor nonconformance. On the other hand, after finding the missing signature and receiving assurances that the event was an isolated case of plain oversight, you find that changes in control documents are performed without appropriate signatures or proper authorization throughout the organization. At that point, you should record the incident as a major noncompliance.

The difference between the first and second situations is that in the first case the lapse was an isolated error, whereas the second case implies a breakdown of the system and as such a major noncompliance.

2. Closing Meeting. The closing meeting is sometimes called the postaudit conference (exit) meeting. The closing meeting must take place regardless of how rushed all the parties are. The meeting itself is attended by all managers of the audited activities as well as by all auditors. It is not recommended that the only auditee representative be the quality assurance manager; he or she may filter or distort the information.

The purposes of the closing meeting are to

Review the audit scope.
Review the audit limitations.
Present the summary of results.
Identify all action requests.
Clarify details and emphasize findings.
Announce the registration eligibility.
Present the manuscript report.
Explain follow-up and response time (if applicable).
Announce the postregistration (surveillance) requirements.

If there is a follow-up report, then the contents of the report may contain the following:

Purpose and scope of the audit.
Participants.
Background information.
Summary of results.

Identified weaknesses.

Responses to action requests.

Evaluation of responses.

Timetable for reaudit (if necessary).

Disposition on the certification.

The report should state the items of concern very carefully. Some guidelines are

Use management terms whenever possible.

Use industry jargon whenever possible.

Put comments in order of importance.

Report results in a language that is concise, exact, and easy to understand.

Call attention to truly exemplary practice whenever possible.

The audit report should avoid emotional words and phrases, personal bias, nit-picking, and management overload.

What is the result (product) of phase 3? In this phase the audit team produces a physical report that includes the findings of the audit and the recommendation whether or not the auditee should be certified.

Phase 4 Closure

All audits come to an official close with Phase 4. A typical closure may be a review of the noncompliances and the auditee's reaction to those noncompliances, or it may be a revisit to the organization by the registrar. In the first case a desk audit (review) may be necessary, whereas the second case may require a more formal approach, such as a physical audit.

The closure of any audit focuses on four specific areas.

1. Evaluation of the noncompliances and the action requested. As a general rule, it is the responsibility of the lead auditor to evaluate the auditee's responses. The evaluation deals with

- Evaluating and closing all corrected items.
- Reauditing the items that need on-site verification.
- Accepting or rejecting the corrections.
- Assess the chance of success if partial acceptance is required because of time limitations or some other legitimate reason.

2. Follow-up on the corrective action. All noncompliances require action by the auditee. The corrective action is a formal way to recognize the problem and to solve it in a systematic way. There are four basic steps in any corrective action.

- Identifying the root cause of the problem with tools such as brainstorming, cause-and-effect diagrams, statistical process control (SPC) charts, and process flow diagrams.
- Specifying actions to correct the problem in the short term.
- Specifying actions to correct the *root* cause in such a way that the problem will not repeat. This is the solution for the long term.
- Identifying responsibilities and the timetable for corrective action. The lead auditor is responsible for evaluating both the timeliness and the effectiveness of the resources applied to the corrective actions. Most Registrars require a 30 to 60 day (45 days average) buffer zone for the corrective actions for major noncompliances.

3. Retention of audit documents. Finally, the closure in any audit must consider the retention of both official and unofficial records.

Official records are generally retained for three to five years. However, in some industries the retention period may be defined from cradle to grave, as for example in the nuclear industry. The following items are official audit records.

Notification letter.

Audit plan (if separate document).

Preassessment questionnaire.

Checklist.

On-site audit/evaluation.

Auditee's response.

Closure letter.

Auditors qualifications (optional).

Unofficial records are retained for 6 to 12 months. Unofficial audit records include the auditor's workpapers, supporting documents, and additional correspondence.

4. Communication with management. Part of the responsibility of the lead auditor is to make sure that management gets the message (the results of the audit) and incorporates these results into the corrective actions identified in the quality system. This is a prescription of the ISO 9001 clause 4.17. It is expected that improvements will occur through corrective action initiatives and that the system will become more effective.

COMMON PROBLEMS IN CONDUCTING AUDITS

Just like any other endeavor, audits are subject to mistakes, problems, and misunderstandings. Some of the most basic and avoidable problems are

- Inadequate planning and preparation for the audit. The more you plan and prepare, the better the chances for a successful audit. You can never plan or prepare enough.
- Lack of clearly defined scope and objective. You must know the boundaries and plan the objectives of what you are trying to accomplish. Take time to evaluate alternate proposals.
- Inadequate procedures. It has been reported (Irwin Professional Publishing 1993; QIM 1993) that one of the most frequent inadequacies for certification is lack of documentation. Without proper documentation, quality awareness, and the contribution of the operator, it is impossible to have a complete, accurate, and current quality system documentation.
- Lack of properly trained auditors. Without appropriate knowledge in how to perform the audit, the results of the audit may be worthless. It takes special skill and knowledge to perform an audit correctly. Investment in training is a must.
- Lack of operator involvement. Without the cooperation of all the employees in any organization, the audit will not be effective and will not fulfill the spirit of the ISO. Without their cooperation, procedures and instruction may not be current and correct.
- Lack of follow-up. Without systematic follow-up, the audit and its results will become just one more activity in the organization. Active follow-up must be cultivated and encouraged at all times. Appropriate feedback must be given and corrective actions must be communicated throughout the organization.

A GUIDE TO THE GUIDE

The person charged with the responsibility to guide the auditors in the auditee's facilities is the guide. This is a very important responsibility and the success or failure of the audit may depend on the way the guide carries out the assigned tasks. The guide must understand both the mechanical aspects and the behavioral aspects of the audit.

The Mechanical Aspects

These are the logistic considerations of the audit. The guide must be familiar with physical area where the audit will occur and should know how to get there by the shortest path.

The guide is also expected to know (1) the standard in which the company is being certified, (2) details of the organization's quality system, and (3) management policy as it relates to the quality system and operating procedures.

The Behavioral Aspects

The guide's responsibility is to accompany the auditors at all times and answer their questions when asked. If a guide does not know the answer, he or she

Should not give an opinion.

Should not admit not knowing the answer.

Should know the source where the answer may be found.

The guide is the expert in the particular area; however, one of the guide's responsibilities is to help the auditors and the organization perform a successful audit. As such, a guide should try to accommodate the auditor and help the organization at the same time. Examples of how this policy may prove beneficial follow.

• If the auditor is about to ask a specific question of an operator and the guide knows that the operator does not have the answer, the guide should advise the auditor of the fact (and in some cases offer an explanation).

• A guide is not authorized or qualified to disagree with the auditor when the auditor identifies a noncompliance. However, based on his or her knowledge of both the standard and the process, you may diplomatically question a noncompliance if the guide suspects that the auditor does not understand the specific process or that the auditor is applying the wrong standard to the particular situation. If the noncompliance is not changed the guide should report to the ISO coordinator or the department management. Under no circumstances should the guide argue with the auditor.

• The guide should not sign the noncompliance or the ACAR if he or she disagrees with the finding. The auditor is merely doing his or her job. The auditor is asking you to be a witness of the finding, not whether you agree that the finding is indeed a noncompliance.

• The guide should always answer the questions of the auditor in a matter of fact and never editorialize or give a personal view.

• The guide's cooperation with the auditor will save time and facilitate a productive audit. The organization requested the audit, and the objective is not only to be certified against a specific standard but also to improve the quality system.

• The guide's job is to help the auditor; the auditor is responsible for carrying out the audit.

• Finally, it is the auditor's job to find noncompliances; it is not the guide's job to supply them.

COMMUNICATIONS

All auditors talk, observe, and listen; in fact, one may say that the act of auditing is a matter of communication. The job of all auditors is to collect information based on objective evidence. However, the better the auditor is at communicating (both verbally and nonverbally), the more effective the audit will be. There are at least three ways auditors can communicate, and each method has its own advantages. The three ways are verbal (one or two way), nonverbal (mannerisms and body language), and observation.

1. Verbal. In a one-way communication the auditor issues notices, procedures, letters, etc. When the auditee responds to the item, then the communication becomes two way. The auditor may prefer one-way communication because it is fast and because it gives the originator a measure of protection and feeling of security, as the communicated message is not questioned. Two-way communication is slower, less orderly, and certainly noisier. In two-way communication the receivers will understand the message better and will feel more motivated to actively participate because they can check their understanding of what is required.

In the course of the audit, the auditor must always be alert to the communication rules that will make or break the audit. Some of the "always" rules are

Be cognizant of your own abilities.

Seek to be understood and to understand.

Be a good listener.

Simplify and clarify the message.

Make sure that the message has been understood.

Examine the purpose of the message.

Remember that the message may have long-term effects.

Consider the human and physical setting.

Make sure that your actions suit the message.

Ask to be sure, before communicating. (If you are not sure, ask for clarification before you proceed to the next item.)

In case some of the communication rules seem well beyond the duty of an auditor, let us examine the issue of communication. People communicate to get something done, affect somebody's attitude, and reinforce the message. To accomplish these three goals, the auditor must

- Know the audience and be sensitive to age, sex, ethnicity, etc.
- Know the specific situation and why he or she is present.
- Know the message and organize the message in a way that communicates to the entire audience. The message should be informative rather than demeaning. It should address the experience level and knowledge of the audience.

2. Nonverbal. An auditor must be cognizant of all unusual changes in mannerism and body language in the course of the audit. There is no guarantee that these changes are meaningful, but a thoughtful follow-up question may prove invaluable in uncovering problem areas.

3. Observation. Observation is the major skill in any auditor's profile, the bread and butter of the trade. It takes much discipline in listening and communicating thoughts and actions to do a good job in observation. The auditor is asked to record what he or she observes without any bias. Without good observations there cannot be a good audit.

The following table describes some common communication mistakes.

Incorrect	Correct
Assuming	Be complete and factual.
Asking any question	Ask open-ended questions with specific focus.
Acting as though you are the expert	Be flexible; be enthusiastic; reinforce appropriate behavior; clarify your role.
Using jargon	Use everyday language; paraphrase; give feedback frequently and especially when asked.
Jumping around	Be systematic and logical; be well-organized; be positive; point out possibilities.
Being very formal	Be personable and friendly; be willing to discuss issues.
Using incorrect grammar, diction, punctuation, or pronunciation	Learn to use the language effectively; make the language work for you.
Using pronouns and other words incorrectly	Learn when to use *it is* as opposed to *it's*; learn the difference between *datum* and *data*. For a thorough review of proper language, use any writer's handbook, a thesaurus, or even a dictionary.

COST OF QUALITY AND LIABILITY

Two of the most misunderstood concepts of the standards and the auditing process are cost of quality and liability. Neither of these topics are part of the certifiable standards (ISO 9001, ISO 9002, or ISO 9003). However, both are explicitly mentioned in the ISO 9004 (clauses 6 and 19, respectively).

One of the questions auditees usually ask is how the evaluation of cost and liability is going to take place. The answer, of course, is very simple. Although the certifiable standards do not provide a direct link between cost, liability, and quality, the ISO 9004 identifies such a requirement.

A good auditor can identify both these issues by going around to other clauses of the certifiable clauses for hints and directions. For example, in the case of cost of quality, an auditor may get to the same information through clauses 4.9 (process control), 4.8 (product identification and traceability), 4.13 (control of nonconforming product), and 4.14 (corrective and preventive action). In the case of liability, an auditor may get to similar or the same information through clauses 4.4 (design control), and 4.8 (product identification).

INTERNAL VERSUS EXTERNAL AUDITORS

As we mentioned earlier the internal auditor (usually not certified by an outside body) conducts the audits for his or her organization, and the results of the audit are not recognized for certification. The internal auditor more often than not is an employee of the auditee. The external auditor is usually certified by an outside body and conducts the audit as an impartial entity. The results of this kind of audit, if run under the jurisdiction of a Registrar, may be recognized for certification. An external auditor is never an employee of the auditee.

CERTIFICATION VERSUS NONCERTIFICATION OF AUDITORS

Whether you are certified in the art of auditing is an academic point. What is essential is that you demonstrate competence and specific knowledge of what you are about to audit. If you are interested in becoming a professional auditor, then the requirement of certification is mandatory. If, on the other hand, you want to be an auditor for your organization, then certification is not necessary. The ISO 9001 clause 4.17 states that internal audits must be performed; it does not specify that the auditors must be certified. The moral of this clause is that knowledge of the organization and the product line and auditing skills are indeed requirements for a good internal audit. If that is all that is expected, then certification is a moot point.

To attain certification in auditing is a personal goal and a worthy pursuit. You must attend a recognized course and complete the requisites. For a current requirement list contact the American Society for Quality Control. Nevertheless, certification is not a requirement for internal audits or for unofficial audits to your supplier base.

Many commercial programs in auditing are available. Their only requirement is that you pay the seminar fee and attend the usual two-day class recommended by the RAB or some other certifying body. (We may add that the content of the certifiable course and the noncertifiable course is practically the same. The major differences are the higher fees, the test, the limited number of locations, and the limited class size (usually a maximum of 20 students) for the certifiable course. A certifiable class will qualify you to perform official audits if you pass the exam at the end of the course—provided you also have the appropriate experience and the other requisites for the certification.

ETHICS

Ethics is the discipline that deals with what is good and what is bad, with moral duty and obligations. Additionally, ethics may be defined as those principles of conduct that govern an individual or a group.

From the audit perspective, ethics involves a built-in moral compo- nent. This component, in conjunction with the self-correcting mechanisms of the audit (the objective and systematic evidence), guards the moral integrity of the auditors. Without this moral integrity auditors can inter- pret, conduct, or declare to be true things that are not so. Moral integrity is precisely what will keep the system and the auditors honest and correct. Ethical principles of auditing practices; the activity of auditing (both the process and priority); the treatment of the auditee; and the allocation of proper, appropriate, and correct credit for discoveries are most essential in any audit. The quality audit is no exception.

Additional ethical principles, which are often unrecognized, should guide the analysis of the audit data. Let me explain. I was assigned to be the lead auditor in an ISO 9001 audit in Houston, Texas. Just after the opening meeting and before the actual audit, one of the auditors approached me and asked, "Dean, can I bother you for a moment?" I thought, of course, that the auditor had a question regarding the audit itself, the standard, or something relating to the audit. To my surprise, the auditor, with a most serious expression, asked, "I have worked with many lead auditors, and every one of them has guidelines for the first audit. What I want to know is how many noncompliances you want me to deliver for this audit?" I disqualified him on the spot.

I hope the example illustrates the subtlety of the auditor's question. He was not going to be objective in the audit. I am sure he would have delivered whatever number of noncompliances I identified. He would not have conducted an impartial audit, and his results (data driven as they may have been) would have been useless.

A few more examples of poor auditing practices may delineate the point of ethics and understanding of audits. The first example is from training—a single-group pretest-posttest design. Between the pretest and the posttest, a treatment was administered to all subjects, a treatment that was expected to increase the scores of the dependent variable. Suppose 4 of the 25 subjects obtained lower scores on the posttest than on the pretest. In other words, the treatment did not have a positive effect on all the subjects. These lower scores were removed from the data, and a correlated means t-test was calculated based upon the remaining 21 score pairs. The table probability associated with the obtained value of the t statistic was less than 0.05, and the auditor, or the trainer in this case, concluded that the treatment was effective.

The second example is from a supplier survey. The auditor or the Quality Assurance engineer analyzes the responses from a supplier survey. The analysis led to the calculation of over 100 chi-square tests of independence. Of these, 20 were statistically significant at $p < 0.05$. In the report of the analysis, the auditor reported only the significant tests, making no mention of the more than 80 chi-square tests that did not yield significant values of the statistic.

Few auditors would fail to recognize the poor practices illustrated in these examples. However, it is very important to add that in neither example was the auditor intentionally deceptive. Furthermore, either auditor would be both surprised and righteously offended at insinuations of fraudulent practices. With these examples, we have tried to illustrate the lack of consideration of ethical principles in the analysis of the data and the subtle nature of our tendency as auditors to deceive ourselves about the objective evidence. Always remember that figures do not lie; liars figure.

In the course of an audit—especially one that runs five or more days—there is abundant opportunity to test the ethics of even the best auditors. There are always minor shadings, manipulations, and distortions as well as fraudulent practices. However, auditors must protect the auditee whenever the evidence is not sufficient or questionable—to the point of always giving them the benefit of the doubt and always trying to be consistent, fair, and objective in evaluations. The excuse that everybody distorts things just a little bit and everybody knows it is totally unacceptable. We must do everything in our power to have appropriately trained auditors who know the standards, their intent, the methodology of the audit, and the wisdom to seek both advice and criticism about the audits they perform.

One of the author's area of ethical concerns is the evaluation of data, especially in the chemical or pharmaceutical industries or other industries that deal in batches. The issue of batch process is quite common, so from an auditor's point of view the questions are when, how, where, and what to sample. As it turns out, the answers to these very simple questions can be very troublesome for both the auditor and the auditee if they are not familiar with random and representative samples.

Tukey (1980) suggested four general processes in which the researcher (auditor) influences the data.

- The generation of appropriate questions. This is where a good checklist may prove worthwhile.
- The process of research (audit) design. This is where the planning of the audit will prove priceless.
- The monitoring of data collection. This is where the data has to be challenged as to its appropriateness and applicability.
- The process of data analysis. This is where, from the author's experience, most of the inconsistencies and erroneous results happen. In fact, since this area is of profound interest to both the auditor and the auditee, let us examine it further.

The American Statistical Association (ASA) developed ethical guidelines for statistical practice (Ad Hoc Committee on Professional Ethics, 1983). Five elements of these guidelines are directly pertinent to the ethics of data analysis. First, the results and findings should be presented honestly and openly. Surprises and contradictory findings must be avoided. Second, deceptive or untrue statements in the reports should be avoided. Third, the boundaries of inference should always be clear. Fourth, clear and complete documentation of data editing, statistical procedures, and assumptions must be provided. Fifth, all statistical procedures should be applied without concern for a favorable outcome.

Against the backdrop of the ethical guidelines suggested by the ASA, seven categories of questionable practices are described below. These should not be interpreted as a complete list of ethical problems, but rather as a sample of commonly encountered practices.

1. Selectivity of data (cooking the data) or altering or discarding data that appears to be anomalous. The idea comes from Dunnette (1966) who proposes that auditors tend to support their hypotheses. Very famous cases of cooking the data have been reported by Birch (1990), Westfall (1973), McNemar (1960) and others.

2. Use of data-driven hypotheses. This is when an auditor may look at patterns in the data and then decide what hypotheses to test.

3. Use of postmortem analyses. This technique of data analysis guarantees specific findings based on subset analysis in the quest for significance. This can be interpreted as nit-picking or the auditor is after you.

4. Probability pyramiding and selective reporting. This technique guarantees results by analyzing the data with every analysis known. Sooner or later one will identify significance. Diaconis (1985) and Nehrer (1967) have reported this problem of multiplicity.

5. Type I and Type II calculations bias. Friedlander (1964) pointed out this subtle bias resulting from the interaction between calculation errors and hypotheses. Specifically, our commitment to our results leads us to recheck our calculations and/or observations only in some circumstances and to avoid such rechecking in others. When the original calculations of statistics do not support our hypotheses, we will recheck the computations. However, when the initial analysis of the data supports our hypotheses, we fail to see the need for such a check and potential errors are undetected.

6. Confusion of probability level and the strength of relationships. Here the results will be interpreted the same way for both the small and large samples whether there is a relationship or not. Examples are given by Dunnette (1966), Thompson (1988), and McNemar (1960).

7. Confusion between exploratory and confirmatory approaches to analysis. Tukey (1980) and Brush (1974) have addressed this issue quite extensively. In summary, this issue has to do with the formation of the hypothesis in the exploratory study or analysis. However, regardless of what the study or analysis show, the hypothesis must be subjected to independent, confirmatory inquiry.

One may wonder at this point why an auditor would have a bias, and if the bias exists, where did it come from? This is a fair question, but not so easy to answer. As auditors we take pride in what we do—no question about it. We are professionals, and we are eager to do the best possible job. However, in the process of doing our best, we become like tunnel-visioned parents who can see no fault with their offspring. We convince ourselves that the empirical data would speak in favor of our theories if only we could analyze them properly or longer. From this perspective, our audit efforts become directed toward supporting our theories rather than testing them. (A good example of this is when auditors audit their pet areas, say document control or design or procurement, with extra interest. Their excuse may be that these areas are more demanding or complicated or more time consuming, but they like to spend time auditing the favored area.)

Another area of creeping bias is the pressure—whether real or imaginary—to find noncompliances. Publications and consultants alike announce the likelihood of trouble spots of the audit on the first, second, or whatever try, and in addition, they point out alleged trouble-spot areas. As a consequence, auditors feel that if they pass the auditee on the first try, something went wrong, that they did not do their job. In addition, if they did not find anything wrong in the highlighted areas of possible errors or noncompliances, their professionalism is challenged.

This undue emphasis on statistical performance for the organization, the auditor, and the Registrar begins with the introductory training in the ISO standards. Even though the training and statistics are supposed to guide and direct, they take on an aura of their own and in the end work against both the auditor and the auditee.

A third possibility of ethical problems is the way the auditor defines success of audit activities. Some auditors want to be known as hard, or difficult, or easy, or likable, and they stop at nothing to convince everyone of their perception. They interpret hard or difficult as fair and unbiased. How unfortunate. These auditors have missed the essence of the ISO, which focuses on substantiating the system and also on the corrective action and continual improvement of the organization. Audits should follow the rules of randomness, consistency, and fairness and not be concerned with the popularity of the auditor.

RECOMMENDATIONS FOR IMPROVING ETHICAL PRACTICES

As we already have mentioned, auditors are professional individuals who are asked to evaluate objective evidence and offer a decision based on their findings. In the process of evaluation, the results are sometimes clouded for both individuals and organizations to the point where hard feelings and conflicts occur.

To avoid hard feelings and conflicts, we recommend the following strategy:

- Focus on honesty throughout the audit.
- Develop an awareness of the subtlety of ethical issues in data analysis.
- Train auditors to audit not to nit-pick or spy.
- Develop checklists to guide you during the audit, but do not use checklists as tools to dwarf initiative, inquisitiveness, and creativity.
- Develop openness during the audit and evaluation of results.
- Avoid any situation in which the auditor was previously employed by the auditee, regardless of the reason for separation.

- Avoid any situation in which the auditor was previously employed by the auditee's competitor, regardless of the reason for separation.
- Avoid any situation in which the auditor has holdings of stocks or bonds in the auditee's business or that of a competitor of the auditee.
- Avoid any situation in which the auditor was associated with the development of the quality system under evaluation to meet a particular quality standard.

Auditors following guidelines such as the above will enter the audit arena with a strong commitment to fairness, an aversion to bias, and a high level of personal satisfaction. They indeed will do the best to evaluate the auditee.

THE ROLE OF THE CONSULTANT IN THE DOCUMENTATION AND PREASSESSMENT STAGES

The field of quality is becoming very complicated and at the same time very demanding. There are questions regarding the hiring of consultants. However, two questions are essential:

- Do we really need a consultant? Before answering this question, let me remind the reader of the story about Lewis and Clark. Lewis and Clark were considered to be the best surveyors in the land. They certainly knew how to paddle and which way was west. That, however, did not stop them from hiring Sacagawea, a Native American guide familiar with the territory and the dangers that lurked there.

Having giving you a clue to my answer to this question, I must admit that strictly speaking, you do not need a consultant. Your organization can do it all. However, if you do it alone, it is guaranteed that you will repeat mistakes and that you will try things based on intuition and hearsay. Eventually you may succeed. On the other hand, if your organization wants to expand, become more efficient, and save a tremendous amount of resources as part of the implementation and auditing process, then a consultant is the answer. A good consultant can be a coach, a changing agent, and a leader.

- How much is it going to cost? Just like anything else, the cost depends on how you negotiate and what services the consultant renders. Before your organization decides to hire a consultant, do the following:

1. Shop around. Find out what is available and ask questions. Ask for references. Find out about specific experiences and how the consultants will be able to help you.

2. Be careful of promises and quick solutions offered by many consultants. Remember, the ISO/QS total implementation takes time. It is not an overnight success. Be realistic of what you are asking the consultant to do.

3. Be choosy. When your organization is ready to make the decision, pick what is the best for your organization. The best can be defined as being comfortable with the relationship you are about to embark on. Money is not always the best criterion for evaluation. Availability, experience, ability to get along with different people, good communication skills, and above all, a track record are all important and worth considering as part of your selection process.

So, how much is it going to cost? No single algorithm governs the way companies choose consultants. The best we can offer is to recognize that cost, effort, and time are interrelated. They all depend on what, where, how, and why the organizations buy. Remember, however, that quality can and in fact is being bought on a daily basis, from boutiques as well as department stores, and the customer is just as satisfied with the boutique purchase as with that from the department store.

SUMMARY

In this chapter we have addressed the issues of auditing, including the topics of who is involved, the auditing process, common problems, ethics, recommendations for improving ethical practices, and the role of the consultant. In the next chapter we will address the issues of the QS-9000 standard as they relate to documentation and auditing.

REFERENCES

Ad Hoc Committee on Professional Ethics. (1983). "Ethical Guidelines for Statistical Practice: Report of the Ad Hoc Committee on Professional Ethics." *American Statistician*. 37, pp. 5–8.

American Society for Quality Control (1993). *Certification Program for Auditors of Quality Systems*. Milwaukee, WI: ASQC.

ANSI/ISO/ASQC A8402 (1994). *Quality Vocabulary*. Milwaukee, WI: ASQC.

Arter, D. R. (1994). *Quality Audits for Improved Performance*. 2nd ed. Milwaukee, WI: Quality Press.

Irwin Professional Publishing. (June 1993). "ISO 9000 Survey." *Quality Systems Update*. Burr Ridge, IL: Irwin Professional Publishing.

Birch, A. J. (1990). "Deceit in Science: Does It Really Matter?" *Interdisciplinary Science Reviews* 15, pp. 335–343.

Brush, S. G. (1974). "Should the History of Science Be Rated X?" *Science* 183, pp. 1164–1172.

Diaconis, P. (1985). "Theories of Data Analysis: From Magical Thinking through Classical Statistics." In *Exploring Data Tables, Trends and Shapes*. eds. D. C. Hoaglin; F. Mosteller; and J. W. Tukey. New York: Wiley

Duhan, S. (1979). "An Audit Is More Than an Audit." *ASQC Technical Conference Transactions*.

Dunnette, M. D. (1966). "Fads, Fashions and Folderol in Psychology." *American Psychologist* 21, pp. 343–352.

Emmons, S. (1977). "Auditing for Profit and Productivity." *ASQC Technical Conference Transactions* pp. 94–108.

Friedlander, F. (1964). "Type I and Type II Bias." *American Psychologist* 19, pp. 198–199.

Hutchins, G. (1992). *Standard Manual of Quality Auditing: A Step by Step Workbook with Procedures and Checklists*. Milwaukee, WI: Quality Press.

Keeney, K. A. (1995). *The ISO 9000 Auditor's Companion*. Milwaukee, WI: Quality Press.

Keeney, K. A. (1995a). *The Audit Kit*. Milwaukee, WI: Quality Press.

McNemar, Q. (1960). "At Random: Sense and Nonsense." *American Psychologist* 15, pp. 295–300.

Mills, C. A. (1989). *The Quality Audit*. Milwaukee, WI: Quality Press.

Nehrer, A. (1967). "Probability Pyramiding, Research Error and the Need for Independent Replication." *Psychological Record* 17, pp. 257–262.

Parsowith, B. S. (1995). *Fundamentals of Quality Auditing*. Milwaukee, WI: Quality Press.

QIM. (November/December 1993). "ISO Companies Reap Big Benefits." *Quality in Manufacturing* pp. 3–4.

Robinson, C. B. (1992). *How to Make the Most of Every Audit: An Etiquette Handbook for Auditing*. Milwaukee, WI: Quality Press.

Sayle, A. J. (1988). *Management Audits*. Milwaukee, WI: Quality Press.

Thompson, B. (1988). "A Note about Significance Testing." *Measurement and Evaluation in Counseling and Development* 20, pp. 146–148.

Tukey, J. W. (1980). "We Need both Exploratory and Confirmatory Data." *American Statistician* 34, pp. 23–25.

Westfall, R. S. (1973). "Newton and the Fudge Factor." *Science* 179, pp. 751–758.

CHAPTER 6

QS-9000
Quality Requirement

As we already have mentioned, effective September 1994 U.S. automotive companies—Chrysler, Ford, General Motors, and some truck manufacturers—introduced a quality system to harmonize their own individual quality standards. In this chapter we address the implications of this QS-9000 requirement in regard to documentation and audits. This chapter identifies only the additional issues and concerns that the QS-9000 brings to the new quality system. For more information on the QS-9000, see AIAG (1995) and Stamatis (1995).

APPLICATION OF THE QS-9000

Perhaps the most important contribution of the QS-9000 to the automotive industry is the use of the word *effective*. Effective implies that the system must exist in practice, not just on paper, and that its positive effects may be seen throughout the suppliers' records, customer feedback, and employee interviews. This is indeed a revolutionary approach to quality.

The reader may wonder why we use such strong language to describe another quality system. That is just it: This is not "just another quality system." We believe that the days of convenience, of unqualified personnel for audits, of biased criteria, and of issuing awards based on political resolution are gone. They are gone because now two very important characteristics prevent such events.

The first characteristic is that all requirements of the QS-9000 must be incorporated in the quality manual. (Of course, nonapplicable clauses must be stated as such.) The quality manual is now a requirement for a quality system.

The second characteristic is that a third party will judge the effectiveness of the system except in some special situations when a second party may perform the evaluation.

DOCUMENTATION

For all intents and purposes, the documentation process and generation of the quality manual, procedures, and job instructions are the same as those for the regular ISO 9001 standard and were discussed in Chapters 3 and 4. The difference is the addition of new requirements. In this section we will identify these extra requirements. These new requirements must—if applicable—be identified in the quality manual and certainly be collaborated in both procedures and job instructions. The mechanics for incorporating them in the quality manual, procedures, and job instructions are the same as those discussed in Chapter 4. A full-length example of a quality manual based on the QS-9000 requirements is found in Appendix C.

Additional ISO 9001 Requirements

Management Representative (4.1.2.3)

This clause requires that organizational interfaces must be in place to ensure management of appropriate activities during concept development, prototype, and production. In essence the documentation must demonstrate existence of a functional interface throughout the organization. The reader is referred to the *Advanced Product Quality Planning and Control Plan: Reference Manual* (1995).

Business Plan (4.1.4)

Although this item is not subject to a third-party audit, the requirement is that the supplier must utilize a formal documented and comprehensive business plan.

Analysis and Use of Data (4.1.5)

The supplier must document trends in quality, operational performance, and current quality levels for key products and service features.

Customer Satisfaction (4.1.6)

The supplier must have a documented process for identifying customer satisfaction.

Quality Planning (4.2.3)

As part of the documentation process for quality planning, the supplier must utilize the *Advanced Product Quality Planning and Control Plan: Reference Manual* (1995). In addition, the supplier must identify the special characteristics and must note them during the preparation of FMEAs and control plans. For more information on FMEA, see Stamatis (1995a) and *Potential Failure Mode and Effect Analysis: Reference Manual* (1995). In implementing quality planning, it is imperative to establish cross-functional teams and to follow the rules of *Advanced Product Quality Planning and Control Plan: Reference Manual* in addressing concerns and issues applicable to production for new or changed products. Furthermore, cross-functional teams may be used for feasibility reviews, process FMEA, and control plans.

Design and Development Planning (4.4.2)

This clause is only for those suppliers who deal with design and development work. If the supplier is not involved with design, then this clause has no effect on the documentation and the audit. The supplier in this case will be certified to QS-9000 standard with the ISO 9002 designation. The clause defines specific requirements of varying difficulty that the supplier must fulfill. Examples are geometric dimensioning and tolerancing, quality function deployment, failure mode and effect analysis, and finite element analysis.

Design Input (4.4.4)

The supplier must have appropriate resources and facilities to utilize computer-aided product design, engineering, and analysis.

Design Output (4.4.5)

The supplier must demonstrate that the design is the result of a process that utilizes appropriate quality planning tools such as those stated in clause 4.4.2.

Design Verification (4.4.7)

The supplier must have a comprehensive prototype program unless waived by the customer or the item is a standard item. The comprehensiveness will be evaluated through product life, reliability, and durability for a timely completion and conformance to requirements. Furthermore, this clause states that the supplier is expected to show leadership.

Design Changes (4.4.9)
All design changes must be approved, and they must follow the *Production Part Approval Process* (1995).

General Document and Data Control (4.5.1)
Reference documents and appropriate special characteristics must be available at all relevant manufacturing locations.

Document and Data Approval and Issue (4.5.2)
The supplier shall establish a procedure to assure the timely review, distribution, and implementation of all customer-engineering specifications and changes.

General Purchasing (4.6.1)
If the customer has an approved subcontractor list , the supplier shall purchase the relevant materials from subcontractors on the list. In any case, all materials used in part manufacturing must satisfy current governmental and safety, toxic, hazardous materials, and environmental considerations.

Evaluations of Subcontractors (4.6.2)
Suppliers must conduct quality system development for their subcontractors using specific guidelines identified in sections I and II of the QS-9000. Furthermore, suppliers shall require 100 percent on-time delivery performance from subcontractors.

Purchasing Data (4.6.3)
Suppliers must assure compliance with all restricted processes relative to the purchase of products and manufacturing.

Process Control (4.9)
(By far the most demanding clause.) The clause demands that the supplier have a process to ensure compliance with all applicable regulations, comply with customer requirements for designation and control of special

characteristics, and identify key process equipment with a total preventive maintenance system. The system must include (1) a procedure that describes planned maintenance activities, (2) predictive maintenance methods, and (3) scheduled maintenance activities.

Process Monitoring and Operator Instructions (4.9.1)

The supplier must prepare documented process monitoring and operator instructions for all appropriate personnel with responsibilities for the operation of processes. The instructions must follow the guidelines of the *Advanced Product Quality Planning and Control Plan: Reference Manual* (1994).

Preliminary Process Capability Requirements (4.9.2)

Preliminary process capability is required for each supplier- or customer-designated special characteristic for new processes. A reference for following the capability is the *Production Part Approval Process* (1993) and an additional reference for explaining the calculations and rationale of the Ppk is the *SPC: Reference Manual* (1995).

Ongoing Process Performance Requirements (4.9.3)

Ongoing capability is a requirement for characteristics that have been identified in the control plan or when the customer requires it. Furthermore, regardless of the capability requirement or the demonstrated process capability, continuous improvement is required, with the highest priority on special characteristics.

Modified Preliminary or Ongoing Capability Requirements (4.9.4)

If changes are occurring because of customer requests, the appropriate notification must be entered in the control plan.

Verification of Job Setups (4.9.5)

Job setups must have documented instructions and must be available for setup personnel.

Process Changes (4.9.6)

Changes in the production part approval require prior approval. For more information see *Production Part Approval Process* (1995).

Appearance Items (4.9.7)

The supplier is required to provide proof that appearance standards are followed. The standard itself provides four such standards: appropriate lighting, masters for color, maintenance of appearance masters and evaluation equipment, and verification of personnel qualifications.

Inspection and Testing (4.10)

All acceptance criteria will be documented. In addition, the supplier may use accredited laboratory facilities when required.

Receiving Inspection and Testing (4.10.2)

The supplier is given a choice of five items that may be used to control the incoming quality.

Final Inspection and Testing (4.10.4)

A layout inspection and a functional verification are required for all products at a frequency established by the customer.

Inspection, Measuring, and Test Equipment Records (4.11.3)

Records of the calibration and verification activity on all gauges, measuring, and test equipment, including employee-owned gauges, must be kept.

Measurement System Analysis (4.11.4)

Evidence is required that appropriate statistical studies have been conducted to analyze the variation present in the results of each type of measuring and test equipment system. The methods used for such analysis must conform to the *Measurement System Analysis: Reference Manual* (1995).

Inspection and Test Status (4.12)

This clause emphasizes that the location of product in the normal production flow does not constitute suitable indication of inspection and test status unless inherently obvious. Furthermore, the customer may require additional verification or identification.

Control of Nonconforming Product (4.13.1)

Control applies to both suspect and nonconforming product.

Engineering Approved Product Authorization (4.13.4)

Prior written customer authorization is required whenever the product or process is different from that currently approved. *Production Part Approval Process* (1995) may be of help in this area.

General Corrective and Preventive Action (4.14.1)

A supplier must use disciplined problem-solving methods when an internal or external nonconformance to specification or requirement occurs.

Corrective Action (4.14.2)

A supplier must analyze parts returned from the customer, keep appropriate records, and make the records available upon request.

Storage (4.15.3)

The supplier must establish an inventory system and document that system with the intent to continually optimize inventory turnover time.

Packaging (4.15.4)

Customer requirements must be followed for packaging. On the other hand, the supplier must develop a system to label all materials according to customer requirements.

Delivery (4.15.6)

The supplier must establish the following:

- A goal of 100 percent on-time shipments.
- A schedule that is order driven.
- A computerized system for on-line transmittal of advance-shipment notifications, transmitted at the time of shipment unless waived by the customer.

Control of Quality Records (4.16)

Records dealing with approvals, tooling, and purchase orders are to be maintained for the length of time that the part is active plus one calendar year unless otherwise specified by the customer or governmental requirements. Performance records shall be retained for one calendar year unless otherwise specified by the customer. Records of internal quality system audits and management reviews must be retained for three years unless otherwise specified by the customer. Superseded parts required for new part qualification must be retained in the new file. In addition, a suitable working environment must be considered as part of the internal audit process.

Training (4.18)
Training should be viewed as a strategic issue. Therefore, its effectiveness must be evaluated periodically.

Servicing (4.19)
A procedure for communication of information on service concerns must be established and maintained.

Procedures for Statistical Techniques (4.20.2)
The selection of appropriate statistical tools for each process should be determined during advanced quality planning and included in the control plan. Basic concepts of variation, control, capability, and adjustment should be understood throughout the supplier's organization. If there is a need, consult the *SPC: Reference Manual* (1995).

Sector-Specific Requirements

Production Part Approval Process

General (1.1.)   Suppliers must comply with all requirements identified in the *Production Part Approval Process* (1995).

Engineering Change Validation (1.2)   Suppliers must verify that changes are properly validated.

Continuous Improvement

General (2.1)   Suppliers must continually improve their quality, service, and price for all customers. Towards that end, they must develop specific action plans that are important to the customer, and demonstrate stability, acceptable capability, and improvement.

Quality and Productivity Improvements (2.2)   Suppliers must identify opportunities for quality and productivity and implement appropriate improvement projects.

Techniques for Continuous Improvement (2.3)   Suppliers must demonstrate knowledge of the following measures and methodologies and use them appropriately.

- Capability indexes
- Control charts
- Cumulative-sum charting
- Design of experiments
- Theory of constraints
- Evolutionary operation of processes
- Cost of Quality
- Value analysis
- Overall equipment effectiveness
- Problem solving
- Benchmarking
- Parts-per-million analysis

Manufacturing Capabilities

Facilities, equipment, and process planning and effectiveness (3.1)   Suppliers must use cross-functional teams in conjunction with advanced quality planning processes. Methods must be developed for evaluating the effectiveness of the capability.

Mistake Proofing (3.2)   Suppliers must perform mistake proofing analysis in conjunction with FMEAs, capability studies, and service reports.

Tool Design and Fabrication (3.3)   Suppliers must provide technical resources for tool and gauge design, fabrication, and full-dimensional inspection. Customer-owned tools and equipment must be permanently marked.

Tooling Management (3.4)   Suppliers must establish and implement a system for tooling management. The system should include

- Maintenance and repair facilities and personnel.
- Storage and recovery.
- Setup.
- Tool change.

If the work is subcontracted, a tracking system is required.

Customer-Specific Requirements

Chrysler's special requirements deal with

- Parts identified with symbols (i.e., shield, diamond, and pentagon).
- Significant characteristics.
- Annual layout.
- Internal quality audits.
- Design validation/production verification.
- Corrective action plan.
- Packaging, shipping, and labeling.
- Process sign-off.
- Bibliography.

Ford's special requirements deal with

- Control item parts.
  - Control plans and FMEAs.
  - Shipping container labels.
  - Equipment standard parts.
  - Critical characteristics.
  - Setup verification.
- Control item fasteners.
  - Material analysis—heat-treated parts.
  - Material analysis—non-heat-treated parts.
  - Lot traceability.
- Heat treating.
- Process and design changes for supplier responsible designs.
- Engineering specification-test performance requirements.
- Ongoing part quality initiatives.
- Qualification and acceptance criteria for materials.
- Supplier modification of control item requirements.
- System design specification.
- Quality operating system.
- Bibliography.

General Motors's special requirements are not obvious. They are embedded in the supplied bibliography of 18 documents. The reader is encouraged to request additional information at (800) 421-7676 or (810) 758-5400.

Truck Manufacturers' Specific Requirements

The following truck manufacturers have participated in the development of the *Quality System Requirements QS-9000* (1995) and have adopted it for basic quality system requirements.

Mack Trucks, Inc.

Navistar International Transportation Corporation.

PACCAR, Inc.

Volvo GM Heavy Truck Corporation.

The reader is encouraged to seek additional specific requirements in the relevant publications.

OVERVIEW OF THE QS-9000 EVALUATION PROCESS

Conformance is established either through a second-party assessment (customer) or through a third-party assessment (quality systems Registrar). In addition, conformance to the ISO 9001 or ISO 9002 is necessary but not sufficient for the QS-9000 certification because the ISO 9001 has 134 requirements stated as "shall," whereas the QS-9000 has 244 requirements stated as "shall."

Just as in the regular certification process for the ISO, in the case of the QS-9000, only Registrars approved by the Automotive Task Force guidelines are acceptable. As of this writing, the following accreditation bodies have been approved: the RvA, UKAS, RAB, JAS-ANZ, SWEDAC, TGA, SAS, ENAC, SCC, and FINAS. As for Registrars, as of this writing the following have been approved: ABS, BSI, DNV, Entela, RPMG, CRQA, and NSF. For the latest listings of both accreditation bodies and Registrars, the reader is strongly encouraged to call ASQC or to consult the latest copy of the sanctioned QS-9000 interpretation (1995).

A third-party audit proceeds exactly as described in Chapters 1 and 5.

A second-party audit, on the other hand, may proceed as follows.

- The customer may request the following items:
  - Quality manual.
  - Procedures.
  - Self-assessment using the *Quality System Assessment.*
  - Internal audit results.
  - Plan for securing the third-party certification.
- Upon receipt of the requested items, the customer will prioritize the on-site audit generally using the following criteria:
  - Is the quality of the product satisfactory?
  - Is the scope of the QS-9000 registration appropriate?
  - Has the supplier received registration from an approved registrar?
  - Does the quality manual comply with the QS-9000?
  - Does the QSA provide a credible evaluation of the supplier's quality system?

It is very important to realize that suppliers whose product and service quality meet customer requirements and who have third-party QS-9000 registration will not receive redundant audits. On the other hand, suppliers whose product or service quality fails to meet the customer's continuous improvement objectives will be given a high priority for an on-site visit for either problem solving or an audit.

THE QUALITY SYSTEM ASSESSMENT (QSA)

Whereas the *Quality System Requirements: QS-9000* is the tool used to communicate expectations, the QSA is a tool used to document and determine conformance to the QS-9000. In fact, one may even describe the QSA as the official checklist for the QS-9000 standard. Its fundamental importance is that the QSA promotes consistency between activities and personnel and facilitates the evaluation for the QS-9000 conformance during the assessment and audit.

An assessment is a systematic investigation of the documented quality system and the implementation of the quality system to determine its effectiveness. That effectiveness is measured during three events. The first is the documentation review, the second is the on-site audit, and the third is the analysis and report. During the documentation review, a comparison of the documentation to the QS-9000 requirements takes place. During the on-site audit, a comparison of the quality documentation to the implementation of the quality system takes place. During the analysis and report a review of the findings takes place. In the first case we look for adequacy, in the second we look for effectiveness, and in the third we determine conformance to the QS-9000.

To appreciate the QSA, one must understand the meaning of the terms *quality system* and *effectiveness*. A simple, yet powerful, definition for a quality system is the totality of the organizational structure, responsibilities, procedures, processes, and resources working together to implement quality management. Effectiveness, on the other hand, focuses on the desired result and whether the result can be measured. Sometimes, effectiveness even stresses the actual production of or the power to produce the desired result.

The application of the QSA is quite versatile. It can be used as

- A self-assessment (first party) tool.
- An instrument to assess a supplier's operations (second party).
- An instrument by a quality systems Registrar (third party).
- An instrument of supplier qualification.

The instrument itself is made up of 168 key questions based on each of the clauses of the standard, and it serves as the official checklist. These 168 questions contain 109 subquestions focusing on very specific items within the clauses. Please notice that there is not a 1:1 relationship between the QS-9000 and the QSA. The supplier is responsible for the implementation of all applicable requirements in QS-9000 and all specified requirements in their quality documentation.

THE AUDIT

Although the procedure and the process for the physical audit for the QS-9000 is essentially the same as that of the ISO discussed in Chapter 5, there are some very distinct differences. The differences have to do with definitions and the actual evaluation process.

Definitions

The following definitions are based on the QSA document page 2.

Adequacy. The supplier's documentation meets or exceeds the QS-9000 intent given the scope of the supplier's operation.

Conforms. No major or minor nonconformities found in the audit.

Inadequacy. The supplier's documentation does not meet the QS-9000 intent given the scope of the supplier's operation.

Minor nonconformance. A noncompliance with the QS-9000 that judgment and experience indicate is not likely to result in the failure of the quality system or reduce its ability to assure controlled processes or products. Furthermore, it may be either a failure in some part of the supplier's documentation relative to QS or a singled observed lapse in following one item of a company's quality system.

Major nonconformance. The absence or total breakdown of a system to meet a requirement of the QS (several minor nonconformities against one requirement can represent a total breakdown); any noncompliance that would result in the probable shipment of nonconforming product (a condition that may result in the failure or materially reduce the usability of the products or services for their intended purpose); or a noncompliance that judgment and experience indicate is likely either to result in the failure of the quality system or to materially reduce its ability to assure controlled processes and products.

Evaluation

The QSA provides a very different evaluation from that of the ISO. Where the ISO is based on a simple pass/fail system, the QSA provides for pass/ fail and a variable score method. The customer decides which method to use. The explanation of the evaluation is given in a very detailed manner on pages 3 and 4 of the QSA document. Here we summarize the process.

- The pass/fail method. An overall "pass" is given when no major or minor nonconformities are found during the audit. An overall "fail" is given when more than one major nonconformity is found during the audit. An "open" status is given when major and minor nonconformities exist. If they are fixed during 90 days or some other agreed-upon time, the status converts to pass. This situation may require an on-site visit.

- Variable score method. The variable method is based on a zero- to three-point rating for each element based on the following method.

O   Requirement is not met at all or there are major inconsistencies.

M   Requirement is met, but there are minor inconsistencies.

C   Requirement is met and implemented effectively.

Cl   Requirement is met, effectively implemented, and improvement is recorded for the last 12 months.

Scoring

0   One or more questions with a result of O, or more questions with result of M.

1   One to three questions with a result of M.

2   No O or M results.

3   No O or M results and one or more Cl.

The final score is calculated by dividing the total-clause score by the number of clauses answered and multiplying the result by 50. To pass the QSA, a minimum score of two is required on every applicable clause

A final note: The auditor and the lead auditor should be very familiar with both the ISO 9001 standard and the references that the QS-9000 identifies, especially in the customer requirements bibliography. Unless the auditor and lead auditor are familiar with these documents, the audit will not meet the intent of the standard and it will be just another quality system.

SUMMARY

In this chapter we have addressed the additional QS-9000 requirements for certification from both a documentation and auditing perspective. Attention was given to the overall application of the QS-9000, the QSA document, the specific additional requirements of each of the three sections, and the auditing process.

In the following eight appendixes, the reader will find a comparison of documentation requirements, two complete quality manuals, procedures and instructions, guidelines for generating checklists, examples of checklists, miscellaneous information, and a typical curriculum for an auditor and lead auditor.

REFERENCES

All the AIAG references are official distributors of the Chrysler, Ford, GM Task Force.

Chrysler, Ford, GM International Automotive Sector Group (IASG). (November 9, 1995). *Sanctioned QS-9000 Interpretations*. ASQC. Milwaukee, WI. (1994). *Quality System Assessment* (QSA). Chrysler, Ford, GM through AIAG. Southfield, MI.

Chrysler, Ford, GM International Automotive Sector Group (IASG). (November 9, 1995). *Sanctioned QS-9000 Interpretations*. ASQC. Milwaukee, WI. (1995) *Quality System Requirements: QS-9000*. Chrysler, Ford, GM through AIAG. Southfield, MI.

Chrysler, Ford, GM International Automotive Sector Group (IASG). (November 9, 1995). *Sanctioned QS-9000 Interpretations*. ASQC. Milwaukee, WI. (1994). *Advanced Product Quality Planning and Control Plan: Reference Manual*. Chrysler, Ford, GM through AIAG. Southfield, MI.

Chrysler, Ford, GM International Automotive Sector Group (IASG). (November 9, 1995). *Sanctioned QS-9000 Interpretations*. ASQC. Milwaukee, WI. (1993). *Potential Failure Mode and Effects Analysis: Reference Manual*. Chrysler, Ford, GM through AIAG. Southfield, MI.

Chrysler, Ford, GM International Automotive Sector Group (IASG). (November 9, 1995). *Sanctioned QS-9000 Interpretations*. ASQC. Milwaukee, WI. (1993). *Production Part Approval Process*. Chrysler, Ford, GM through AIAG. Southfield, MI.

Chrysler, Ford, GM International Automotive Sector Group (IASG). (November 9, 1995). *Sanctioned QS-9000 Interpretations*. ASQC. Milwaukee, WI. (1992). *Measurement System Analysis: Reference Manual*. Chrysler, Ford, GM through AIAG. Southfield, MI.

Chrysler, Ford, GM International Automotive Sector Group (IASG). (November 9, 1995). *Sanctioned QS-9000 Interpretations*. ASQC. Milwaukee, WI. (1991). *Fundamental SPC: Reference Manual*. Chrysler, Ford, GM through AIAG. Southfield, MI.

Stamatis, D. H. (1995). *Integrating QS-9000 with Your Automotive Quality System*. Milwaukee, WI: Quality Press.

Stamatis , D. H. (1995a). *Failure Mode and Effect Analysis: FMEA from Theory to Execution*. Milwaukee, WI: Quality Press.

Documentation

The intent of part 1 of this appendix is to help the reader organize the documentation needed for the ISO certification. The matrix that follows is generic. However, it does provide basic cross-references to the relevant ISO 9001 and ISO 9004 clauses. In addition, it provides some guidelines that constitute minimum requirements for the documentation (procedures), as well as for the controlled documentation (records), for each element. Obviously, specific organizations may need additional requirements or may not need every requirement identified here. Appendix D contains the required records and procedures, as well as several specific examples.

Part 2 of this appendix provides the reader with an extensive list of appropriate tools to substantiate the documentation and summarizes each tool's purpose.

Part 3 contains a very generic internal preassessment audit questionnaire to help uncover deficiencies before the Registrar conducts an audit. This survey must be looked upon as a guideline only and not as the official checklist for an audit.

PART 1   DOCUMENTATION MATRIX

ISO 9001 Clauses (The Most Comprehensive)	ISO 9004 Clauses (Advisory Quality System)	Standard Documentation (Procedures)	Control Documentation (Records)
4.1 Management Responsibility	4.0 Management Responsibility	• Policy and objectives statements • Organization charts • Role and responsibility statements • Job descriptions • Training plans and descriptions	• Training records • All changes

4.2 Quality System	4.4 Quality System through 5.3.4 Quality Records	• Quality manual • Quality plans • Quality records • Clarification of all standards of acceptability	Note: Clause 4.2 documentation requirement
4.3 Contract Review	N/A	• Contract review procedures	• Sign-off sheets for each stage of the contract cycle: quote, proposal, contract, sales order, work order, purchase order
4.4 Design Control	8.0 Quality in Specification and Design	Project life cycle procedures: • Standard steps in design or development projects • Role and responsibility assignments • Deliverables: specifications, designs, etc. • Verification • Change control	• Project plan: task list, budget, schedule, task descriptions responsibilities • Project documents: requirements, design specifica-tions, test plans • Design and order review results and follow-up records • Test results • Discrepancy descriptions and log • Change requests • Documentation of follow-up on changes, issues, and discrepancies
4.5 Document and Data Control	17.0 Quality Records	• Procedure on how to create, approve, distrib-ute, change, and eliminate docu-mentation	• Master list of documents and their current location, version, and approval level • Document change logs • Approval

4.6 Purchasing	9.0 Quality Purchasing	Purchasing procedures: • Selection of subcontractors • Acquisition • Verification of product • Handling noncompliance • Review of purchasing products • Accounts payable	• Requests for proposal/bids • Vendor evaluation reports • Approved vendor list(s) • Purchase contracts • Purchase orders • Specification • Documentation of test/inspection results • Documentation of returns or corrections of discrepancies
4.7 Control of Customer-Supplied Product	N/A	• Procedure for receipt, verification, storage, maintenance, use, return, and accounting for product, supplies, or equipment received from the client	• Contract • Specifications • Documentation of test/inspection results • Documentation of returns or corrections of discrepancies • Inventory and utilization records • Maintenance records
4.8 Product Identification and Traceability	11.0 Control of Processes	• Procedures for identifying the product and its components • Procedures for identifying an individual occurrence of a product to enable tracing it back through production • Master lists of serial numbers or other identifiers	• Design documentation • Process records such as traveler tags and engraved or painted-on serial numbers • Batch control records (e.g., a list of item numbers in a batch) • Shipping records • Records of purchased or client-supplied parts or material

4.9 Process Control	10.0 Quality of Processes	• Overview process flow description • Procedures and work instructions for every process that may affect quality • Standards of workmanship • Procedures for machine preventive maintenance • Procedures for monitoring that the process is being performed according to operating procedures and standards • Procedures for monitoring the effectiveness and performance of the process	• Product control records and statistics • Preventive maintenance logs and reports • Employee training records * Inspection logs and results
4.10 Inspection and Testing	12.0 Product Verification	Testing and inspection standards and procedures for • Verification of incoming material and equipment • Verification of interim (in-process) results • Verification of final product	• Test logs • Test results • Records of discrepancies and actions
4.11 Control of Inspection, Measuring, and Test Equipment	13.0 Control of Inspection, Measuring, and Test Equipment	• Procedures for the control, calibration, and maintenance of measuring and test equipment • Contents of procedures for calibration: equipment type, identifying number, location, frequency of check, method of check, acceptance criteria, action upon unacceptable results	• Calibration status records for equipment • Maintenance records • Calibration records • Inspection results

4.12 Inspection and Test Status	11.7 Control of Verification Status	• Procedures for identifying the inspection and test status (if verified; if in conformance) of product (including interim product and final product)	Status, indicators (tags, markings, etc.,) on product or on accompanying documentation • Records of the release of nonconforming product that identifies the responsible authority
4.13. Control of Nonconforming Product	11.8 Control of Nonconforming Product 14.0 Control of Nonconforming product	Procedure to ensure that nonconforming product is not inadvertently used • Procedures for review of nonconforming product • Procedures for disposition (rework, acceptance by concession, or rejection) of nonconforming product	• Documentation of labeled and segregated products (including interim or in-process product) • Documentation of the disposition of nonconforming product (rejection report, reacceptance report, etc.)
4.14 Corrective and Preventive Action	15.0 Corrective Action	Procedures, role, and responsibility • Investigating the cause of nonconforming product • Cause removal analysis • Initiating preventive action • Initiating and documenting procedural change to correct deficiencies	• Process review results • Follow-up reports
4.15 Handling Storage, Packaging, Preservation, and Delivery	10.4; 16.1; 16.2 Handling, Storage, and Delivery	Procedures for • Handling materials and products • Storage • Packaging • Delivery	• Inventory records • Product-tracking • Delivery records

4.16 Control of Quality Records	5.3; 17.2; 17.3 Documentation of the Quality System; Quality Records; Quality Records Control	Procedures for the identification, collection, storage, retrieval, and disposition of the events in the quality system	• Inspection reports • Test data • Audit reports • Calibration results • Process control results
4.17 Internal Quality Audits	5.4 Auditing the Quality System	Procedures, role, and responsibility for holding audits to determine if the process is being performed in accordance with plans and if the quality system is effective • Audit plan	• Audit reports identifying deficiencies and suggesting corrective action • Audit responses acknowledging or refuting discrepancies • Reports of the resolution of differences • Documentation of corrective action to "close out" all discrepancies
4.18 Training	18.1 Training	• Training plans to identify the training requirements for each position, process, or skill level • Training descriptions (objectives, type, materials, length, contents, prerequisites, validation method, audience)	• Training schedules • Employee training records • Validation results
4 19 Servicing	16.4 Servicing	• Procedure for performing service activities • Procedures to verify that service activities are being performed acceptably	• Service-call reports • Change requests • Trouble reports • Closure records on change requests and trouble reports • Client surveys • Response-time records • Test and maintenance reports on field equipment

4.20 Statistical Techniques	20.0 Use of Statistical Methods 6.0 Financial Considerations of Quality Systems 19.0 Product Safety 7.0 Quality in Marketing	• Procedures to identify the statistical techniques needed to verify the acceptability of the process and the product	• Measurement results • Statistical reports, charts, etc.

PART 2   TOOLS USED IN THE DOCUMENTATION PROCESS

ISO 9001	Tool	Reason
4.1 Management Responsibility	Survey sampling	To assess the extent and depth of understanding of the quality policy
	Work sampling	To determine time requirements
	Descriptive statistics	To verify activities
	Design of Experiments (DOE)	To improve the structure of the organization
	Quality Function Deployment (QFD)	To determine if the organization meets the customer's requirements
	Process capability	To provide a tool to assess operations during management review
4.2 Quality System	Process capability	To access the capability of the system to meet requirements
	QFD	To determine if the system meets customer's requirements
	Descriptive statistics	To describe the components of the system
	Control charts	To determine when processes need updating
	Statistical sampling	To evaluate effectiveness of documentation and compliance with documentation
4.3 Contract Review	Statistical process control (SPC)	To determine when to reuse specifications
	Acceptance sampling	To determine if contract requirements are met
4.4 Design Control	Classical DOE	To identify and evaluate significant design parameters
	Taguch DOE (tolerance design)	To set tolerances and determine parameter settings
	Shanon DOE	To identify and evaluate robustness
	Control charts	To monitor design parameters
	FMEA	To evaluate potential design problems
	Graphical techniques	To clarify process dynamics
	Regression	To study design parameters
4.5 Document and Data Control	Process flow charts	To describe the flow of processes and tasks
	Pareto chart(s)	To set or study priorities
	Spreadsheet(s)	To keep track of document changes
	Sampling	To estimate the extent of compliance with controls

4.6 Purchasing	Control charts	To review the performance of subcontractors
	Graphical techniques	To review and analyze the performance of subcontractors
	Process capability indexes	To evaluate subcontractors
	Acceptance sampling	To evaluate shipments received from subcontractors
4.7 Control of Customer-Supplied Product	Control charts	To evaluate and control the product
	Statistical estimation	To evaluate the extent of product conformance
	Acceptance sampling	To evaluate the product
4.8 Product Identification and Traceability	Flowcharts	To illustrate process flows
		To assist in evaluating traceability
4.9 Process Control	Control charts	To evaluate and control processes
	Sampling techniques	To determine sampling requirements, including sample size, location, and frequency
	Pareto chart(s)	To evaluate priority of various defects
	Time series	To evaluate autocorrelated data
4.10 Inspection and Testing	Acceptance sampling	To make decisions regarding acceptability of product
	Pareto chart(s)	To study defect patterns in relation to each other
	Bulk sampling	To evaluate lots of bulk materials
	Process capability	To evaluate processes and shipments of product
	Control charts	To monitor shipments
	Time series	To study trends
	Graphical techniques	To monitor inspection results
4.11 Control of Inspection, Measuring, and Test Equipment	Measurement error studies	To evaluate measuring devices
	Process capability studies	To evaluate gauge capability
	Calibration studies	To review calibration results
	Concept of bias and precision, reproducibility, and repeatability	To evaluate test equipment
	Control charts	To monitor calibrations
	Time series	To evaluate trends
4.12 Inspection and Test Status	Graphical techniques	To analyze test results
	Control charts	To evaluate test results
	Sampling	To estimate extent of nonconformance
4.13 Control of Nonconforming Product	Control charts	To monitor and control product
	Graphical techniques	To evaluate and monitor nonconforming product
4.14 Corrective and Preventive Action	Control charts	To evaluate defect patterns
	DOE	To evaluate causes of nonconforming product and determine best corrective actions
	Exploratory data analysis	To help evaluate causes of problems
	Correlation and regression analysis	To search for root causes of problems and best corrective actions
4.15 Handling, Storage, Packaging, Preservation, and Delivery	Statistical modeling	To search for root causes of problems
	Pareto charts	To study defect patterns
	Cause-and-effect diagrams	To analyze and search for root causes of problems
	Control charts	To control handling, delivery, packaging, storage, and preservation problems

4.16 Control of Quality Records	Sampling Graphical techniques	To evaluate outgoing packaging To evaluate shipment, packaging, and handling problems
4.17 Internal Quality Audit	Descriptive statistics Control charts Sampling	To monitor records To monitor and control records To estimate extent of conformance
4.18 Training	Spreadsheets Descriptive statistics	To evaluate and monitor training To evaluate training results
4.19 Servicing	Sampling Control charts	To estimate extent of conformance to servicing specifications To control servicing problems
4.20 Statistical Control	Everything and anything that is appropriate and applicable to substantiate consistency, control, and capability in processes	To monitor processes for consistency, control, and repeatability

For QS-9000*

Section II

1.1 Production Part Approval Process (PPAP)	The PPAP is very prescriptive as to requirements	To control the initial product based on the customer requirements set forth in the purchase contract To define feasibility of production To review design To provide the requirements of advanced quality planning (FMEA and so on)
2.1 Continuous Improvement	The QS-9000 is very prescriptive as to requirements	To monitor and evaluate processes for continual improvement
3.1 Manufacturing Capabilities	The QS-9000 is very prescriptive as to requirements	To make sure that the manufacturing capabilities are satisfied based on mistake proofing, tooling management, tool design, fabrication, facilities, equipment, process planning, and effectiveness

* It is very important to note that the customer may require and define in the purchasing contract other tools and requirements for specific products, processes, and situations.

PART 3   A TYPICAL INTERNAL PREASSESSMENT SURVEY

These questions are intended to be used only as guidelines in a given organization. They are designed to identify any shortcomings in your system and to allow you to plan accordingly. They are not meant to be used as a formal checklist for any organization, since the official checklist is prepared by the representatives of the Registrar. The list is based on C. Grossman, "ISO 9000 Readiness Survey," *Quality in Manufacturing*, January–February 1995, pp. 34–35.

1. Does your company have a written quality policy that describes management's commitment to quality and objective for achieving quality in every part of the company's operation?

2. Has your management group endorsed the quality policy and communicated the policy to all employees?

3. Is there an approved organization chart showing who is responsible for all work that affects the quality of the product or service that your company produces?

4. Are the functions and job specifications for personnel who affect the quality of the product or service clearly defined?

5. Are the technical and personnel resources that are needed for the inspection, testing, and monitoring of the production of the product or service made available by management?

6. Are the technical and personnel resources that are needed for the inspection, testing, and monitoring of the product or service during its life cycle made available by management?

7. Are periodic audits of the quality system completed as often as necessary to keep each part of the system in control?

8. Are periodic audits of the manufacturing processes completed as often as necessary to keep each process in control?

9. Are periodic audits of the product or service that your company produces completed as often as necessary to ensure that the quality of the product meets customer requirements?

10. Are the results of the audit communicated to management and to those employees who affect quality?

11. Has your company appointed a coordinator to be responsible for monitoring the quality system and calling attention to the deficiencies?

12. Are quality reviews held at appropriate intervals?
13. Are the results of the audits recorded and maintained?
14. Are procedures written for each activity that affects quality? are they appropriately maintained? are they easily accessed by the employees?
15. Does your company have a plan for achieving and maintaining quality?
16. Does your company audit and evaluate its progress in achieving the objectives listed in the quality plan?
17. Are customer needs identified and communicated to all employees who affect the quality of the product?
18. Do employees know what they have to do on the job to provide the desired level of quality in the product or service?
19. Are the customer requirements for product and service quality adequately defined in the contract with the customer?
20. Are customer contracts reviewed for accuracy?
21. Are records of the customer reviews maintained?
22. Are incomplete and ambiguous requirements resolved before design or production?
23. Are all applicable and appropriate documents reviewed before they are released for use?
24. Do you have an obsolescent policy? Do you follow it?
25. Do your procedures and instructions describe what is actually done on the job?
26. Do you have document control? Do you follow it?
27. Do you have a certification program for your suppliers? If not, how do you approve your suppliers?
28. Do you keep performance records from your suppliers? Do you perform regular analysis with the data? Do you communicate the information to your supplier base?
29. Does someone check all incoming supplies and equipment to verify that you have indeed received the correct resources to do the job and that they meet the defined requirements?
30. Do you maintain a list of approved suppliers?
31. Do you audit your suppliers?

32. Do you use systematic methods to identify and plan production processes and (if appropriate) equipment and product installation processes?

33. Do your employees use their own tools?

34. Do you do calibration?

35. Do you have written setup and process instructions?

36. Do you have preventive maintenance?

37. Do you have written standards for workmanship and criteria for meeting the standards?

38. Do your employees follow job procedures and instructions?

39. Do your employees follow unwritten procedures or instructions?

40. Do the procedures and instructions describe the way employees do their jobs now?

41. Do you record tooling repairs to ensure process control?

42. Do you have written procedures to ensure that incoming products are not used or handled before an inspection or other form of verification proves that these products meet specified requirements?

43. Are inspection procedures carried out in accordance with written instructions and your company's quality plan?

44. Do you have written procedures to identify incoming material that may have been released before it was inspected because of urgent production purposes?

45. Do you maintain a receiving inspection history or log?

46. Does your company collect and maintain records to prove that you have met customer requirements?

47. Do you have written instructions for inspecting and testing?

48. Are nonconforming products identified and separated so that they are not sent to customers?

49. Are there written procedures to verify that all final inspections and tests are completed before products are sent to customers?

50. Are there written procedures for calibration and maintenance of inspection, measurement, and test equipment that show calibration frequency?

51. Do you have a system to identify the inspection or test status of products during manufacturing?

52. Is there a documented procedure for identifying and separating rejected material to prevent inadvertent use of nonconforming products?

53. Is there a method of recording the rejected material and the disposition of such material? Are there documents to support that the method is being followed?

54. Is there a method for requesting a deviation from the customer? Is it being followed? Is there documentation to support the practice?

55. When a waiver of change or a deviation has been authorized by the customer, is that information recorded and maintained?

56. Is there an analysis of nonconformities?

57. Are there procedures for ensuring that effective corrective actions are carried out?

58. Are there procedures from preventing damage to products as they are handled?

59. Are in-stock products inspected at periodic intervals?

60. Is there a written procedure for identifying, collecting, indexing, filing, maintaining, and disposing of quality-related records?

61. Are quality records maintained so that the achievement of their required levels of quality can be demonstrated to customers and to your management team?

62. Are quality records stored in an accessible place?

63. Are quality records accessible to your customers for their review?

64. Do you have a retention policy? Is it written? Is it being followed?

65. Are quality audits performed as defined in your procedures?

66. Do the appropriate personnel take timely corrective actions? Are their actions recorded?

67. Do training and development plans exist for all employees who have an impact on the organization, product, or service?

68. Are records maintained to show who attended training, when they attended, and their success in learning the skills?

69. Are there written procedures and instructions for follow-up service? Does appropriate maintenance exist for these procedures? Do they meet the requirements?

70. Is there a method of establishing the need for statistical techniques? How do you maintain control in your processes?

Quality Policy Examples

In this appendix we present examples of several quality policies. These policies represent different industries and are offered here only as examples.

COMMUNICATIONS COMPANY

Quality excellence is the foundation for the management of our business and the keystone of our goal of customer satisfaction. It is, therefore, our policy to

- Consistently provide products and services that meet the quality expectations of our customers.
- Actively pursue ever-improving quality through programs that enable each employee to do his or her job right the first time.

CHEMICAL COMPANY

Total quality is meeting customer requirements

- Both external and internal.
- For all products and services.
- All the time.

Total quality requires

- Total involvement of all employees.
- Total management commitment.
- Customer and supplier working together.
- Objectives, standards, and systems that conform to the commitment to total quality.
- Continuous improvement.

Total quality is achieved by

- Conforming to requirements.
- Prevention not detection.
- Getting it right the first time and every time.
- Measuring quality performance (including costs).

Total quality is a permanent feature of the company's life. It is monitored, nurtured, and maintained by an ongoing quality improvement program.

AUTOMOTIVE COMPANY

Quality is defined by customers. Customers want products and services that meet their needs and expectations at a cost that represents value.

TYPICAL MANUFACTURING COMPANY

XYZ Manufacturing is committed to conformance with Corporate quality policy and any additional quality policies of organizations in the reporting chain.

XYZ's quality policy is to manufacture products of high quality at a reasonable price.

UNIVERSITY

ABC University, one of the nations s leading urban universities, will emerge as a premier public research university offering comprehensive, high-quality instruction, research opportunities, and public service based on the expectations of the diverse population we serve.

HEALTH CARE FACILITY

RST Hospital, a member of the ABC Health and Hospitals Corporation, is an integral member of the DEF community. It is our mission to provide quality health care to residents of our community. Beyond our mandated service area, we will always provide first-rate care to anyone in need of medical attention, regardless of race, religion, nationality, or ability to pay. As such, we provide a wide range of services:

- 24-hour emergency care.
- Primary care outpatient services.
- State-of-the-art inpatient medical care, within a caring and patient-oriented environment.

Through our role as a teaching hospital, RST is dedicated to the development and dissemination of medical knowledge to patients and health professionals.

RST will provide the best public health, and whenever appropriate, social services to the community that it serves.

ENVIRONMENTAL POLICY

The management of XYX company has adopted a general policy of operating the service under control of an environment management system, installed and operated according to the BS 7750 standard. It is a company policy to operate continuously to these standards, as they apply, and to seek annual certification from an accredited body.

TYPICAL CONSULTING COMPANY

Our mission is to provide practical and cost-effective solutions to management problems caused by change and development in client companies. These clients will be from a variety of industries including manufacturing, automotive, plastic, print, steel, electronics, medical devices, health care, and defense. These clients will use the full range of our resources and expertise in design, development, manufacturing, and general management. The expertise we offer is based on the systematic collection and analysis of facts and relevant data augmented and constructed to form practical proposals on which to base sound business decisions.

The work must benefit the client in ways that can be understood and stand the tests of rigorous application. The work must be of the highest standards of our profession and reflect the dedication of our staff members. The work must be profitable to our company, demonstrably cost effective as a yardstick of our own efficiency, and provide the funds necessary for growth and sound corporate health.

Quality Manuals

In this appendix we provide two complete quality manuals. The first one is based on the ISO and the FDA's good manufacturing processes (GMP) requirements, and the second one is based on the QS-9000. The reader is warned that these sample manuals are only examples and should be used as guidelines in developing individual quality manuals. In the first example, the quality manual of a medical device company illustrates the multiple requirements that are necessary for a complete document to satisfy the ISO 9001 requirements. The second quality manual is based on the QS-9000 to illustrate the structure and flow of the automotive requirements.

Document No: QM XYZ 001
Revision: 00
Date: May 1, 1995
Supersedes: New
Section: 0
Page 1 of 1
Authorized By:_____

XYZ, INC. QUALITY SYSTEM MANUAL

Based on ISO 9001 and GMP

Sample Manual

TITLE:

Table of Contents

Document No: QM XYZ 001
Revision: 00
Date: May 1, 1995
Supersedes: New
Section: 0
Page 1 of 3

TITLE: Document No: QM XYZ 001

                                       Revision: 00

Table of Contents   Date: May 1, 1995

                                   Supersedes: New

                                       Section: 0

                                   Page 2 of 3

TITLE:	Document No: QM XYZ 001
	Revision: 00
Table of Contents	Date: May 1, 1995
	Supersedes: New
	Section: 0
	Page 3 of 3

5.0*   APPENDIXES

5.1   *XYZ Organizational Chart*

5.2   *Cross-Reference between ISO-9001 Regulations and XYZ Quality System*

5.3   *Cross-Reference between FDA GMP Regulations and XYZ Quality System*

` The appendix listing is for display only; this sample document does not contain the actual appendixes.

TITLE:	**Document No: QM XYZ 001**
	Revision: 00
Introduction	**Date: May 1, 1995**
	Supersedes: New
	Section: 1.0
	Page 1 of 1

1.0   INTRODUCTION

1.1   XYZ Medical Technology Quality Policy

XYZ will provide products and services that meet or exceed the expectations of our internal and external customers through our total commitment to continuous improvement in everything we do.

Quality is our primary concern for each product throughout its entire life cycle, from design to manufacturing to shipping to customer follow-up. Since quality cannot be inspected into a product, it is XYZ's policy to educate personnel at all levels on how their performance contributes to product quality. All XYZ employees are responsible for the work they perform to ensure that we satisfy our customers' expectations.

1.2   Scope of the *XYZ Quality System Manual*

The *XYZ Quality System Manual* describes the policies, procedures, and quality system structure that XYZ employs to ensure the design, production, and distribution of safe and effective medical devices. The XYZ quality system was created to reflect a quality program consistent with the regulations and standards outlined by FDA's good manufacturing practices (GMP) and the ISO 9001 (International Organization for Standardization).

TITLE:	Document No: QM XYZ 001
	Revision: 00
References	Date: May 1, 1995
	Supersedes: New
	Section: 2.0
	Page 1 of 2

2.0   REFERENCES

2.1   Quality Standards

The following quality standards were consulted and employed during the establishment and continuing improvement of the XYZ quality system:

- ISO 9001 (ANSI/ASQC-1994) *Quality Systems—Model for Quality Assurance in Design/Development, Production, Installation, and Servicing*
- ISO 9004-1 (ANSI/ASQC-1994) *Quality Management and Quality System Elements Guidelines*
- ISO/DIS 10013 *Guidelines for Developing Quality Manuals*
- GMP regulations as promulgated under section 520 of the Food, Drug, and Cosmetic Act and defined in the Code of Federal Regulations, title 21, part 820
- DOH Quality Systems for Orthopaedic Implants 1990 Good Manufacturing Practice

TITLE: Document No: QM XYZ 001

                                 Revision: 00

References   Date: May 1, 1995

                                 Supersedes: New

                                 Section: 2.0

                                 Page 2 of 2

2.2   XYZ QUALITY SYSTEM DOCUMENTS

This manual contains the XYZ policies and practices for the manufacture of high quality products. In cases where more detail is needed, the reader can consult other procedures in the XYZ quality documentation system. The appendixes of this manual contain cross-references to the ISO 9001 and the FDA GMP requirements as well as to the XYZ documents that correspond with and demonstrate compliance to these standards. Upon issuance of this manual, these tables were up-to-date. However, documentation is constantly being added and revised. The reader may consult the XYZ QA documentation department for an updated listing of documents.

TITLE:

Quality System Terminology

Document No: QM XYZ 001
Revision: 00
Date: May 1, 1995
Supersedes: New
Section: 3.0
Page 1 of 6

3.0   XYZ QUALITY SYSTEM TERMINOLOGY

3.1   Terms and Definitions

Customer   The organization or individual receiving products or services. The customer may be external or internal to the firm. Internal clients are not purchasers, but they receive products and services from internal functions and are the customers of those functions.

Device history record   A compilation of records containing the complete production history of a finished device.

Device master record   A compilation of records containing the design, formulation, specifications, complete manufacturing procedures, quality assurance requirements, and labeling of a finished device.

Finished product/device   An orthopedic implant or instrument that has completed all stages of manufacture including packaging, labeling, and sterilization where applicable.

TITLE:	Document No: QM XYZ 001
	Revision: 00
Quality System Terminology	Date: May 1, 1995
	Supersedes: New
	Section: 3.0
	Page 2 of 6

Labels/labeling   Written or printed matter in words, symbols, diagrams, or pictures applied to a device and to any of its containers or supplied with the device by the manufacturer.

Lot   A defined quantity of raw materials, intermediate product, work in process, or finished devices.

Manufacturer   The organization, in this manual XYZ, providing a product to the customer; also the organization that is the subject of the standards; that is, the first party.

Manufacturing environment   The facilities, environmental conditions, equipment, and process materials used during manufacture.

Manufacturing procedure   The manufacturing steps required to produce a component or finished product.

Medical device   Any instrument, apparatus, appliance, material, or other item, used alone or in combination, and any accessories or software (essential) for its proper functioning intended for human use in the

- Diagnosis, prevention, monitoring, treatment, or alleviation of disease or injury.
- Investigation, replacement, or modification of the anatomy or of a physiological process, which does not achieve its principal intended action by pharmacological, chemical, immunological, or metabolic means but may be assisted in its function by such means.

TITLE: Document No: QM XYZ 001

                                                          Revision: 00

Quality System Terminology   Date: May 1, 1995

                                                    Supersedes: New

                                                       Section: 3.0

                                                      Page 3 of 6

Orthopedic implant   A medical device that is surgically implanted in the body to aid in the repair of bone and/or related tissues and to replace these tissues either temporarily or permanently.

Process materials   Materials such as wax, coolant, glass beads, and sand that are used in manufacturing processes but are not intended to be part of the finished product.

Quality   The set of features, functions, and characteristics of a product or service that are relevant to its ability to satisfy the needs of the user and/ or customer.

Quality assurance   All the planned and systematic activities implemented within the quality system, and demonstrated as needed, to provide adequate confidence that an entity will fulfill requirements for quality.

TITLE:	Document No: QM XYZ 001
	Revision: 00
Quality System Terminology	Date: May 1, 1995
	Supersedes: New
	Section: 3.0
	Page 4 of 6

<u>Quality system</u>   The organizational structure, responsibilities, procedures, processes, and resources for implementing quality management.

<u>Quarantine</u>   The status of material or product awaiting release by the person responsible for quality assurance.

<u>Quarantine area</u>   An area, isolated by physical barriers or other effective means, that is used for the storage of product while subject to quarantine.

<u>Raw materials</u>   Any material or fabricated component used singly, or in conjunction with other raw materials and/or components, in the assembly or fabrication of parts or in the total production of products.

<u>Recall</u>   A communication to customers with instructions to return devices to the manufacturer or to destroy them.

<u>Specified requirements</u>   Requirements prescribed by the purchaser in a contract, or requirements prescribed by the supplier that are not subject to direct specification by the purchaser.

TITLE:	Document No: QM XYZ 001
	Revision: 00
Quality System Terminology	Date: May 1, 1995
	Supersedes: New
	Section: 3.0
	Page 5 of 6

Sterile package   The protective containers designed to maintain the sterility and integrity of the components up to the time of use and to permit, where appropriate, aseptic removal of its contents. Once opened, the package cannot be resealed easily and clearly reveals that it has been opened.

Supplier   The subcontractor that provides products or services to the manufacturer.

Traceability   The ability to determine from which lot a particular item originates. The ability to determine the origin or disposition of any given lot of products or raw materials.

3.2   Standard Abbreviations

DHR   device history record

DMR   device master record

FMEA   failure mode effects analysis

GMP   good manufacturing practice

TITLE: **Document No: QM XYZ 001**

                                         Revision: 00

Quality System Terminology   **Date: May 1, 1995**

                                      Supersedes: New

                                         Section: 3.0

                                      Page 6 of 6

ISO   International Organization for Standardization

MDR   medical device reporting

NIST   National Institute of Standards and Technology

QA   quality assurance

QI   quality instructions

SPC   statistical process control

XYZ   company name

TITLE:	Document No: QM XYZ 001
	Revision: 00
Quality System Practices and Controls:	Date: May 1, 1995
Management Responsibility	Supersedes: New
	Section: 4.1
	Page 1 of 3

4.0   QUALITY SYSTEM REQUIREMENTS

4.1   Management Responsibility

4.1.1 XYZ Quality Policy

It is the responsibility of XYZ management to provide the personnel and resources necessary to maintain the requirements of the XYZ quality policy and the XYZ quality manual.

4.1.2 Organization

4.1.2.1 Responsibility and Authority   XYZ has an organizational structure with established levels of responsibility and authority that will provide quality products to our customers and reduce conflicts of interest among departments and functions. (An organizational chart is provided in the appendix.) This organizational structure allows independence and authority of the quality function, an essential element for ensuring that we deliver quality products to our customers. In addition, all personnel are authorized to make decisions within their realm of responsibility to ensure that operations are carried out in accordance with the policies and procedures of the quality manual and the entire XYZ quality system.

TITLE:	Document No: QM XYZ 001
	Revision: 00
Quality System Practices and Controls:	**Date: May 1, 1995**
Management Responsibility	**Supersedes: New**
	Section: 4.1
	Page 2 of 3

4.1.2.2 Resources and Personnel   All managers and supervisors are responsible for ensuring that only trained personnel are assigned to verification activities such as receiving inspection, in-process inspection, final inspection, and document review functions. Personnel working in these areas shall be allowed sufficient time to do the work and shall receive documented procedures on how to do the work.

Audits of verification activities will be performed by personnel independent of those having direct responsibility for the work being performed.

4.1.2.3 Management Representative   The overall responsibility for quality assurance at XYZ, Inc. rests with the chairman and chief executive officer, who has delegated full authority for product quality and regulatory compliance activities to the quality assurance manager.

The quality assurance manager has the following authority and responsibility:

- Ensures organizationwide compliance with this manual.
- Approves or disapproves the shipment of products.
- Ensures that all testing, inspection, labeling, packaging, sterilization, and other manufacturing processes comply with applicable requirements.
- Reports any nonconforming conditions to appropriate managers for resolution.

TITLE: **Document No: QM XYZ 001**

Revision: 00

Quality System Practices and Controls: **Date: May 1, 1995**

Management Responsibility   **Supersedes: New**

Section: 4.1

Page 3 of 3

4.1.3   Management Review Requirements

The quality system at XYZ is designed to satisfy the requirements of ISO 9001. Management will review the system at least annually to ensure conformance and effectiveness. These reviews, including minutes of meetings, shall be documented.

Related Documentation (Insert all appropriate and applicable documentation.)

TITLE: Document No: QM XYZ 001

                                                              Revision: 00

Quality System Practices and Controls: Date: May 1, 1995

Quality System   Supersedes: New

                                                           Section: 4.2

                                                          Page 1 of 1

4.2   Quality System

Purpose   The quality system is the means by which XYZ implements its stated quality policy and procedures. This system comprises the structure and resources necessary to implement quality management.

Policy   The XYZ quality system is designed to interact with all activities that are related to the quality of our products to ensure that they meet customer expectations. In all elements of the product life cycle, from initial concept through design to manufacturing and then to implementation in patients, the emphasis is on prevention of defects rather than detection during inspection or after a problem occurs.

The quality system exercises adequate and continuous control over all activities that affect product quality. The system is documented by the Quality Manual and operational procedures. These procedures are written in a clear and concise manner to indicate methods to be used and criteria to be satisfied. Changes to these procedures are controlled and documented so that adherence to our Quality System is maintained.

Related Documentation (Insert all appropriate and applicable documentation.)

TITLE: Document No: QM XYZ 001

Revision: 00

Quality System Practices and Controls: Date: May 1, 1995

Contract Review   Supersedes: New

Section: 4.3

Page 1 of 1

4.3   Contract Review

Purpose   The contract review at XYZ is established at the time of order by the customer. It is maintained through reviews of the specific manufacturing processes and is documented in the quality records of the processes.

Policy   The policy of XYZ for contract review is to make sure that the requirements of the customer are adequately defined and documented. The definition and documentation will be available to all concerned through the appropriate quality records. In case of changes and/or amendments, proper authorization is expected and proper documentation will be maintained.

Contract review at XYZ company is the documentation process of establishing the requirements of the customer so that XYZ can meet those wants, needs, and expectations. It is designed to make sure that the customer and the XYZ corporation will develop a win-win attitude about each other and establish a long-term working relationship.

Related Documentation (Insert all appropriate and applicable documentation.)

TITLE: **Document No: QM XYZ 001**

Revision: 00

Quality System Practices and Controls: **Date: May 1, 1995**

Design Control   **Supersedes: New**

Section: 4.4

Page 1 of 8

4.4   Design Control

Purpose   Design control verifies and ensures that specified product requirements are met. The purpose of preproduction quality assurance (the
design validation process) is to provide a high degree of confidence that
medical device designs are reliable, safe, and effective prior to their release for routine production.

Policy   A formally documented product specification will be written and
approved prior to authorization of any product development project. All
new or redesigned products shall be subjected to design validation and
design reviews prior to their release to manufacturing for routine production.

4.4.1   General

Procedures to control and verify that product designs meet specified product requirements shall be formally documented and periodically reviewed
to ensure that they are effective.

TITLE: Document No: QM XYZ 001
                                                Revision: 00
Quality System Practices and Controls: Date: May 1, 1995
Design Control   Supersedes: New
                                                Section: 4.4
                                                Page 2 of 8

4.4.2   Design and Development Planning

A comprehensive product development plan and schedule shall be prepared for each design project. The project schedule shall identify the responsibility for each design and development activity. Design reviews shall be an integral element of the design and development process.

4.4.3.   Organizational and Technical Interfaces

Organizational and technical interfaces between the FDA (GMP) exist at the XYZ company and are defined ahead of design as part of the contract review. The results of such interfaces are always recorded and kept as part of the quality records

4.4.4   Design Input

Input to the project design process shall consist of a formally documented and approved product specification. This document prescribes the design and performance requirements to meet customer needs and forms the basis of all design validation activities. It must be a comprehensive statement of all requirements, including product descriptions, materials, test requirements, manufacturing costs, clinical/regulatory requirements, etc. (list others here) The product specification and an approved project authorization request must exist before the formal design process is initiated.

TITLE:

Quality System Practices and Controls:
Design Control

Document No: QM XYZ 001
Revision: 00
Date: May 1, 1995
Supersedes: New
Section: 4.4
Page 3 of 8

4.4.5   Design Output

Output from the design process will include (1) a comprehensive design development file, (2) approved product drawings, (3) a sufficient number of engineering reports to fully document all the design validation tests that were conducted, (4) complete production process procedures, and (5) quality instructions.

The design development file shall include, but not be limited to, engineering analyses, failure modes and effects analyses, design review minutes, project correspondence, and technical references. Product drawings will fully describe manufacturable products. Design validation shall ensure that the product is safe, effective, and meets all requirements described in the product specification.

TITLE: Document No: QM XYZ 001

                                                  Revision: 00

Quality System Practices and Controls: Date: May 1, 1995

Design Control   Supersedes: New

                                                  Section: 4.4

                                                  Page 4 of 8

4.4.6   Design Review

At appropriate stages as defined by XYZ and the customer design, reviews will be conducted and documented. For the actual policy on design
review see pages 6, 7, and 8 of this section.

4.4.7   Design Verification

At appropriate stages design verification shall be performed based on
contractual, technical, and regulatory requirements (see also section 4.4.8).

4.4.8   Design Validation (Verification)

Design validation shall include demonstration that design acceptance criteria outlined in the product specification have been met. Test performance is to be documented in engineering reports for future reference and
use with regulatory submissions. The design must be validated with product
that fully represents all production process variables and must be considered for revalidation if any production process variable is subsequently
changed.

    Design reviews will be attended by associates independent of the
department (or persons) that developed the product. The reviews will
address all elements of the Preproduction QA program described in document QM XYZ xxxx. Results of each design review will be formally
documented.

TITLE: **Document No: QM XYZ 001**

                                                        Revision: 00

Quality System Practices and Controls: **Date: May 1, 1995**

Design Control   **Supersedes: New**

                                                        Section: 4.4

                                                      Page 5 of 8

The vice president will analyze complaint trends to verify that the design continues to be safe and effective in clinical use. This is a combined responsibility of the quality assurance and product development departments.

4.4.9   Design Changes

Design changes are to be identified, documented, and reviewed for effect on all device master record documents before the change is approved for implementation. Also, effect of design changes on design validation and process validation shall be evaluated with appropriate tests to ensure that the design will still be safe and effective after the changes are implemented. The product configuration change procedure shall control all design changes.

TITLE:	Document No: QM XYZ 001
	Revision: 00
Quality System Practices and Controls:	Date: May 1, 1995
Design Control	Supersedes: New
	Section: 4.4
	Page 6 of 8

Preproduction Quality Assurance
Purpose

The purpose of preproduction quality assurance is to provide a high degree of confidence that medical device designs are reliable, safe, and effective prior to releasing them to production for routine manufacturing. As part of the formal preproduction quality assurance program, the design review serves three purposes.

- To confirm the adequacy of the product design by independent evaluations performed by persons other than the original product development engineers.
- To assure that the product is economically producible.
- To maximize protection against design omissions that might adversely affect the product's quality, safety, and efficacy.

TITLE:	Document No: QM XYZ 001
	Revision: 00
Quality System Practices and Controls:	Date: May 1, 1995
Design Control	Supersedes: New
	Section: 4.4
	Page 7 of 8

Policy

Prior to release to manufacturing for routine production, all new products or redesigned products will be subject to design review, attended by associates independent of the department (or persons) that developed the product. The review will address all elements of the preproduction QA program described in document PREP-0001.

Operations (for Design Review)

Prior to routine production, senior management or the site QA team will appoint an ad hoc design review group. The chairperson of the group is a senior officer of the company. The group consists of a minimum of three persons representing at least manufacturing, quality assurance/quality engineering, marketing and the product steward, with an engineering representative in an advisory role.

　　The design is evaluated by criteria established by management. As a minimum, the following questions shall be addressed in evaluating the design.

TITLE: Document No: QM XYZ 001

                                                              Revision: 00

Quality System Practices and Controls: **Date: May 1, 1995**

Design Control   **Supersedes: New**

                                                          Section: 4.4

                                                          Page 8 of 8

Can the product consistently perform its assigned function?

Are there any characteristics that make the product unsafe in any way?

Can available production equipment or equipment scheduled for procurement replicate the design?

Are existing facilities and testing facility adequate?

Do suppliers of materials and components have the capability to deliver quality items on schedule?

Is production economically feasible?

Does the product design satisfy all regulatory requirements?

Has a design FMEA been performed?

The design review topics and action steps shall be outlined in a formal report that is referenced in the device development file. The review team advises management of the outcome of all design reviews; management makes final decisions regarding production start-ups.

Related Documentation (Insert all appropriate and applicable documentation.)

TITLE:	Document No: QM XYZ 001
	Revision: 00
Quality Systems Practices and Controls:	**Date: May 1, 1995**
Document and Data Control	**Supersedes: New**
	Section: 4.5
	Page 1 of 2

4.5   Document and Data Control

Purpose   Document control helps to assure that employees and suppliers of XYZ have the necessary paperwork to perform their jobs.

Policy   Control of all documents relative to the requirements of ISO 9001, GMP, and DOH is a function of the XYZ quality assurance department. When practical, the originators keep and maintain their documents, that is, the appropriate research and development function keeps and maintains design documents.

4.5.2   Document and Data Approval and Issue

Prior to issue, a representative from each affected department or function reviews and approves a document. When deemed necessary, training for employees affected by a new or revised document occurs before the document is implemented or distributed. The affected department maintains a database and distribution lists of controlled documents.

TITLE:	**Document No: QM XYZ 001**
	Revision: 00
Quality Systems Practices and Controls:	**Date: May 1, 1995**
Document and Data Control	**Supersedes: New**
	Section: 4.5
	Page 2 of 2

4.5.3   Document and Data Changes/Modifications

All changes to documents go through a formal change control system. This system includes documenting the changes to be made, gaining approval of changes from representatives of all departments affected by the change, upgrading the revision level of the document, and distributing revised copies to owners of the previous version.

Related Documentation (Insert all appropriate and applicable documentation.)

TITLE: **Document No: QM XYZ 001**

Revision: 00

Quality System Practices and Controls: **Date: May 1, 1995**

Purchasing   **Supersedes: New**

Section: 4.6

Page 1 of 5

4.6   Purchasing

Purpose   Supplier qualification ensures that products and services procured from contracted sources conform to XYZ established specifications and requirements. Specifications established by the supplier must comply with XYZ requirements.

Policy   Suppliers are considered to be extensions of XYZ manufacturing. Accordingly, XYZ recognizes the importance of controlling the quality, efficacy, and safety of components, raw materials, and services acquired from suppliers, and exercises appropriate controls.

4.6.1   General
Suppliers must demonstrate their ability to meet XYZ's process/product specifications for designated characteristics by submitting to a first-article inspection for new products/processes and by using acceptable statistical methodology on a lot-by-lot basis.

TITLE: **Document No: QM XYZ 001**

Revision: 00

Quality System Practices and Controls: **Date: May 1, 1995**

Purchasing   **Supersedes: New**

Section: 4.6

Page 2 of 5

4.6.2   Evaluation of Subcontractors

Only those suppliers whose competence is verified will be approved as sources by XYZ. This competence may be demonstrated by a satisfactory performance history, or by assessment for being capable of satisfactory performance in the case of new suppliers. Suppliers will have an established quality assurance program to ensure meeting XYZ requirements. Suppliers are required to notify the appropriate XYZ representative(s) prior to making any changes that may affect the design, processing, performance, or quality requirements of an XYZ product or service.

TITLE:	Document No: QM XYZ 001
	Revision: 00
Quality System Practices and Controls:	**Date: May 1, 1995**
Purchasing	**Supersedes: New**
	Section: 4.6
	Page 3 of 5

4.6.3   Purchasing Data

All suppliers must have an "approved supplier" status prior to a purchase order being issued or a service being provided. Prior to a purchase order being issued to a supplier, its technical accuracy and completeness is reviewed by the appropriate functions. The review includes, but does not exclude, the following requirements:

- Reference to current specification revision.
- Product/process conformance verification.
- Unit identification.
- Unit cost.
- Number of units.
- Delivery schedule.
- Purchase order control number.

TITLE: **Document No: QM XYZ 001**

Revision: 00

Quality System Practices and Controls: **Date: May 1, 1995**

Purchasing   **Supersedes: New**

Section: 4.6

Page 4 of 5

4.6.4   Verification of Purchased Product

XYZ reserves the right to conduct inspection and testing on all purchased products. The procedures for these inspections and tests will be written and include the following:

- Characteristics to be inspected.
- Inspection sampling requirements.
- Inspection and testing methods used to assess conformance.

In the event a purchased item does not conform to the specification requirements, it is clearly identified an segregated from the conforming units. The supplier is promptly notified and directed to take corrective action.

TITLE: Document No: QM XYZ 001

Revision: 00

Quality System Practices and Controls: Date: May 1, 1995

Purchasing   Supersedes: New

Section: 4.6

Page 5 of 5

The results of all receiving inspection and testing are recorded and periodically reviewed to evaluate trends of suppliers quality performance.
When corrective action is required, details of the requested action are retained as an element of the supplier's history record.

Related Documentation (Insert all appropriate and applicable documentation.)

TITLE:	Document No: QM XYZ 001
	Revision: 00
Quality System Practices and Controls:	**Date: May 1, 1995**
Control of Customer-Supplied Product	**Supersedes: New**
	Section: 4.7
	Page 1 of 2

4.7   Control of Customer-Supplied Product

Purpose   The acceptability of finished product depends upon final in-spection criteria (e.g. form, fit, and function) and also depends upon other regulatory compliance, quality assurance, and GMP aspects that may not be measurable in the final product. In order to define these less tangible criteria, a uniform policy has been established (See Document No. QM XYZ xxxx, *General Supplier Requirements: Purchase of Finished Product*).

Policy   On a predetermined basis, it will be considered acceptable to test preshipment samples as a criterion for final product release. The indi-vidual final product testing standard will be used as the protocol or accep-tance regimen. In cases where products are quarantined at external sources and where the lot(s) are judged to meet release criteria prior to receipt of the lot(s) quantity at XYZ, it will be permissible to move such goods when received directly to approved stock only when a quality control release notice is issued prior to said receipt.

It is the responsibility of shipping and receiving to verify receipt quantities. The quality control release notice will be based upon quanti-ties produced and tested. Any discrepancy in count will subject the received shipment to quarantine until such time as counts have been reconciled (see Document No. QC ZYX xxxx, *Receiving Inspection Procedure*).

TITLE: Document No: QM XYZ 001

                                                          Revision: 00

Quality System Practices and Controls: Date: May 1, 1995

Control of Customer-Supplied Product   Supersedes: New

                                                          Section: 4.7

                                                          Page 2 of 2

In the event that it is necessary to store supplier items, arrangements are made to assure that like items are segregated and to prevent damage or adulteration. Received items are used on a first-in/first-out basis, and shelf life requirements, if any, are satisfied.

Related Documentation (Insert all appropriate and applicable documentation.)

TITLE:	Document No: QM XYZ 001
	Revision: 00
Quality System Practices and Controls:	Date: May 1, 1995
Product Identification and	Supersedes: New
Traceability	Section: 4.8
	Page 1 of 1

4.8   Product Identification and Traceability

Purpose   To identify where appropriate and applicable all in-process and final product throughout the stages of production, delivery, and installation. Appropriate documentation will be generated, maintained, and stored.

The identification system will monitor traceability and reflect both XYZ and FDA requirements.

Policy   The policy of XYZ company is to develop, implement, and maintain an identification and traceability system that is unique for each product produced (individual and batches) and to provide appropriate records.

Requirements   To facilitate both the identification and traceability of all products and batches within the jurisdiction of the XYZ company, the following tools are used:

- Six-digit identifier assigned by the customer information control system.
- Color-coded labels for different products.
- Material identification code.
- Appropriate records and forms.

Related Documentation (Insert all appropriate and applicable documentation.)

TITLE:	Document No: QM XYZ 001
	Revision: 00
Quality System Practices and Controls:	Date: May 1, 1995
Process Control	Supersedes: New
	Section: 4.9
	Page 1 of 6

4.9   Process Control

Purpose   The primary purpose of production and process control is to prevent product defects, thus minimizing nonconforming products. The second purpose is to detect defects as early as possible and thus reduce production costs by instituting corrective action as early in the process as possible.

Policy   Continuous control of the manufacturing operations while production is in progress, with less emphasis on in-process inspection and testing, is the keystone of the company's quality assurance discipline. This control encompasses personnel, methods, machines, and materials.

Requirements   Written procedures (flow charts, standard operating procedures, and instructions) must be available at the work stations so that employees may have access to them. In addition, information about product and process characteristics must be available for employee use.

Controls   Appropriate parameters as defined by the customer, XYZ, and the FDA should be identified and controlled in assessing conformance to requirements. Process capability must be demonstrated for critical product characteristics on an ongoing basis. Production and processes are controlled by the following elements.

- Preparation and implementation of supporting technical documentation. This consists of drawings, specifications, procedures, process sheets, quality instructions (QI) sheets, and setup sheets.

TITLE: Document No: QM XYZ 001

                                                Revision: 00

Quality System Practices and Controls: Date: May 1, 1995

Process Control   Supersedes: New

                                                Section: 4.9

                                               Page 2 of 6

- Planned manufacturing flow. Production operations, equipment layout, and work areas are designed to prevent product mix-ups and to achieve orderly and efficient material flow.
- Maintenance of device history records. A history record is maintained for each product lot. Among other functions, this document records or references the following specifics:
  - Identification of products by lot number.
  - Identification of pertinent drawings.
  - Identification of material(s), components, tools, machinery, or measuring equipment.
  - Description of operations, their sequence, and assignment of production units responsible for each operation, including sterilization and cleaning.
  - Inspection, testing, and labeling history.
  - Changes in any aspect of operations and identification of person(s) directing such changes.
- Automated manufacturing and test equipment when economically or otherwise practical. The performance of automated equipment is evaluated prior to production and is monitored to assure its sustained performance within established tolerances.
- Utilization of personnel trained and skilled in their assigned function.
- Utilization of statistical process control (SPC) techniques at the point of production.
- In-process controls, inspections, and tests (QA).

TITLE:	Document No: QM XYZ 001
	Revision: 00
Quality System Practices and Controls:	Date: May 1, 1995
Process Control	Supersedes: New
	Section: 4.9
	Page 3 of 6

4.9.1   General: Buildings, Environmental Control, Cleaning, and Sanitation

Purpose

The purpose of the control procedures in the XYZ quality system are to:

- Ensure orderly and efficient operations by means of efficient building layout and maintenance.
- Preclude mix-ups of any kind.
- Establish an environment that is safe and conducive to efficient operations.
- Maintain cleanliness to the degree that products cannot be contaminated.

Policy

The buildings, environmental control, cleaning, and sanitation operations of the company are integral elements of its overall manufacturing quality assurance capability. In terms of size, construction, location, and equipment reliability, these facilities are designed for the controlled and efficient production of safe and effective products. The adequacy of buildings is regularly re-evaluated in light of new needs. Conformance to hygienic requirements is maintained by a scheduled, supervised, and documented cleaning program.

TITLE:	Document No: QM XYZ 001
	Revision: 00
Quality System Practices and Controls:	**Date: May 1, 1995**
Process Control	**Supersedes: New**
	Section: 4.9
	Page 4 of 6

Requirements

Building space is allocated and equipment is located for the purpose of (1) achieving orderly sequencing of operations, (2) segregating incoming and in-process materials and components from discards, and (3) providing segregated storage for finished products pending shipment.

Controlled areas are provided and clearly marked. Ingress to these areas is limited to authorized personnel.

Environmental controls are established and monitored; environmental data are recorded. Environmental controls (e.g., lighting, ventilation, temperature, humidity, air pressure, and flow) are maintained commensurate with the function of each area of the plant. The adequacy of these controls and needs for additional controls are periodically monitored and evaluated.

Other aspects of physical control include the following:

- Laboratories are separate from manufacturing areas. Laboratories are equipped to perform special and routine testing.
- Inspection and test stations for final product evaluation are appropriately equipped and monitored.
- Technical documentation and records are stored in assigned areas.

TITLE: Document No: QM XYZ 001

Revision: 00

Quality System Practices and Controls: Date: May 1, 1995

Process Control   Supersedes: New

Section: 4.9

Page 5 of 6

Cleanliness is accomplished by

- Following written cleanliness procedures and schedules compatible with manufacturing specifications and with the character of the product.
- Providing protective attire to personnel working in operational, laboratory, and testing areas.
- Excluding food, beverages, and tobacco products from all controlled manufacturing spaces.
- Planning accessibility of equipment for cleaning.
- Disposing of trash, byproducts, discards, and other refuse promptly.
- Enforcing written and scheduled cleanliness procedures, including vermin and pest control.
- Posting cleanliness requirements and warnings at key locations in the plant.

Support equipment (e.g., handling devices) is selected and operated so as to preclude damage to end products or components.

Manufacturing and test equipment is designed (or acquired) in accordance with criteria aimed at minimizing the possibility of products or components being adversely affected (e.g., tearing materials, defacing labels, soiling packages). In addition, the following safeguards apply.

TITLE: Document No: QM XYZ 001
                                                    Revision: 00
Quality System Practices and Controls: Date: May 1, 1995
Process Control   Supersedes: New
                                                    Section: 4.9
                                                    Page 6 of 6

- Performance characteristics and tolerance limits are posted, or are otherwise readily accessible, for all equipment used directly for fabrication or testing.
- Maintenance and cleaning of equipment is planned and scheduled as an element of the total maintenance program.
- Heat treatment processes, for example, annealing that is carried out in house, are continually monitored and documented with special procedures. Records of heat treatment are maintained.
- Heat treatment that is vended out is vended only to companies having continual monitoring facilities and/or documented procedures.

Related Documentation (Insert all appropriate and applicable documentation.)

TITLE: **Document No: QM XYZ 001**

                                                    Revision: 00

Quality System Practices and Controls: **Date: May 1, 1995**

Inspection and Testing   **Supersedes: New**

                                                    Section: 4.10

                                                    Page 1 of 4

4.10   Inspection and Testing

Purpose   Prior to packaging, final product inspection and testing are performed to assure that characteristics pertinent to device safety, efficacy, and aesthetics conform to all requirements.

Policy   Final inspection and testing encompass characteristics not previously inspected or tested as well as characteristics that are reviewed for aesthetics. Unless sampling is otherwise specified, final inspections and tests are conducted on each unit of product in accordance with written procedures incorporated directly into the device master record or referenced in that record. Products are shipped only after all documents have been reviewed and have been found to be complete and accurate.

4.10.1   General

XYZ Corporation has established and maintains documented procedures for inspection and testing activities in order to verify that the specified requirements for the products are met. Control plans are used when appropriate.

4.10.2   Receiving Inspection and Testing

All materials purchased for XYZ corporation are released for use when conformance to requirements has been established. Conformance to requirements may be demonstrated by any one of the following items:

- Use of approved supplier.
- Data supplied by the supplier.
- Sample inspection and testing.
- Use of certified supplier.

   Materials that have not been fully tested are used for production only under the following conditions:

TITLE:	Document No: QM XYZ 001
	Revision: 00
Quality System Practices and Controls:	Date: May 1, 1995
Inspection and Testing	Supersedes: New
	Section: 4.10
	Page 2 of 4

- Material is identified.
- Use is authorized appropriately.
- Product is manufactured using material that can be traced and recalled if completion of the test program indicates nonconformance.

4.10.3   In-Process Inspection and Testing

In-process inspection and testing is performed throughout the XYZ company to verify conformance to internal requirements and to allow early corrective action should any nonconformance be detected. Only product conforming to requirements is released to the next stage of manufacturing. Where the product is required for production and complete conformance to requirements has not been established, a conditional release is given subject to satisfactory completion of inspection and testing. Traceability of conditionally released product is maintained to allow rejection or rework of product subsequently found to be nonconforming. Product not conforming to requirements is clearly identified either physically, in computer records, or both.

4.10.4   Final Inspection and Testing

Final inspection and testing in XYZ company is carried out on parts or fully manufactured products to verify compliance with final product specifications. Each product characteristic is verified as early as possible in the production sequence. Different characteristics are subject to final inspection and testing at different stages of manufacturing and as defined by the quality assurance of the XYZ company, the customer, and the FDA. Some of the following practices may be applicable:

TITLE: **Document No: QM XYZ 001**
                                              Revision: 00
Quality System Practices and Controls: **Date: May 1, 1995**
Inspection and Testing   **Supersedes: New**
                                              Section: 4.10
                                              Page 3 of 4

- The product and its particular characteristics to be inspected are clearly identified on the DMR and DHR.
- Instruments necessary to conduct inspections and tests are listed in the DMR by name and number.
- Characteristics may be sampled in accordance with statistically valid sampling procedures such as MIL-STD-105E.
- Shipment of each lot of product must be approved by initials or a stamp on the DHR by the designated quality assurance person and by the general manager or by their formally designated representatives.
- Samples from lots that have been shipped are retained for inspections and tests to be conducted after specified time intervals to assure that the products delivered to users conform to original inspection and testing criteria.

4.10.5   Inspection and Test Records

The results of inspection and tests, including information regarding the disposition of the product, are recorded and quality trends are analyzed. The results of final product inspection and tests are stored and preserved as elements of the DHR, and are retained for two years or for the expected life of the product plus one year, whichever is longer.

TITLE: Document No: **QM XYZ 001**
                                                                Revision: 00
Quality System Practices and Controls: **Date: May 1, 1995**
Inspection and Testing   **Supersedes: New**
                                                               Section: 4.10
                                                              Page 4 of 4

Quality assurance or its equivalent as mandated by management implements inspection and test requirements; maintains records; approves or
disapproves shipment and advises general manager; analyzes quality trends,
and informs engineering and operations of these trends and of problems
that need resolution. Persons assigned to quality assurance functions are
trained specialists in particular fields of inspection and testing. To create
and maintain quality-assurance skills, management provides on the job
and classroom training and encourages participation in professional meetings.

Related Documentation (Insert all appropriate and applicable documentation.)

TITLE: Document No: QM XYZ 001

                                                        Revision: 00

Quality System Practices and Controls: Date: May 1, 1995

Control of Inspection, Measuring,   Supersedes: New

and Test Equipment   Section: 4.11

                                                        Page 1 of 4

_____

4.11   Control of Inspection, Measuring and Test Equipment

Purpose   The purpose of inspection and calibration is to assure that measurement equipment is in usable condition, is precise and accurate, and yields reliable data.

Policy   Measurement equipment used to evaluate or control product or process characteristics shall be inspected and calibrated at scheduled intervals in accordance with written procedures.

Requirements   Detailed instructions about measurement and calibration. All critical test equipment shall have a minimum (or as required) gauge and research and development study once per quarter.

Written Descriptions

Procedures are prepared in writing for the inspection and calibration of each piece of measurement equipment. Such procedures may be those specified by the equipment manufacturer or developed by XYZ.

TITLE: **Document No: QM XYZ 001**

                                                            Revision: 00

Quality System Practices and Controls: **Date: May 1, 1995**

Control of Inspection, Measuring,   **Supersedes: New**

and Test Equipment   **Section: 4.11**

                                                          Page 2 of 4

Schedules

Whether purchased or fabricated by XYZ, each piece of measurement
equipment is inspected and qualified prior to initial use. Thereafter, equipment is inspected and recalibrated at specified intervals in accordance with
the equipment manufacturer's recommendations or at intervals based on
experience in using similar equipment.

Records

The following information is recorded for each type of measurement equipment:

- Identification by number, name, and description.
- Location.
- Calibration procedure.
- Interval of calibration and inspection.
- Dates of each calibration and inspection.
- Identification of calibration technician or source.
- Results of measurements, deficiencies, repairs, or adjustments.
- Due date for next calibration and inspection.

TITLE: Document No: QM XYZ 001

Revision: 00

Quality System Practices and Controls: Date: May 1, 1995

Control of Inspection, Measuring,   Supersedes: New

and Test Equipment   Section: 4.11

Page 3 of 4

Labels

Each piece of equipment bears an identification label that states (where space permits) or references the following information:

- Equipment identification.
- Date of last calibration and inspection.
- Identification of calibration technician or source.
- Due date for next calibration and inspection.

Standards

Measurement equipment is calibrated against standards traceable to the National Institute of Standards with an accuracy 10 times greater than the item being measured.

Accuracy

To the extent practical, all measurement equipment should discriminate to a capability of accuracy to 1/10 or less of the allowable tolerance band of the parameters being evaluated.

TITLE: Document No: QM XYZ 001
                                                   Revision: 00
Quality System Practices and Controls: Date: May 1, 1995
Control of Inspection, Measuring,   Supersedes: New
and Test Equipment   Section: 4.11
                                               Page 4 of 4

Environment

To the extent necessitated by the character or a calibration operation, the environment (e.g., temperature, humidity, lighting, vibration, and cleanliness) is controlled.

Related Documentation (Insert all appropriate and applicable documentation.)

TITLE:	Document No: QM XYZ 001
	Revision: 00
Quality System Practices and Controls:	Date: May 1, 1995
Inspection and Test Status	Supersedes: New
	Section: 4.12
	Page 1 of 1

4.12   Inspection and Test Status

Purpose   The purpose of inspection and test status is to ensure that we ship to our customers only product that has successfully passed all required inspections and tests.

Policy   Authorized signatures, stamps, tags, work orders, and inspection records identify the inspection and test status of all products and accompany the product in accordance with established operational procedures. These forms indicate the conformance or nonconformance of products to the specifications with regard to the inspections and tests performed. In addition, a final documentation review occurs before any conforming products are released to distribution.

Requirements   All inspection and test records shall be documented and maintained for a minimum of three years. All changes to the inspection and testing procedures shall be authorized by the regulatory and quality assurance departments.

Related Documentation (Insert all appropriate and applicable documentation.)

TITLE:	Document No: QM XYZ 001
	Revision: 00
Quality System Practices and Controls:	Date: May 1, 1995
Control of Nonconforming Product	Supersedes: New
	Section: 4.13
	Page 1 of 2

4.13   Control of Nonconforming Product

Purpose   To ensure that items found to be nonconforming are promptly identified, segregated, and dispositioned to prevent their inadvertent use, shipment, or mixing with conforming product.

Policy   Nonconforming product is defined as any incoming raw material, in-process product, or final product that fails to conform to specified requirements. Such product is clearly identified either physically or in computer records in order to segregate it from conforming product. The nonconforming product is then held pending a disposition decision being made by the affected XYZ department(s).

Requirements   Nonconforming products shall be identified and segregated from the production flow or installation process to prevent their inadvertent use, shipment, or mixing with conforming product. Inspection function personnel identifying deficiencies shall ensure that the deviation or discrepancy is clearly described relative to the acceptance criteria and notify all appropriate personnel.

TITLE: **Document No: QM XYZ 001**

Revision: 00

Quality System Practices and Controls: **Date: May 1, 1995**

Control of Nonconforming Product   **Supersedes: New**

Section: 4.13

Page 2 of 2

4.13.2   Review and Disposition of Nonconforming Product

The responsibility for review and authority for disposition of nonconforming materials and products are defined in quality reference documents. XYZ company allows four release decisions.

- Routine releases when conformance to all specifications has been demonstrated.
- Conditional or partial release when further action is required at a subsequent stage.
- Restricted or concessional release when conformance to requirements is borderline and product disposition requires special control.
- Product is condemned or returned to suppler(s).

Related Documentation (Insert all appropriate and applicable documentation.)

TITLE:	Document No: QM XYZ 001
	Revision: 00
Quality System Practices and Controls:	Date: May 1, 1995
Corrective and Preventive Action	Supersedes: New
	Section: 4.14
	Page 1 of 4

4.14   Corrective and Preventive Action

Purpose

The XYZ corrective action and complaint control system serves the following purposes:

- To receive, acknowledge, and act on requests for corrective action, complaints or other information provided by internal and external customers.
- To acquire as much information as possible as a basis for product improvement.
- To verify product safety and efficacy at the user level.
- To assure that products returned to XYZ for repair or rework meet product specification criteria.

Policy   XYZ values customer opinion. When requests for corrective action, complaints, or suggestions for product improvement are received regarding any aspect of product manufacturing, distribution, or performance, XYZ take prompt and objective action. The quality assurance function maintains records of specific and significant complaints, including their disposition. The quality assurance function serves as the coordinator on matters related to product efficacy, safety, and quality for internal and external customers. Returned, reworked, or upgraded products are processed to assure that their quality, safety, and efficacy are equal to newly manufactured products.

TITLE: Document No: QM XYZ 001

                                                        Revision: 00

Quality System Practices and Controls: Date: May 1, 1995

Corrective and Preventive Action   Supersedes: New

                                                       Section: 4.14

                                                       Page 2 of 4

4.14.1   General

XYZ Corporation has established and maintains documented procedures for implementing correction and prevention as well as complaint control systems throughout the organization as needed.

4.14.2   Corrective Action

When nonconforming products are identified, the cause of their occurrence shall be investigated, corrective action taken, and preventive measures initiated. When corrective action is necessary, controls shall ensure the intended action has been performed and is effective. There shall be a system to implement and document any change to existing procedures as a result of corrective actions.

TITLE:	Document No: QM XYZ 001
	Revision: 00
Quality System Practices and Controls:	Date: May 1, 1995
Corrective and Preventive Action	Supersedes: New
	Section: 4.14
	Page 3 of 4

4.14.3   Preventive Actions

Technical Liaison

Field representatives report formally and informally on the reactions of customers to end products/medical devices from a technical point of view. They also report problems encountered in product utilization. XYZ specialists consult regularly with users on technical matters and conduct technical and training seminars to assure continuing two-way dialogue.

Processing of Comments and Complaints

All written comments and significant complaints received by XYZ are filed and assigned to the appropriate department for further evaluation and recommendations for their disposition. Needed corrective action is promptly taken, and the results of this action are recorded.

Customer Liaison

A designated person or organizational unit is responsible for assuming that comments and complaints are processed on schedule and that related actions are fully implemented.

TITLE:	Document No: QM XYZ 001
	Revision: 00
Quality System Practices and Controls:	**Date: May 1, 1995**
Corrective and Preventive Action	**Supersedes: New**
	Section: 4.14
	Page 4 of 4

Processing Returned Products

The company monitors all products returned for repair or rework to assure that the products are identified in the manufacturing flow and that they are reworked/reprocessed and retested to standards equivalent to newly manufactured products. In addition, quality assurance or an assigned function is responsible for initiating such action as appropriate to preclude future returns.

Related Documentation (Insert all appropriate and applicable documentation.)

TITLE: Document No: QM XYZ 001

                                                     Revision: 00

Quality System Practices and Controls: Date: May 1, 1995

Handling, Storage, Packaging,   Supersedes: New

Preservation, and Delivery   Section: 4.15

                                                     Page 1 of 5

4.15   Handling, Storage, Packaging, Preservation, and Delivery

Purpose   Handling, storage, packaging, preservation, and delivery controls are designed to retain products in the same condition as when manufactured and to make it possible to ascertain the location of products subsequent to production. The procedures specified for labeling and packaging protect the product against damage, assure that labels are correct, prevent label mix-ups, facilitate traceability and inventory control, and transfer clear and pertinent information to users for correct product utilization. The sterility control program assures that products represented by XYZ as sterile conform to established sterility standards when delivered to users.

Policy

The identity and traceability of products are maintained from shipment to point of delivery. XYZ's storage, shipping, and handling practices prevent product deterioration or damage.

TITLE: Document No: QM XYZ 001

                                                  Revision: 00

Quality System Practices and Controls: Date: May 1, 1995

Handling, Storage, Packaging,   Supersedes: New

Preservation, and Delivery   Section: 4.15

                                               Page 2 of 5

XYZ fully recognizes that the effectiveness of product packaging and the accuracy and completeness of labeling are prerequisites for orderly and controlled product storage and distribution and for correct and safe product utilization. Accordingly, packaging and labeling procedures are designed, specified, and implemented with the same attention to detail as applies to product. The central mechanisms for control of packaging and labeling are the device master record and device history record.

When product sterilization is required, it is accomplished in accordance with planned procedures incorporated into the device master record. Packaging is designed to maintain the integrity of sterility from the point of sterilization to the point of use. The sterility control procedure applies to XYZ and its suppliers of sterilization services.

4.15.1   General
Distribution Documentation

All shipments of devices are identified by control. Records identify to whom lots are consigned, quantity, and ship date.

Product Sterilization

Products are cleaned according to procedure before sterilization. Product sterilization is then performed as scheduled and as specified in the device master record. During sterilization processing, products are identified and controlled by sterilization lot numbers to preclude intermingling of sterilized and nonsterilized products.

TITLE: Document No: QM XYZ 001
                                                   Revision: 00
Quality System Practices and Controls: Date: May 1, 1995
Handling, Storage, Packaging,   Supersedes: New
Preservation, and Delivery   Section: 4.15
                                                Page 3 of 5

The capacity of sterilization processes and the adequacy of the surrounding environment are validated before routine sterilization is initiated. The results of this validation are recorded on the device master record. Changes in sterility control procedures are made only by authorized persons, and a record of these changes, including effective dates, is recorded and initialed on the device master record.

4.15.2   Handling
Methods and means will be provided to ensure that handling of the products does not cause damage or deterioration.

4.15.3   Storage
After production, products are stored and quarantined in assigned locations under conditions that preclude mix-ups, damage, or deterioration. Products are shipped to customers on a first-in/first-out (FIFO) basis.

TITLE: Document No: QM XYZ 001

Revision: 00

Quality System Practices and Controls: Date: May 1, 1995

Handling, Storage, Packaging,   Supersedes: New

Preservation, and Delivery   Section: 4.15

Page 4 of 5

4.15.4   Packaging

Packaging is designed to resist product damage during handling, storage, and distribution. The labeling and packaging locations are examined to assure that only products qualified for packaging and labeling are positioned in such locations. The conformance of labels and packaging to established procedures is verified routinely. Procedures are specified on the DMR and DHR. Product labels are printed on a per-order basis at the time of packaging. Accessibility to the labels is limited to manufacturing personnel with assigned labeling duties. The product lot number is identified on the label, and the accuracy of this number is verified. Storage and handling of packaging and packaging materials are performed in accordance with instructions incorporated into the device master record.

TITLE: **Document No: QM XYZ 001**

                                                                           Revision: 00

Quality System Practices and Controls: **Date: May 1, 1995**

Handling, Storage, Packaging,   **Supersedes: New**

Preservation, and Delivery   **Section: 4.15**

                                                                        Page 5 of 5

4.15.5   Preservation

The integrity of the product will be preserved as defined by the customer's requirements or the prescribed procedures of the particular product.

4.15.6   Delivery

The quality of the product shall be protected after final inspection and test. Where contractually specified, this protection shall be extended to include delivery to destination.

Related Documentation (Insert all appropriate and applicable documentation.)

TITLE:	Document No: QM XYZ 001
	Revision: 00
Quality Systems Practices and Controls:	Date: May 1, 1995
Control of Quality Records	Supersedes: New
	Section: 4.16
	Page 1 of 4

4.16   Control of Quality Records

Purpose   Quality records serve the following purposes:

- To provide internal control and documentation of the XYZ quality assurance system.
- To verify that products conform to established requirements.
- To allow traceability of the manufacturing history and disposition of a device.
- To provide a defense in the event of product liability litigation.

Policy   For general management and operational purposes, three types of records are maintained: technical, administrative, and financial. Of the three types of records, technical records are the most pertinent to the quality system, and of the technical records, the device master records and the device history records are the most significant to the quality system. Administrative records include numerous documents of which only personnel records are directly related to quality assurance. Financial data are not an element of the quality system and are confidential.

TITLE:	Document No: QM XYZ 001
	Revision: 00
Quality Systems Practices and Controls:	Date: May 1, 1995
Control of Quality Records	Supersedes: New
	Section: 4.16
	Page 2 of 4

Both internally and externally, accessibility to all records is controlled on a need-to-know basis. Guidelines for accessibility to confidential records may be found in the *XYZ Information and Security Policy and Procedure* manual.

4.16.1   General

Confidentiality and Accessibility

When representatives of regulatory agencies, outside companies, or other outside parties have a valid and confirmed need to know for specific records, management may authorize accessibility or release of the records. Certain parties, such as suppliers, may be required to sign a confidential disclosure agreement. Confidential data and information are clearly marked as such prior to release. Employees are directed to inform all visitors and correspondents of the XYZ procedures for protecting the confidentiality and accessibility of records.

TITLE: Document No: QM XYZ 001

                                            Revision: 00

Quality Systems Practices and Controls: **Date: May 1, 1995**

Control of Quality Records   **Supersedes: New**

                                            Section: 4.16

                                            Page 3 of 4

Technical Support Data

Technical support data includes drawings, specifications, standards, test and control procedures, change control entries, sampling methods, and any other information that technically supports day-to-day operations. These data and their locations are referenced in the device master record and are thus retrievable when needed.

Quality System Records

The totality of XYZ quality system inspection, audit, and test data constitutes the quality system records.

4.16.2   Device Master Record

The device master record, directly or by reference, identifies production and quality assurance specifications and the procedures by which a product is controlled. Depending on the stage of product manufacturing, the device master record includes packaging and labeling procedures.

TITLE: Document No: QM XYZ 001

Revision: 00

Quality Systems Practices and Controls: Date: May 1, 1995

Control of Quality Records   Supersedes: New

Section: 4.16

Page 4 of 4

The DMR delineates, in sequence, the procedures, specifications, and controls by which a device is fabricated, inspected, tested, packaged, labeled, sterilized, stored, and distributed. In doing so, the DMR assures effective, efficient, and orderly operation.

4.16.3   Device History Record Requirements

The device history record identifies each lot of product and provides a complete product history, both qualitatively and quantitatively. The device history record serves as a historical record of each production lot and provides product traceability. A DHR accompanies each lot of product from initiation of production to shipment and documents the specifics of manufacturing operations including process steps, test and inspection information, and personnel performing the operations.

Related Documentation (Insert all appropriate and applicable documentation.)

TITLE: **Document No: QM XYZ 001**

                                                           Revision: 00

Quality System Practices and Controls: **Date: May 1, 1995**

Internal Quality Audits   **Supersedes: New**

                                                        Section: 4.17

                                                       Page 1 of 3

4.17   Internal Quality Audits

Purpose   XYZ's system audits serve three purposes:

- To confirm compliance to management-prescribed policies and practices.
- To facilitate internal system improvements.
- To review the effectiveness of the operations.

Policy   Under the direction of senior management, internal audits of operations and technical procedures are periodically conducted.

Audits are performed by persons not administratively responsible for the functions being audited, with the exception of senior managers who have companywide responsibility. The results of audits along with any requests for corrective action are distributed to responsible functional managers.

TITLE: Document No: QM XYZ 001

                                                            Revision: 00

Quality System Practices and Controls: Date: May 1, 1995

Internal Quality Audits   Supersedes: New

                                                          Section: 4.17

                                                          Page 2 of 3

Requirements

Each audit is conducted in accordance with explicit directions that

- Specify the operation or area to be audited.
- Define the purpose and scope of the audit.
- Provide a checklist of details to be reviewed.
- Designate the audit team membership (if applicable) and the lead auditor responsible for performance of the audit.
- Establish a schedule for initiation and completion of the audit

Audit teams may, at management's option, be appointed ad hoc. They are then dissolved upon completion of the assigned tasks. Persons responsible for a function being audited are excluded from audit committees.

TITLE: **Document No: QM XYZ 001**

Revision: 00

Quality System Practices and Controls: **Date: May 1, 1995**

Internal Quality Audits   **Supersedes: New**

Section: 4.17

Page 3 of 3

Records are maintained to show operations or functions audited, the identity of the lead auditor and membership of the audit team (where applicable), significant results, and results of the corrective actions that have been implemented. The details of the auditor's (or audit team's) observations are communicated by written report to senior management.

Related Documentation (Insert all appropriate and applicable documentation.)

TITLE: **Document No: QM XYZ 001**

Revision: 00

Quality System Practices and Controls: **Date: May 1, 1995**

Training   **Supersedes: New**

Section: 4.18

Page 1 of 2

4.18   Training

Purpose   To achieve our policy goal of continuous improvement in everything we do, XYZ recognizes the value and benefit of training and educating employees on an ongoing basis. It is our belief that when we invest in training and educating our employees, quality products and customer satisfaction are the returns.

Policy   XYZ is committed to the professional development of its employees through training and retraining to improve current skills and/or introduce new skills. XYZ encourages its employees to take educational courses to increase their effectiveness in their current positions and prepare them for increased or new responsibilities.

Requirements

On the Job Training—Training, when necessary, will be provided for all personnel involved in activities affecting quality and quality verification. This training will include quality awareness.

TITLE: Document No: QM XYZ 001

                                                            Revision: 00

Quality System Practices and Controls: Date: May 1, 1995

Training   Supersedes: New

                                                         Section: 4.18

                                                        Page 2 of 2

Training and Retraining—XYZ offers both on-site and off-site training programs in a wide variety of subjects, such as quality assurance, GMP, first aid, and safety. Employees will be scheduled to attend these sessions as needed or as recommended by the supervisor or manager.

Training Development Department—XYZ has a training and development department that facilitates, conducts (when practicable), and documents in-house training of XYZ employees.

Educational Assistance—XYZ will reimburse the cost of tuition, books, entrance exam fees, and lab fees for

- Courses taken as an undergraduate degree.
- Courses taken as an advanced degree candidate.
- Nondegree courses that are directly related to an employee's current work or a to company position to which an employee may aspire.

Related Documentation (Insert all appropriate and applicable documentation.)

TITLE:	Document No: QM XYZ 001
	Revision: 00
Quality Systems Practices and Controls:	**Date: May 1, 1995**
Servicing	**Supersedes: New**
	Section: 4.19
	Page 1 of 1

4.19   Servicing

The ISO 9001 clause 4.19 on servicing is not considered applicable to orthopedic implants; however, XYZ does provide servicing on the surgical instruments we manufacture.

Purpose   XYZ will repair and modify our surgical instruments as a service to our customers in order to maintain the instruments in high quality condition.

Policy   Upon request and when applicable, our policy is to respond to our customers' needs in a way that is safe, efficable, and provides customer satisfaction.

Requirements   We shall produce and make available comprehensive instructions covering on-site servicing activities.

Related Documentation (Insert all appropriate and applicable documentation.)

TITLE:	Document No: QM XYZ 001
	Revision: 00
Quality System Practices and Controls:	Date: May 1, 1995
Statistical Techniques	Supersedes: New
	Section: 4.20
	Page 1 of 1

4.20   Statistical Techniques

Purpose   The use of proven statistical techniques is a reliable method for making sound decisions for purposes of determining adequate inspection sampling, process capability, and for controlling excessive variation while the manufacturing operations are in progress.

Policy   Standardized statistical methods will be documented and used to establish lot acceptance sampling plans for product inspection and testing, and statistical process control charting techniques will be used to control excessive variation for designated product characteristics of process parameters.

Requirements

XYZ will identify and document acceptance sampling plans to verify the acceptability of product characteristics or process capabilities. These plans will be reviewed periodically to determine their adequacies in detecting nonconforming product or process characteristics.

Document No: QM ABC 001
Revision: 00
Date: August 1, 1995
Supersedes: New
Section: 0
Page 1 of 1
Authorized By:_____

ABC, INC. QUALITY MANUAL

Based on QS-9000 Standard

Sample Manual

Title: ABC's	Document No: QM ABC 001
Quality System Practices and Controls:	Revision: 00
Table of Contents	Date: August 1, 1995
	Supersedes: New
	Section: 0
	Page 1 of 2

0.0	Table of Contents
0.1	Master Document Control (not included here)
0.2	Authorized signatures (not included here)

Section I:	ISO 9000-Based Requirements

1.0	Introduction
1.1	ABC Quality Policy
1.2	Scope of the ABC Quality System Manual
1.3	Company Profile

2.0	References
2.1	Quality Standards
2.2	Quality System Documents

3.0	Quality System Terminology
3.1	Terms and Definitions
3.2	Standard Abbreviations

4.0	Quality System Practices and Controls
4.1	Management Responsibility
4.1.1	Quality Policy Requirements
4.1.2	Organization
4.1.2.1	Responsibility and Authority
4.1.2.2	Resources
4.1.2.3	Management Representative, Organizational Interface
4.1.3	Management Review
4.1.4	Business Plan
4.1.5	Analysis and Use of Company-Level Data
4.1.6	Customer Satisfaction
4.2	Quality System
4.2.1	General
4.2.2	Quality System Procedures
4.2.3	Quality Planning
	. . .
	. . .

Title: ABC's	**Document No: QM ABC 001**
Quality System Practices and Controls:	**Revision: 00**
Table of Contents	**Date: August 1, 1995**
	Supersedes: New
	Section: 0
	Page 2 of 2

Section II: Sector-Specific Requirements

1.0   Production Part Approval Process
2.0   Continuous Improvement
3.0   Manufacturing Capabilities

Section III: Customer-Specific Requirements

1.0   Chrysler Requirements
2.0   Ford Requirements
3.0   General Motors Requirements
4.0   Truck Manufacturers Requirements

5.0   Appendixes (May include the following, even though these items are not
        included here.)
5.1   ABC Organizational Chart
5.2   Cross-Reference between QS-9000 Requirements and the ABC Quality
        System
5.3   Cross-Reference between Individual Automotive Requirements and the
        ABC Quality Manual
5.4   Miscellaneous

TITLE: ABC's	Document No: QM ABC 001
Quality System Practices and Controls:	Revision 00
	August 1, 1995
Introduction	Supersedes: New
	Section 1.0
	Page 1 of 1

1.0   INTRODUCTION

1.1   ABC Quality Policy

ABC will provide products and services that meet or exceed the expectations of our customers (internal and external) through our total commitment to continuous improvement in everything we do. We are committed to world class quality for everything we do—from design to manufacturing to shipping to customer follow-up. To implement this policy we are educating all our employees on how their performance contributes to product quality, and we encourage measurement characteristics to track our improvement. In addition we are committed to empowering all our employees with the appropriate authority and responsibility to get the job done right the first time.

1.2   Scope of the ABC Quality Manual

The ABC Quality Manual describes the policies and quality system structure employed by ABC to ensure that design, production, and delivery are in good order. The quality system was created to reflect a quality program consistent with the ISO 9001 standard and the automotive requirements known as QS-9000.

1.3   Company Profile

ABC was founded in 1947 with the sole purpose of supplying the automotive industry with decorative striping. The company started out with 50 employees and by 1995 had grown to 1,568 employees. Gross sales in 1994 were $868 million.

The company has grown not only in financial terms and number of employees but also in product line and facilities. ABC operates 15 plants throughout the USA, Canada, Mexico, Germany, and Brazil and has extended its product line to include seating and mirror technology.

TITLE: ABC's	Document No: QM ABC 001
Quality System Practices and Controls:	**Revision 00**
	August 1, 1995
References	**Supersedes: New**
	Section 2.0
	Page 1 of 1

2.0   REFERENCES

2.1   Quality Standards

The following quality standards and guidelines have been used in developing this quality manual:

- *ISO 9001 Quality Systems—Model for Quality Assurance in Design/ Development, Production, Installation and Servicing*
- *ISO 9004 Quality Management and Quality System Elements Guidelines*
- *Quality System Requirements: QS-9000*
- *ISO/DIS 10013 Guidelines for Developing Quality Manuals*

2.2   Quality System Documents

This manual contains the policies of ABC for the design and manufacture of high quality products. In case more detail is needed, the reader is encouraged to consult the procedures and instructions manuals in the ABC quality documentation system. The appendixes of this manual contain reference tables and requirements that correspond with and demonstrate compliance to these standards. Because documentation is constantly changing to reflect the requirements of the customer, the reader may consult the ABC QA documentation department for an updated listing of documents.

TITLE: ABC's	Document No: QM ABC 001
Quality System Practices and Controls:	Revision 00
	August 1, 1995
Quality System Terminology	Supersedes: New
	Section 3.0
	Page 1 of 1

3.0   QUALITY SYSTEM TERMINOLOGY

3.1   Terms and Definitions

No special terminology or jargon is used. If there is a need for explanation for certain words, the official interpretation is based on the ANSI/ASQC A8402 standard.

3.2   Standard Abbreviations

Within ABC we use many abbreviations, and the reader is encouraged to consult our booklet on acronyms and abbreviations, which is found in every office of the company.

TITLE: ABC's	**Document No: QM ABC 001**
Quality System Practices and Controls:	**Revision 00**
	August 1, 1995
Management Responsibility	**Supersedes: New**
	Section 4.1
	Page 1 of 4

4.0   QUALITY SYSTEM PRACTICES AND CONTROLS

4.1   Management Responsibility

4.1.1   Quality Policy Requirements

It is the responsibility of ABC management to provide the personnel and resources necessary to maintain the requirements of the ABC quality policy and the ABC quality manual.

Specifically, management will

- Provide quality products and services by striving to exceed the defined needs and expectations of our customers.
- Develop a quality system based on the ISO 9001 and QS-9000 standards to foster continuous process improvement and problem prevention instead of problem detection.
- Define and implement our quality system based upon employee empowerment and a commitment to excellence.
- Give all employees the training and support to provide quality products and services to all customers.
- Communicate our mission and quality objectives to all employees, and assign individual responsibilities for quality and accountability.
- Use statistical methods where appropriate to monitor quality performance and to isolate major problems for immediate solution.
- Establish and maintain a working environment that supports the production and delivery of high quality products and services.
- Form relationships with both customers and suppliers that will improve quality in all aspects of product usage and purchased parts.

TITLE: ABC's

Quality System Practices and Controls:

Management Responsibility

Document No: QM ABC 001

Revision 00

August 1, 1995

Supersedes: New

Section 4.1

Page 2 of 4

4.1.2 Organization

4.1.2.1 Responsibility and Authority ABC has an organizational structure with established levels of responsibility and authority that will provide quality products to our customers and reduce conflicts of interest among departments and functions. A detailed organizational chart is provided in the appendix.

The organizational structure allows independence and authority of the quality function, an essential element for ensuring that quality products are delivered to our customers.

Another important element of the organizational structure is that all employees are responsible for the quality of their work and have the freedom, responsibility, and duty to identify and document quality problems for corrective actions to prevent the occurrence of nonconformities in their product, service, process, or quality system.

4.1.2.2 Resources All resource requirements are defined in the procedures and instructions manual as needed. As for the ability of workers to perform their designated tasks, their qualifications may be found either in the training department or in their respective departments.

4.1.2.3 Management Representative The management representative has the authority and responsibility to ensure that the quality system is effectively implemented and maintained in accordance with the ISO/QS requirements and to report to the company's chief executive on the performance of the quality system at the time of the management review.

Organizational Interfaces ABC is committed to the philosophy of teams and as such is always encouraging cross-functional and multidisciplinary teams for continuous improvement.

4.1.3 Management Review The quality system at ABC is designed to satisfy the requirements of both the ISO 9001 and QS-9000. Management, therefore, will review the system at least once every 12 months to ensure conformance and effectiveness. The process and the results of the reviews will be documented.

TITLE: ABC's	Document No: QM ABC 001
Quality System Practices and Controls:	**Revision 00**
	August 1, 1995
Management Responsibility	**Supersedes: New**
	Section 4.1
	Page 3 of 4

4.1.4 Business Plan   The senior vice president is responsible for ensuring that business goals and plans are implemented and adhered to as described in ABC's business plan. The business plan details short- and long-term goals for specific areas of the business, including

- Market-related issues.
- Financial planning and cost.
- Growth projections.
- Plant/facilities plans.
- Cost objectives.
- Human resource development.
- Research and development plans, projections, and projects with appropriate funding.
- Projected sales figures.
- Quality objectives.
- Customer satisfaction plans.
- Key internal quality and operational performance measurable.
- Health, safety, and environmental issues.

The senior vice president is also responsible for ensuring that the business plan is developed, documented, tracked, revised, reviewed, and communicated as defined in the appropriate procedure. Goals and plans are developed as a result of the analysis of company-level data, competitor and other benchmark data, customer satisfaction data, and current and future customer needs and expectations.

4.1.5   Analysis and Use of Company-Level Data

The quality staff is responsible for ensuring that trends in quality, current levels of quality for key product and service features, and key indicators for operational performance are documented in the quarterly business performance report. The information documented in these reports is used as an input to the tracking, analysis, and subsequent revision of the business plan.

TITLE: ABC's	Document No: QM ABC 001
Quality System Practices and Controls:	Revision 00
	August 1, 1995
Management Responsibility	Supersedes: New
	Section 4.1
	Page 4 of 4

To make sure that appropriate data are used, each department manager prepares monthly performance reports that document key internal quality, and operational indicators. The reports are submitted to senior management for review and become key inputs to the business performance report. The manager of quality assurance, in consultation with the department head, initiates a corrective action procedure or preventive action procedure, as appropriate, based on the results of the monthly reports in order to ensure that prompt action is taken on customer-related problems and that weaknesses in the quality system are addressed.

4.1.6   Customer Satisfaction

The marketing department is responsible for documenting and tracking trends and current levels of customer satisfaction according to the determination, reporting, and review of customer satisfaction procedures. This responsibility includes determining customer satisfaction, and collecting competitive and other benchmark data for comparative purposes. The results of these activities are key inputs to the business performance report and business plan.

Related Documentation (Insert all appropriate and applicable documentation.)

TITLE: ABC's	Document No: QM ABC 001
Quality System Practices and Controls:	**Revision 00**
	August 1, 1995
Quality System	**Supersedes: New**
	Section 4.2
	Page 1 of 2

4.2   Quality System

4.2.1   General

ABC's quality system is defined through a four-tier documentation system. Its purpose is to ensure that all products and services conform to the requirements as defined by our customers and our own management. The four levels of the documentation system are

- The quality manual that defines the policy and companywide structure and methods for maintaining the quality system.
- Procedures that define who does what, when it is done, and what documentation is used to verify that the quality event was performed as required.
- Work instructions that define the detail of the procedures.
- Records and forms. Records provide the assurance that the required product or service was achieved. Forms refer to tags, labels, stamps, printed sheets, and all other means to identify the status of specific material, equipment, and other items in the organization.

4.2.2   Quality System Procedures

ABC maintains documented quality system procedures to satisfy both the ISO and QS requirements and to meet the company's need to effectively manage and control the quality system.

4.2.3   Quality Planning

The quality assurance department is responsible for defining the specific quality practices throughout ABC company.

The manager of quality assurance has the direct responsibility and authority to define, implement, and maintain the quality system. That responsibility extends but is not limited to control plans as defined in APQP and control plan, special characteristics, the use of cross-functional teams, feasibility reviews, and the use of FMEAs.

TITLE: ABC's	Document No: QM ABC 001
Quality System Practices and Controls:	**Revision 00**
	August 1, 1995
Quality System	**Supersedes: New**
	Section 4.2
	Page 2 of 2

ABC defines special characteristics as those characteristics that may affect safety or compliance with government regulations, are closely tied to customer satisfaction, or require special monitoring and control for any other reason. It is ABC's responsibility to familiarize its suppliers with the appropriate identification and use of the special characteristics.

Related Documentation (Insert all appropriate and applicable documentation.)

TITLE: ABC's	**Document No: QM ABC 001**
Quality System Practices and Controls:	**Revision 00**
	August 1, 1995
Contract Review	**Supersedes: New**
	Section 4.3
	Page 1 of 1

4.3   Contract Review

4.3.1   General
Contract reviews are conducted and documented as appropriate throughout ABC company.

4.3.2   Review
The marketing and purchasing vice presidents have the primary responsibility for ensuring that all contracts are reviewed prior to submission and that they are adequately defined and documented. Furthermore, at this stage of the review, the engineering and quality departments may be consulted as to the capability of ABC to fulfill the order.

In case of verbal orders, ABC's personnel ensure that the order requirements are agreed to before their acceptance. Appropriate procedures exist for such cases.

4.3.3   Amendments to a Contract
It is the marketing department's responsibility to coordinate all amendments to the contract with the customer and ABC personnel. When changes do occur, they are reviewed, approved, and communicated to the appropriate personnel within ABC company.

4.3.4   Records
All information pertinent to contract reviews is maintained and documented by company name, order number, and customer name and/or code.

Related Documentation (Insert all appropriate and applicable documentation.)

TITLE: ABC's   Document No: QM ABC 001
Quality System Practices and Controls: Revision 00
                                              August 1, 1995
Design Control   Supersedes: New
                                                Section 4.4
                                               Page 1 of 3

4.4   Design Control

4.4.1   General

ABC maintains procedures and instructions that define, control, and verify the design activities as specified in the requirements.

4.4.2   Design and Development Planning

The product manager is responsible for defining a product design, development plan, and implementation that describes the major activities of the project. It is also the product manager's responsibility to assign the design and verification activities to appropriate personnel. A plan is created for each new product design or major redesign of existing products, and the plan is reviewed and approved before detailed design or development begins. The plan is also updated as the product evolves through the stages of design, development, and release for manufacturing.

4.4.3   Organizational and Technical Interfaces

The ABC company uses project managers in the engineering department for the deployment of new products. As such, the responsibility for organizational and technical interfaces in design control falls under his or her jurisdiction. Some of the responsibilities include but are not limited to

* Defining the appropriate channels for communication.
* Encouraging proper documentation and review.
* Defining the appropriate organizational interfaces.
* Establishing appropriate cross-functional teams.

4.4.4   Design Input

All design input requirements are identified, specified, communicated, and reviewed by the appropriate personnel within the ABC company. During this review, the appropriate specification sheet is developed and concerns about incomplete, ambiguous, or conflicting requirements by those responsible for their definition and specification are addressed and documented.

TITLE: ABC's	Document No: QM ABC 001
Quality System Practices and Controls:	Revision 00
	August 1, 1995
Design Control	Supersedes: New
	Section 4.4
	Page 2 of 3

ABC company uses computer-aided design, engineering, and analysis in its design activities. The CAD/CAE systems are capable of two-way interfacing with customer systems.

4.4.5   Design Output
The vice president of engineering (or the appropriate product manager or project manager) is responsible for ensuring that design output is documented and expressed in terms of requirements, calculations, analysis, or other means that can be verified against design input requirements.

4.4.6   Design Review
ABC conducts formal design reviews. They are planned and documented at the following six design stages according to internal engineering procedures.

1. Concept.
2. Definition.
3. Design.
4. Fabrication and assembly (prototype).
5. Testing/verification.
6. Documentation and postmortem review.

Design reviews are coordinated by the product manager and/or the project manager and always include cross-functional teams concerned with the design stage being reviewed. Records of all reviews are maintained in the design project folder for a minimum of three years.

4.4.7   Design Verification
The vice president of engineering (or an assigned product manager or project manager) is responsible for ensuring that activities for verifying the design are defined, planned, executed, and documented by the appropriate personnel according to the prescribed procedures. Design verification will be conducted at least during the following stages prior to release:

TITLE: ABC's	Document No: QM ABC 001
Quality System Practices and Controls:	**Revision 00**
	August 1, 1995
Design Control	**Supersedes: New**
	Section 4.4
	Page 3 of 3

- At the appropriate prescribed stage of design (see clause 4.4.6).
- During performing product performance, life, reliability, durability, and other qualification tests as appropriate and tracking the testing to ensure timely completion and conformance to requirements.
- Following a prototype development.
- At the end of a specific analyses, comparisons with similar proven designs (if available), QFD (Quality Function Deployment) studies, and other competitive or benchmark standards.

4.4.8   Design Validation

The vice president of engineering or an assigned project manager is responsible for ensuring that all final product meets or exceeds specifications prior to release for next stage processing or shipping. Design validations are conducted and documented for the product after completion of a successful design verification.

4.4.9   Design Changes

All design changes and modifications are identified and transmitted through a nonconforming action report (NCAR) or engineering services request (ESR). Design changes are initiated and coordinated by the product manager, product engineer, or project manager, and all changes and modifications are reviewed and approved by the authorized personnel and the customer (when required) prior to re-release. The design changes are part of the document control system, and the procedures follow the guidelines in the *Production Part Approval Process Reference Manual*. In the case of changes to proprietary designs, the impact on form, fit, function, performance, and durability are determined in consultation with the customer.

Related Documentation (Insert all appropriate and applicable documentation.)

TITLE: ABC's	Document No: QM ABC 001
Quality System Practices and Controls:	**Revision 00**
	August 1, 1995
Document and Data Control	**Supersedes: New**
	Section 4.5
	Page 1 of 2

4.5   Document and Data Control

4.5.1   General

ABC company identifies and controls documents and data in all media that relate to the ISO/QS requirements, as well as documents and data supplied by the customer or other sources and used to provide products and services. Whenever appropriate, special characteristics are identified.

4.5.2   Document and Data Approval and Issue

It is the responsibility of the quality assurance manager to ensure that all quality system documents (quality manual, quality system procedures, and the quality system-related work instructions) have the following controls in place:

- All documents in the quality system are current.
- All control documents are properly signed.
- All revisions are properly signed and distributed.
- All obsolete documents have been removed from the system.
- All control documents have been reviewed appropriately and approved by the department manager prior to distribution and use.
- All documents and their copies are numbered and assigned to an individual or area of use.
- All control documents may be found in the master control document manual with the current names and locations of all holders.

ABC has established procedures to assure the timely review, distribution, and implementation of all customer engineering standards, specifications, and changes.

4.5.3.   Document and Data Changes

All document and data changes and modifications are made, reviewed, approved, identified, and communicated based on the following criteria:

TITLE: ABC's	Document No: QM ABC 001
Quality System Practices and Controls:	**Revision 00**
	August 1, 1995
Document and Data Control	**Supersedes: New**
	Section 4.5
	Page 2 of 2

- Document and data changes and modifications are reviewed and approved by the same personnel or departments that performed the original review and approval unless specifically designated otherwise.
- Where applicable, the nature of the changes are identified in the document or the appropriate attachments according to the means specified in the related procedures for developing procedures and work instructions.
- ABC uses a master control document manual to indicate the current revision of documents, and thereby prevent the circulation and use of obsolete documents (see Section 4.5.2).

Related Documentation (Insert all appropriate and applicable documentation.)

TITLE: ABC's	Document No: QM ABC 001
Quality System Practices and Controls:	Revision 00
	August 1, 1995
Purchasing	Supersedes: New
	Section 4.6
	Page 1 of 2

4.6   Purchasing

4.6.1   General

The manager of purchasing is responsible for ensuring that all purchased products and subcontracted services from suppliers (including customer-designated vendors) that have an impact on the quality of ABC's products or services conform to specified requirements. These control activities are conducted according to the following documented procedures:

- Materials for ongoing production of product for a customer with an approved subcontractor list are purchased only from suppliers on the list. Requests for additional suppliers must be submitted to the customer's materials engineering activity and approved prior to placing any orders.
- All materials used in manufacturing must satisfy current governmental and safety constraints on restricted, toxic, and hazardous materials as well as environmental, electrical, and electromagnetic considerations applicable to the country of manufacture and sale.

4.6.2   Evaluation of Subcontractors

ABC requires its subcontractors to follow prescribed quality procedures in providing parts and or services. The qualification process is the responsibility of the purchasing manager. The following activities are the minimum:

- Establishing an approved supplier list (ASL) on the basis of defined criteria related to a supplier's ability to meet ABC's requirements for quality, cost, and delivery.
- Maintaining the ASL based upon supplier performance and reviews of supplier capability versus ABC's requirements.
- Scheduling and conducting supplier analyses and evaluations via a second- or third-party audit against QS-9000.
- Maintaining records of supplier capability, delivery, and performance.

TITLE: ABC's	**Document No: QM ABC 001**
Quality System Practices and Controls:	**Revision 00**
	August 1, 1995
Purchasing	**Supersedes: New**
	Section 4.6
	Page 2 of 2

4.6.3   Purchasing Data

The purchasing manager is responsible for ensuring that purchase orders are reviewed and approved for adequacy of specified requirements.

4.6.4   Verification of Purchased Product

4.6.4.1 ABC's Verification at Supplier's Premises   The manager of purchasing is responsible for ensuring that verification arrangements and the methods for product release are clearly defined in the purchasing documents in those situations where personnel from ABC verify purchased product at the supplier's premises.

4.6.4.2 Customer Verification of Subcontracted Product   It is the policy at ABC to allow the customer to inspect and verify that any subcontracted (vendored) product conforms to specified requirements provided such verification is specified in the purchasing contract. Verification by the customer does not

- Absolve ABC of its responsibility to provide acceptable product.
- Preclude the reality of, or the customer's right to, reject of the product at a subsequent time.
- Serve as evidence of effective quality control by the supplier.

Related Documentation (Insert all appropriate and applicable documentation.)

TITLE: ABC's	Document No: QM ABC 001
Quality System Practices and Controls:	**Revision 00**
	August 1, 1995
Control of Customer-Supplied Product	**Supersedes: New**
	Section 4.7
	Page 1 of 1

4.7   Control of Customer-Supplied Product

ABC has established and maintains current documented procedures for ensuring that all component parts, subassemblies, and test materials supplied by our customers are verified against specified requirements, identified, and maintained in adequate storage until required for use or incorporated into our products.

Related Documentation (Insert all appropriate and applicable documentation.)

TITLE: ABC's	Document No: QM ABC 001
Quality System Practices and Controls:	Revision 00
	August 1, 1995
Product Identification and Traceability	Supersedes: New
	Section 4.8
	Page 1 of 2

4.8   Product Identification and Traceability

ABC establishes and maintains a documented procedure for identifying raw materials and supplies, component parts, subassemblies, and finished products by means of applicable drawings, specifications, and other documents from receipt and throughout all stages of production, delivery, and installation. Product identification is maintained and controlled.

For incoming material the following procedures apply:

* The material coordinator is responsible for ensuring that all incoming materials are clearly identified either individually (where appropriate) or as a lot while they are located at incoming inspection, in transit to storage, or in use in production.
* The material coordinator maintains records that identify incoming materials by their part numbers and their corresponding purchasing documents, such as specifications, inspection requirements, acceptance criteria, and other pertinent data.
* ABC uses computer technology (where applicable) to record the receipt of materials, maintain accurate and timely records on inventory location and age, and update inventory status on a real time basis.

For in-process material: The process supervisor is responsible for ensuring that in-process materials are clearly identified.

* All orders are tagged by means of a job/operation sheet that identifies the material (part number and description), shows its routing, and denotes its current state of processing.
* Floor stock items are identified by part number and part description.
* Stocked component parts are identified by part number and drawing revision number.

For finished products: The shipping supervisor is responsible for ensuring that finished products manufactured at ABC are identified by means of a model number, serial number, and other pertinent data as required by the contract.

TITLE: ABC's	Document No: QM ABC 001
Quality System Practices and Controls:	Revision 00
	August 1, 1995
Product Identification and Traceability	Supersedes: New
	Section 4.8
	Page 2 of 2

General traceability: ABC maintains records for each finished product that include the applicable specification sheets, bills of materials, engineering drawings, and contract specifications used for manufacture. Records on traceability are maintained for a period of five years. All traceability documents are controlled.

Related Documentation (Insert all appropriate and applicable documentation.)

TITLE: ABC's	Document No: QM ABC 001
Quality System Practices and Controls:	**Revision 00**
	August 1, 1995
Process Control	**Supersedes: New**
	Section 4.9
	Page 1 of 4

4.9   Process Control

Managers of departments involved in production processes that directly affect quality of intermediate and end products are responsible for ensuring that these processes are identified, planned, and executed under controlled conditions. Controlled conditions are defined to include the following requirements:

- Documented procedures and/or work instructions for production, installation, and servicing where their absence would adversely affect quality.
- Suitable equipment and working environment to include compliance with government safety, environmental, and hazardous material regulations.
- Compliance with reference standards, codes, quality plans, and documented procedures.
- Monitoring and control of suitable process and product characteristics, with an emphasis on those characteristics designated as "special" by the customer or by ABC, during production, installation, and servicing. Special characteristics are designated, documented, and controlled as required by the customer.
- Approval of processes and equipment, as appropriate.
- Criteria for workmanship that are either written or expressed by means of representative samples.
- Equipment maintenance practices to ensure suitable and continuing process capability, as described in the preventive maintenance procedure, and performed according to regularly updated and maintained schedules of maintenance activities for key process equipment. The maintenance program at ABC includes predictive maintenance activities based upon reviews of equipment-related information, such as manufacturers recommendations, capability studies, SPC results, tool wear, fluid analysis, etc.

TITLE: ABC's	Document No: QM ABC 001
Quality System Practices and Controls:	Revision 00
	August 1, 1995
Process Control	Supersedes: New
	Section 4.9
	Page 2 of 4

4.9.1   Process Monitoring and Operator Instructions

The quality assurance or project manager, or the product quality planning team, is responsible for ensuring that work instructions for processing are developed from the sources given in the *Advanced Product Quality Planning and Control Plan Reference Manual* and documented in the appropriate procedures. Furthermore, the manager of each department with process monitoring and operator instructions is responsible for ensuring that these work instructions are current, appropriate, understandable, sufficiently detailed, and accessible at the work station, and that they are reviewed at the time of management reviews. All instructions will include the appropriate reference.

4.9.2   Preliminary Process Capability Requirements

Either quality assurance or the process team of each individual process is responsible for ensuring that a preliminary process capability study plan that covers each of the special characteristics identified in the control plan is developed and reviewed with the customer and that the plan follows the guidelines given in the *Production Part Approval Process Reference Manual* and the *Fundamental Statistical Process Control Reference Manual*. Unless customer requirements dictate otherwise, a Ppk target of 1.67 is established for preliminary results (up to 30 days) and chronically unstable processes. For processes that produce attributes data, the data collected during preliminary production runs is used to prioritize improvements and to establish control charting parameters based on the *Production Part Approval Process Manual*.

If the results are an unacceptable preliminary capability, then the corrective action process (section 4.14) and an evaluation of the mistake-proofing activities are initiated.

4.9.3   Ongoing Process Performance Requirements

At ABC company, the goal of quality assurance is to continually improve and demonstrate that improvement. The established requirements for performance improvement (unless otherwise defined) are

TITLE: ABC's	Document No: QM ABC 001
Quality System Practices and Controls:	Revision 00
	August 1, 1995
Process Control	Supersedes: New
	Section 4.9
	Page 3 of 4

- Cpk target of at least 1.33 for stable processes and normally distributed data. For processes that demonstrate a consistent high Cpk, the control plan may be reviewed and revised to reflect the process performance if the customer agrees.
- Ppk target of at least 1.67 for chronically unstable processes with output meeting specifications and a predicable pattern.
- Parts per million, non-parametric analysis, and/or index techniques to determine performance targets for nonnormal data.
- When these targets are not met and a characteristic is found to be either unstable or non-capable, the reaction plan specified in the control plan and the corrective action process (section 14) are initiated to ensure the process is returned to a stable, capable state. Both the reaction plan from the control plan and the corrective action plan are reviewed and approved by the customer when required.

4.9.4   Modified Preliminary or Ongoing Capability Requirements

At ABC it is our policy that the control plan always reflects any customer-required modifications to the default capability requirements listed in the preceding sections.

4.9.5   Verification of Job Setups

All work instructions for the performance and verification of job setups are available to the responsible personnel and include last-off part comparison (at a minimum) and statistical verification (where required).

4.9.6   Process Changes

All process changes at ABC require written approval by the customer. Process changes at ABC are defined as any change in material, machine, method, manpower, measurement, or environment. For the specific customer requirements we follow *Production Part Approval Process* and keep appropriate records.

TITLE: ABC's	Document No: QM ABC 001
Quality System Practices and Controls:	Revision 00
	August 1, 1995
Process Control	Supersedes: New
	Section 4.9
	Page 4 of 4

4.9.7   Appearance Items

ABC company provides all the control conditions specified in the ISO/QS requirements to meet the appearance criteria.

Related Documentation (Insert all appropriate and applicable documentation.)

TITLE: ABC's   Document No: QM ABC 001

Quality System Practices and Controls: Revision 00

                                                          August 1, 1995

Inspection and Testing   Supersedes: New

                                                          Section 4.10

                                                          Page 1 of 2

4.10   Inspection and Testing

4.10.1   General

ABC has established and properly maintains documented procedures, work instructions, or quality plans that define the required inspection and testing activities and related records used to verify that all product requirements are met prior to product distribution, processing, or use. The acceptance criteria are based on the notion of zero defect; however, the specific requirement(s) of the customer prevail. All criteria are identified in the control plan. When certification is necessary from laboratory facilities, the requirement is also identified in the control plan.

4.10.2   Receiving Inspection and Testing

In most cases the receiving inspection and testing is waived because of either third-party certification or statistical documentation at the time of delivery. (Appropriate documentation is available.) When neither is verifiable, then

- The specific processes (both manufacturing and nonmanufacturing) are responsible for ensuring that the incoming product or service is not used or processed until and when it has been verified as appropriate and conforming to the requirements.
- The amount and nature of receiving inspection and testing depends on the requirements of the customer, the history of the supplier, and the supplier's ability to supply appropriate documentation.
- All verification is done through procedures and specific instructions.
- All appropriate documentation, usage, and storage of inspection records are maintained and available to appropriate personnel.
- Appropriate segregation of nonconforming material is mandatory.
- If the material is needed for an urgent production situation, that specific material is identified so as to allow its recall and replacement in the event the product is determined not to be in compliance with specified requirements at a later time.

TITLE: ABC's	Document No: QM ABC 001
Quality System Practices and Controls:	Revision 00
	August 1, 1995
Inspection and Testing	Supersedes: New
	Section 4.10
	Page 2 of 2

4.10.3   In-Process Inspection and Testing

The quality assurance team or project management is responsible for ensuring that in-process product is held and not used or processed further until it has been inspected, tested, or otherwise verified as conforming to specified requirements except when product is released under positive recall (see section 10.2). It is ABC's policy to direct process activities and resources toward defect prevention rather than to rely simply on traditional methods of defect detection.

4.10.4   Final Inspection and Testing

The compliance department, the quality assurance department, or both are responsible for ensuring that no product is dispatched until (1) all final inspection and testing are complete according to the appropriate documented procedure, work instruction, or quality plan to show evidence of conformance to specified requirements and (2) all data and documentation covering all inspections and tests (incoming, in-process, and final) specified in the quality procedures and control plans are authorized and show that the results meet specified requirements.

Appropriate and applicable documentation, usage, and maintenance of records are maintained and available.

4.10.5   Inspection and Test Records

ABC's inspection and test records are established and maintained to identify the persons performing inspection and test activities and the results of these verification activities. The responsibility for generating, filing, and maintaining inspection and test records is defined in the appropriate procedures

Related Documentation (Insert all appropriate and applicable documentation.)

TITLE: ABC's	Document No: QM ABC 001
Quality System Practices and Controls:	Revision 00
	August 1, 1995
Control of Inspection, Measuring, and	Supersedes: New
Test Equipment	Section 4.11
	Page 1 of 2

4.11   Control of Inspection, Measuring, and Test Equipment

4.11.1   General

The manager of quality assurance is responsible for establishing and maintaining documented procedures and work instructions for ensuring that all inspection, measuring, and test equipment used in any stage of production or installation is controlled, calibrated, and properly maintained to demonstrate the conformance of product to the specified requirements.

Where measurement is necessary, the appropriate test equipment and calibration are accounted for with appropriate and applicable documentation. ABC provides technical data regarding measurement device calibration to its customers (upon request) to allow customers to verify that the measurement devices are functionally adequate.

4.11.2   Control Procedure

The ABC company has a formal, documented procedure and work instructions for regularly certifying the accuracy of every inspection instrument that is used to make quality decisions in the manufacturing process, including instruments owned by employees. Appropriate procedures and instructions are established and are available to authorized personnel and maintained.

All inspection, measuring, and test devices used to verify dimensions or characteristics or to perform functional testing and thereby accept parts, subassemblies, or assemblies are calibrated periodically, with all appropriate documentation maintained and available.

A calibration checklist, the record of calibration, and all activities related to calibration (including those performed by outside sources) are properly maintained and available. The procedures and instructions for such activities may be found in the appropriate manuals.

All internal standards that are used to verify the accuracy of inspection instruments or assembly tools are regularly calibrated by outside labs. Attribute-type gauges are sent to outside labs to be cleaned, repaired, and/or calibrated. All calibration services, whether performed in or outside the plant, are

TITLE: ABC's	Document No: QM ABC 001
Quality System Practices and Controls:	Revision 00
	August 1, 1995
Control of Inspection, Measuring, and	Supersedes: New
Test Equipment	Section 4.11
	Page 2 of 2

certified to use standards that are traceable to the National Institute of Standards and Technology (NIST).

Any inspection, measuring, and test equipment that is not in current calibration is not used. New equipment or equipment with a past-due calibration date is impounded to prevent its use until the calibration has been completed.

All ABC employees who use the measuring and test equipment are responsible for checking the calibration sticker (or equivalent tag/marker) to ensure that the calibration status is current. Should calibration activity disclose the potential that discrepant material has been shipped, the customer shall be notified of all pertinent information. This notification may be followed by a request for waiver.

Calibration activity that discloses the potential for nonconforming material that is still within the facilities of ABC results in the initiation of an ad hoc audit for the purpose of determining whether the potential was realized. If the material is found to be nonconforming, the appropriate procedure is initiated; otherwise, the material continues its normal production course.

4.11.3   Inspection, Measuring, and Test Equipment Records

All ABC's inspection, measuring, and test equipment records are generated and controlled as stated in section 4.11.2. The manager of quality assurance is responsible for the maintenance of all calibration records, including communications to customers regarding the potential for nonconforming product due to out-of-calibration equipment, and for ensuring that the control of measurement equipment meets or exceeds the requirements stated in the *Measurement Systems Analysis Reference Manual*.

4.11.4   Measurement System Analysis

The manager of quality assurance is responsible for maintaining records of gauge repeatability and reproducibility (G R&R) and other applicable statistical studies to analyze measurement system uncertainty. ABC has documented work instructions that include analytical methods and acceptance criteria that meet the requirements specified in the *Measurement Systems Analysis Reference Manual*.

Related Documentation: (Insert all appropriate and applicable documentation.)

TITLE: ABC's	Document No: QM ABC 001
Quality System Practices and Controls:	Revision 00
	August 1, 1995
Inspection and Test Status	Supersedes: New
	Section 4.12
	Page 1 of 1

4.12   Inspection and Test Status

ABC identifies the inspection and test status of all products with markings, authorized stamps, tags, labels, routing cards, inspection records, physical location designations, or other suitable means, which indicate the conformance or nonconformance of the product with regard to the inspections or tests performed. The identification of inspection and test status is maintained, as defined in the company's procedures and work instructions and as required by customers, throughout production and installation of the product to ensure that only product that has passed the required inspections and tests (or has been released under an authorized concession) is dispatched, used, or installed.

The responsibility to identify the inspection and test status of products lies with the manager of the department responsible for performing the inspection or test. These responsibilities are formally stated in the applicable inspection and testing procedures and/or work instructions.

Related Documentation (Insert all appropriate and applicable documentation.)

TITLE: ABC's	Document No: QM ABC 001
Quality System Practices and Controls:	Revision 00
	August 1, 1995
Control of Nonconforming Product	Supersedes: New
	Section 4.13
	Page 1 of 2

4.13   Control of Nonconforming Product

4.13.1   General

The manager of quality assurance is responsible for maintaining documented procedures and work instructions for ensuring that nonconforming product is clearly identified and quarantined or segregated to prevent inadvertent use or installation until the material is reviewed and disposition is determined. The manager of quality assurance is also responsible for maintaining and analyzing data from the nonconforming material.

4.13.2   Review and Disposition of Nonconforming Product

ABC's review policies for nonconforming product are followed by all personnel who detect suspect or nonconforming material. In fact, ABC's policy is that the person producing the product is also responsible for its quality.

When products are found to be nonconforming, they are immediately tagged with a DO NOT USE tag. The product is physically segregated (whenever possible) or is prevented from further processing or use by other means. At that point appropriate personnel are identified and proper action based on the specified procedures and instructions takes place.

A product that is reworked or repaired is reinspected according to ABC's appropriate inspection and test procedure and/or control plan. Pertinent instructions for rework are readily available for all appropriate personnel.

4.13.3   Control of Reworked Product

All rework is controlled by the appropriate and applicable procedures or instructions to either make the product usable or identify it as scrap.

4.13.4   Engineering Approved Product Authorization

The manager of quality assurance is responsible for managing the customer authorization of products or processes, including materials and services provided by suppliers, that differ from those currently approved according to the *Production Part Approval Process Manual*. This responsibility includes:

TITLE: ABC's	Document No: QM ABC 001
Quality System Practices and Controls:	**Revision 00**
	August 1, 1995
Control of Nonconforming Product	**Supersedes: New**
	Section 4.13
	Page 2 of 2

- Obtaining written customer approval that specifies the item(s) and the dates or quantities for which the approval has been granted.
- Responding to requests from the vendor prior to submission to the customer.
- Ensuring that material shipped under customer authorization for a product or process change is identified as such on the shipping container and applicable shipping documentation.
- Assuring that the original (or any superseding) requirements are met for those materials not covered under the authorization or at the time that the authorization expires.

Related Documentation (Insert all appropriate and applicable documentation.)

TITLE: ABC's	Document No: QM ABC 001
Quality System Practices and Controls:	**Revision 00**
	August 1, 1995
Corrective and Preventive Action	**Supersedes: New**
	Section 4.14
	Page 1 of 2

4.14   Corrective and Preventive Action

4.14.1   General

ABC's focus on quality is prevention. As such, the company has established and currently maintains documented procedures and related records for implementing both corrective and preventive action. These procedures specify problem solving actions for eliminating the cause of actual or potential quality system problems and related nonconformities to a degree commensurate with the magnitude of the problem, its potential outcome, and the level of risk involved. When resolving external nonconformities, corrective action shall take place as required by the customer. The management representative for both the corrective and preventive action(s) is the manager of quality assurance.

4.14.2   Corrective Action

ABC's corrective action policy is to identify, analyze, and resolve problems that have been raised by nonconformities. The result of the corrective action is to correct the root cause of the problem and when necessary to revise the company's quality system, procedures, and instructions, as appropriate.

ABC's corrective action follows as a general rule the 8-D approach (other approaches are used as necessary) to resolve the problems identified either internally or externally. All corrective actions are initiated, controlled, and documented through the corrective action request form. Their retention is a three-year period, unless otherwise specified by the customer or governmental regulations. For the appropriate reviews and documentation, see the relevant procedures and instructions. The person responsible for the corrective action is the quality manager.

4.14.3   Prevention Action

ABC's focus on prevention is the basic tenet of quality. Everything we do is founded on the principles of prevention. We look for weaknesses in the quality system and capitalize on these opportunities to improve based on the findings of internal, external, and third-party audits.

TITLE: ABC's	Document No: QM ABC 001
Quality System Practices and Controls:	**Revision 00**
	August 1, 1995
Corrective and Preventive Action	**Supersedes: New**
	Section 4.14
	Page 2 of 2

Appropriate reviews of the use of information, quality record, service re-ports, customer feedback, special studies, etc., are conducted to identify and or eliminate causes of potential nonconformities. The responsibility for prevention is with all employees; however, the manager of quality assurance is responsible for managing the ABC prevention program effectively.

Related Documentation (Insert all appropriate and applicable documentation.)

TITLE: ABC's	Document No: QM ABC 001
Quality System Practices and Controls:	Revision 00
	August 1, 1995
Handling, Storage, Packaging, Preservation,	Supersedes: New
and Delivery	Section 4.15
	Page 1 of 2

4.15   Handling, Storage, Packaging, Preservation, and Delivery

4.15.1   General
At ABC we believe that the managers responsible for handling, storage, packaging, and delivery of materials and products are also responsible for establishing, documenting, and maintaining methods appropriate to satisfy the requirements in manufacturing and those specified by contract. The procedures and instructions relevant to these requirements are documented and available in the appropriate manuals and locations.

4.15.2   Handling
ABC handles and transports product in a manner that prevents loss of product value and satisfies customer and governmental requirements.

4.15.3   Storage
ABC ensures the appropriate management of stored material according to customer requirements, governmental regulations, and internal procedures and instructions. The person responsible for the appropriate storage is the plant manager. The focus of our policy is to control inventory turns, assure stock rotation, appropriately separate "good" from "not usable" material, and continuously maintain minimum inventory levels. Additionally, our policy emphasizes damage prevention and deterioration while in storage.

4.15.4   Packaging
At ABC all products are appropriately packed and identified on the packaging in a manner that allows for ready identification and traceability through all stages of processing and prevents the loss of product value. Customer packaging and labeling requirements are detailed in appropriate contract-related work instructions and guidelines, including Chrysler's *Shipping/Parts Identification Label Standard.*

TITLE: ABC's	Document No: QM ABC 001
Quality System Practices and Controls:	**Revision 00**
	August 1, 1995
Handling, Storage, Packaging, Preservation,	**Supersedes: New**
and Delivery	**Section 4.15**
	Page 2 of 2

4.15.5   Preservation

At ABC all products (incoming and in process) are segregated and preserved as necessary to maintain product quality and value while they are under the company's control.

4.15.6   Delivery

At ABC the vice president of manufacturing (and quite often the plant manager with the aid of the quality manager) is responsible for ensuring that the quality of the final product is protected after final inspection and test according to the appropriate procedure. Where contractually specified, ABC company shall be responsible for packaging and preservation during transit, including delivery to destination.

Delivery performance is one of the key quality indicators for both the ABC company and our customers. As such we track on-time deliveries, production scheduling, and all advanced shipment notifications. When we discover problems or concerns, we initiate a corrective action report; the results of the investigation are communicated to both management and customer(s).

Related Documentation (Insert all appropriate and applicable documentation.)

TITLE: ABC's	**Document No: QM ABC 001**
Quality System Practices and Controls:	**Revision 00**
	August 1, 1995
Control of Quality Records	**Supersedes: New**
	Section 4.16
	Page 1 of 1

4.16   Control of Quality Records

ABC's quality system is documented through the use of quality records. Quality records may be those records that ABC generates or that customers and suppliers provide. The responsibility for establishing, collecting, filing, indexing, storing, maintaining, and disposing of records is defined in ABC's quality system-related documentation. The retention of the quality records is for at least three years unless the customer or governmental regulations dictate otherwise.

Related Documentation (Insert all appropriate and applicable documentation.)

TITLE: ABC's	Document No: QM ABC 001
Quality System Practices and Controls:	**Revision 00**
	August 1, 1995
Internal Quality Audits	**Supersedes: New**
	Section 4.17
	Page 1 of 1

4.17   Internal Quality Audits

ABC plans and conducts at least two internal quality audits annually according to the ISO/QS and customer requirements. The results of the audit are documented and communicated to management and all other appropriate personnel for any appropriate action. The focus of our audits is to verify the effectiveness of our quality system and to discover opportunities for improvement.

The quality assurance manager is responsible for organizing and coordinating the internal audit as well as for maintaining appropriate records for such audits.

Related Documentation (Insert all appropriate and applicable documentation.)

TITLE: ABC's	**Document No: QM ABC 001**
Quality System Practices and Controls:	**Revision 00**
	August 1, 1995
Training	**Supersedes: New**
	Section 4.18
	Page 1 of 1

4.18   Training

At ABC people are the company's most valuable asset. Investing in people (both management and nonmanagement) through effective training is thus a key corporate strategy for achieving the company's mission and quality policy. Therefore, it is our policy to identify the training needs and provide for the training of all personnel performing activities affecting quality. Documentation for all the training is maintained and may be found in the personnel department.

The effectiveness of training is established through needs assessment for the appropriate training and then through course evaluations, follow-up surveys, and documented improvements in the affected areas.

At ABC we value training so much that all company managers have a contributing responsibility in assessing training needs, providing on-the-job reinforcement of skills, and evaluating the effectiveness of training for the personnel they directly manage. Furthermore, to reinforce this responsibility we have empowered our employees to request training at any time the employee believes that training is essential to maintain the standards and his or her job responsibility.

Related Documentation (Insert all appropriate and applicable documentation.)

TITLE: ABC's	Document No: QM ABC 001
Quality System Practices and Controls:	**Revision 00**
	August 1, 1995
Servicing	**Supersedes: New**
	Section 4.19
	Page 1 of 1

4.19   Servicing

ABC maintains documented procedures for providing contracted services that meet specified requirements and yield high levels of customer satisfaction and for reporting on the results of such services to appropriate activities throughout the organization. Servicing at ABC takes the following forms:

- Managing customer interfacing.
- Managing customer complaints.
- Providing service parts and appropriate training.
- Providing field service on contractual basis where applicable.

The responsibility of servicing belongs to the marketing department (except where otherwise identified; for example, quality issues belong to the quality department). The sales manager and or quality manager will coordinate the customer service activities and ensure that appropriate records to document customer service performance are maintained.

Related Documentation (Insert all appropriate and applicable documentation.)

TITLE: ABC's	Document No: QM ABC 001
Quality System Practices and Controls:	**Revision 00**
	August 1, 1995
Statistical Techniques	**Supersedes: New**
	Section 4.20
	Page 1 of 2

4.20   Statistical Techniques

4.20.1   Identification of Need

ABC recognizes that statistical techniques are valuable for assessing, controlling, and improving our quality system and processes. The concepts of variation, control (stability), capability, and overadjustment are communicated and understood throughout our company. For our processes we utilize both qualitative and quantitative data. Therefore, the specific need and application for statistical techniques and the establishment of specific methods and instructions for improvement of a specific process are assumed by all area managers with the collaboration of the quality manager and or quality engineer. The resolution of the appropriate tool is established through quality planning. The selection of the appropriate statistical tools for individual processes is documented in the control plan.

4.20.2   Applications and Procedures

ABC uses both statistical and nonstatistical methods to maintain process control, monitor defect prevention, assess machine capabilities and levels of quality, and identify areas for quality improvement. Examples of some of the specific tools that our company utilizes are

- Brainstorming.
- Process flow chart.
- Histogram.
- Pareto chart.
- Scatter plot.
- Force field analysis.
- Variable and attribute charts.
- Design of experiments (classical, Taguchi).
- FMEA.
- Gauge repeatability and reproducibility.

TITLE: ABC's	Document No: QM ABC 001
Quality System Practices and Controls:	**Revision 00**
	· **August 1, 1995**
Statistical Techniques	**Supersedes: New**
	Section 4.20
	Page 2 of 2

The specific application of these tools depends upon the individual process; the reader is encouraged to see the individual process for further information.

Related Documentation (Insert all appropriate and applicable documentation.)

TITLE: ABC's	Document No: QM ABC 001
Quality System Practices and Controls:	Revision 00
Sector-Specific Requirements	August 1, 1995
Production Part Approval Process	Supersedes: New
	Section II: 1.0
	Page 1 of 1

SECTION II:
SECTOR-SPECIFIC REQUIREMENTS

1.0 Production Part Approval Process

1.1 General

ABC documents, reviews, submits, revises, and maintains records for production part approvals according to the requirements given in the *Production Part Approval Process Manual*. Production part approval is obtained by part number, revision level, manufacturing site, material vendor(s), and production process environment. The customer is notified of changes to any of these factors and written authorization is obtained when required. The responsibility for production part approval extends to materials and services provided by ABC's suppliers.

1.2 Engineering Change Validation

The vice president of manufacturing is responsible for ensuring that all changes are suitably validated according to the guidelines provided in the *Production Part Approval Process Manual*.

Related Documentation (Insert all appropriate and applicable documentation.)

TITLE: ABC's	Document No: QM ABC 001
Quality System Practices and Controls:	**Revision 00**
Sector-Specific Requirements	**August 1, 1995**
Continuous Improvement	**Supersedes: New**
	Section II: 2.0
	Page 1 of 1

Continuous Improvement

2.1   General

It is the joint responsibility of the management representative and the manager of quality assurance to ensure that the concepts of continuous improvement and the principles of ISO/QS are communicated throughout the ABC company and that personnel receive the appropriate education and training in continuous improvement tools and techniques.

It is the policy of ABC company to strive to continuously improve in the areas of quality, service, delivery, and price for all customers as evidenced by and tracked in the appropriate documentation and customer satisfaction indexes.

Action plans for the improvement of key processes in production, business, and support functions are developed and documented in the business plan in an effort to continuously reduce variation and increase productivity and efficiency. Special emphasis is given to those processes identified as most important to ABC's customers.

2.2   Quality and Productivity Improvements

Improvement projects and plans are documented in the business plan and are developed based upon the indicators tracked in the appropriate documentation. Appropriate measurables for the improvement projects are defined during project planning and are tracked and revised as appropriate throughout the life of the project.

2.3   Techniques for Continuous Improvement

The ABC management representative and manager of quality assurance are jointly responsible for ensuring that all personnel understand and apply the principles of continuous improvement. In addition, a management representative and manager of quality assurance are also responsible for ensuring that appropriate education and training in advanced methods and techniques for continuous improvement are given. The tools and methods used at ABC company meet, and in most cases exceed, the requirements of the standards.

Related Documentation (Insert all appropriate and applicable documentation.)

TITLE: ABC's	Document No: QM ABC 001
Quality System Practices and Controls:	Revision 00
Sector-Specific Requirements	August 1, 1995
Manufacturing Capabilities	Supersedes: New
	Section II: 3.0
	Page 1 of 2

Manufacturing Capabilities

3.1   Facilities, Equipment, and Process Planning and Effectiveness

ABC's objective is to optimize process and material flows, floor plans, and use of floor space. The product quality planning team is responsible for evaluating the effectiveness of the manufacturing system during the advanced quality planning process and for ensuring that a cross-functional team approach is used in developing the plans for facilities, equipment, and processes.

The specific responsibility for the evaluation of effectiveness belongs to the vice president of manufacturing who ensures the implementation, documentation, and review of regular assessments of the manufacturing system. Some factors for the evaluation are plant layout, work flow, automation and human factors issues, planned and predictive maintenance programs, balancing of operators and lines, storage and buffer inventory levels, and value-added labor content.

3.2   Mistake Proofing

ABC company is committed to problem prevention rather than relying simply on problem detection. Therefore, mistake-proofing activities take place throughout the planning process as well as during problem resolution. The results of design and process FMEAs, reliability studies, the use of CAD systems, capability studies, the preventive action process, and service reports are used to identify areas in which to apply mistake-proofing methodologies.

3.3   Tool Design and Fabrication

The manager of design engineering is responsible for establishing and implementing documented procedures and work instructions for tool and gauge design, fabrication, and complete dimensional inspection. He or she is also responsible for ensuring that appropriate technical resources and facilities exist for these activities. Customer-owned tools and gauges are permanently identified as such.

TITLE: ABC's   Document No: QM ABC 001

Quality System Practices and Controls: Revision 00

Sector-Specific Requirements   August 1, 1995

Manufacturing Capabilities   Supersedes: New

                                                        Section II: 3.0

                                                        Page 2 of 2

3.4   Tooling Management

The plant manager is responsible for establishing and implementing documented procedures and work instructions for tool and gauge maintenance, repair, storage, recovery, setup, and replacement. The manager is also responsible for ensuring that appropriate technical resources and facilities exist for these activities.

Related Documentation (Insert all appropriate and applicable documentation.)

TITLE: ABC's	Document No: QM ABC 001
Quality System Practices and Controls:	Revision 00
Customer-Specific Requirements	August 1, 1995
	Supersedes: New
	Section III
	Page 1 of 3

SECTION III:
CUSTOMER-SPECIFIC REQUIREMENTS

In this section of the manual you should include the specific requirements that Chrysler Corporation, Ford Motor Corporation, General Motors, and Truck Manufacturers have defined as important and are not covered as part of earlier sections.

This section of the manual is customized for each company. Therefore, we provide only very generic guidelines. Make sure before you embark on writing or modifying your quality manual, that you confer with your customer's quality supplier representative and both of you agree on what to include in this section.

1.0   Chrysler Requirements

Unique requirements are

- A system that identifies safety characteristics, special characteristics, critical tooling characteristics, and significant characteristics.
- Continuous conformance by conducting an annual layout inspection.

Redundant requirements are

- Internal quality audits (see ISO 9001: section 4.17).
- Design validation/product verification (see ISO 9001: section 4.4).
- Corrective action plan (see ISO 9001: section 4.14).
- Packaging, shipping, and labeling (see ISO 9001: section 4.15).
- Process sign-off (see ISO 9001: section 4.9).

2.0   Ford Requirements

Unique requirements are

- Appropriate control item parts and critical characteristics with the inverted delta.

TITLE: ABC's	**Document No: QM ABC 001**
Quality System Practices and Controls:	**Revision 00**
Customer-Specific Requirements	**August 1, 1995**
	Supersedes: New
	Section III
	Page 2 of 3

- Control plans and FMEAs.
- Equipment and standard parts.
- Heat treating.
- Quality operating system (QOS).

Redundant requirements are

- Setup verification (see ISO 9001: sections 4.4 and 4.9).
- Process changes and monitoring (see ISO 9001: section 4.9).
- Engineering specification, prototypes, and qualifications for materials (see ISO 9000: section 4.4).
- Labeling (see ISO 9001: section 4.15).

3.0   General Motors Requirements

Unique requirements are

- Technology program.
- Key characteristic designation system.
- Continuous improvement.
- Run at rate.
- Specifications for part and bar codes.
- Control plans.
- Layout inspections.

Redundant requirements are

- Process approval (see ISO 9001: section 4.9).
- Match check material (see ISO 9001: sections 4.6 and 4.9).
- Traceability (see ISO 9001: section 4.8).
- Problem reporting (see ISO 9001: section 4.14).
- Evaluation of supplier (see ISO 9001: section 4.6).

TITLE: ABC's	Document No: QM ABC 001
Quality System Practices and Controls:	Revision 00
Customer-Specific Requirements	August 1, 1995
	Supersedes: New
	Section III
	Page 3 of 3

- Production containment procedure (see ISO 9001: section 4.9).
- Packaging, shipping, delivery, and labeling (see ISO 9001: section 4.15).
- Prototyping (see ISO 9001: section 4.4).

4.0   Truck Manufacturers Requirements

No specific requirements are identified in this section.

Procedures and Instructions

This appendix summarizes the critical characteristics of all procedures and provides several examples of procedure formats that meet the requirements for most quality systems, including the ISO 9000 and standards. Furthermore, it identifies both the records and procedures that are required by ISO 9001.

SUMMARY OF THE STRUCTURE

Procedures may take several forms, and the exact form depends on the specific organization. However, all procedures follow this general outline:

Purpose: Why?	Describes the reason for writing the procedure. Most often the reasons are to establish the requirements, the responsibilities, and methods for conducting a specific activity.
Scope: Where?	Defines the departments, divisions, groups, individuals, etc., who are expected to abide by the guidelines set out within the procedure and also discloses how much of a subject is covered by the procedure.
Responsibility: Who?	Specifies who or what positions or departments will be expected to
	• Maintain relevant documentation.
	• Conduct the various activities.
	• Follow up on findings and make reports.
Definitions	Provides the actual definitions of acronyms, not what the initials stand for. Defines every term that is unique to the procedure.
Associated documents	Describes all forms and documents used by the procedure itself.

Instructions for forms	Explains when and how to use forms and gives instructions for completing every form. Identifies every user block on the form with a letter or a number.
Procedures	Provides the actual instructions for performing the procedure. One cannot write a procedure unless she or he knows it will work. One will not know if the procedure works unless one can perform the procedure.
Audit statement	Briefly defined who, what, where, why, when, and how often the procedure will be audited.
Audit checklist	An itemized checklist that reflects the actual requirements and expectations of the procedure itself.

Please note that not all these characteristics may be appropriate for all procedures. In fact, in some cases more maybe appropriate. Use them when appropriate and applicable.

Example 1:   Operating Procedure

Title: Material Handling
Reference: OP-402
Page: 1 of 1
Revision: 0
Rev. Date:
Original Date: 9/3/95
Approval: DHS

Purpose: To enable easy access to each coil without damaging adjacent coils.

Responsible for control: Crane operator.

Process standard: There must be a minimum of 24 inches between rows in the coil storage areas.

Reason for control: To ensure material is shipped to our customers free of crane damage.

Measurement: The stocker or coil checker will visually monitor the space between rows.

Auditing procedure: Once per turn the warehouse supervisor will check compliance to the standards and to the IP-102 instructions, and record the results on the audit checklist.

Procedure: If the coils are not spaced far enough apart, the crane operator will arrange the coils to meet the standards. If there is insufficient floor space to move the coils, the operator must notify the warehouse supervisor.

Example 2:   Procedure Process Flow
of the Shipping Department

Title: The Flow of the Shipping Department
Reference: SDFC 4.1.5.
Page: 1 of 1
Revision: 0
Rev. Date:
Original Date: 5/3/94
Approval: DHS

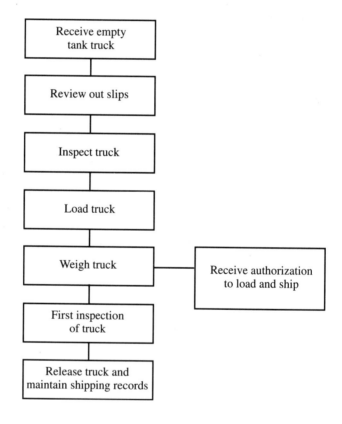

Related material: Quality inspection records
                               Quality shipping records
                               Truck weight records

Example 3:   Procedure Control

Title: Procedure Control
Reference: 91.02
Page: 1 of 2
Revision: 0
Rev. Date:
Original Date: 5/3/94
Approval: DHS

Purpose: This procedure describes how to create and revise procedures in the 991 section of the ABC policy and procedures manual.

Scope: This procedure applies to all procedures in the 91 section of the ABC policy and procedures manual.

Approval: The quality, reliability, and durability (QRD) committee has adopted this procedure and has responsibility for revisions.

Format: The format for procedures in the 991 section is defined by the audit and procedures organization. The procedure format will consist— whenever applicable—of the following sections:

1. Purpose
2. Scope
3. Approval
4. Procedure
5. Flowchart (optional)
6. Attachments (optional)

Procedure: The ABC policy and procedures manual is regulated by the audit and procedures organization of the ABC XYZ department. Manuals are serialized and distributed on the basis of need. A current distribution list is maintained by the audit and procedures organization. Any person or group of persons in the 91 section may write or revise a procedure for the 991 section and submit it to the customer satisfaction staff for processing and submission to the QRD committee.

The QRD committee will review the procedure and decide

- If the procedure should be included in the 91 section of the manual.
- If changes need to be made to the procedure before approving the procedure.

After conducting this review, the QRD committee will recommend that the vice president of operations support, purchasing, and customer satisfaction approve the procedure.

Once approved, the audit and procedures organization will distribute the procedure to all manual holders. The controlled copy of this procedure is maintained by the audit and procedures organization.

Example 4:   Instruction Format

Reference:
Page: ___ **of**____
Revision:
Revised Date:
Original Date:
Approval:
Title:

WORK INSTRUCTION

1.0	Objective:	XXXXXXXXXXXX
		XXXXXXXXXXXX
2.0	Materials/and Tools	XXXXXXXXXXXX
		XXXXXXXXXXXX
		XXXXXXXXXXXX
3.0	Procedure	This section contains the description or the outline of each step.

STEP-BY-STEP ACTION

3.1	Step 1
3.2	Step 2
3.3	Step 3
3.4	Step 4
etc.	

Example 5:   On-Hire Process

Title: On-Hire Process	Authorized by: DHS		Release date: 5/6/94
Company: ABC, Inc.	Reference No.	Revision No.	Page 1 of 1
Responsibility: Operations	Replaces Procedure No. _____ page _____ of _____		

Purpose:

To describe the process of providing a customer with the most suitable tank to meet their needs while satisfying internal and external requirements.

Procedure:

```
┌──────────────────┐          ┌──────────────────────┐
│ Booking request  │────┐     │ Obtain an insurance  │
│    received      │    │     │certificate from      │
└──────────────────┘    │     │   customer           │
         │              │     └──────────────────────┘
         ▼              │                │
┌──────────────────┐    │                ▼
│ Decide what type │    │     ┌──────────────────────┐
│ of tank is needed│    │     │ Contractual documents│
└──────────────────┘    │     │ are drafted and      │
         │              │     │ signed by the        │
         ▼              │     │ customer and ABC     │
┌──────────────────┐    │     │ officials; billing   │
│  Verify credit   │    │     │ code is issued by    │
└──────────────────┘    │     │ contract department  │
         │              │     └──────────────────────┘
         ▼              │                │
┌──────────────────┐    │                ▼
│ Check availability│   │     ┌──────────────────────┐
│   with region    │    │     │ Regional office      │
└──────────────────┘    │     │ completed the booking│
         │              │     │ and notifies the depot│
         ▼              │     └──────────────────────┘
┌──────────────────┐    │                │
│ Discuss terms    │────┘                ▼
│ with customer    │          ┌──────────────────────┐
└──────────────────┘          │ Customer takes        │
                              │ possession of         │
                              │ equipment; regional   │
                              │ office updates        │
                              │ tracking system;      │
                              │ billing cycle is      │
                              │ initiated by regional │
                              │ office                │
                              └──────────────────────┘
                                         │
                                         ▼
                              ┌──────────────────────┐
                              │    End of process     │
                              └──────────────────────┘
```

Associated material:

- On-hire flowchart
- Regional operating instructions
- Contractual agreements

Example 6:   A Procedure That Combines Instructions and Forms

Title: Pending Contract
Reference: PR ABC 110
Page: 1 of 3
Revision: 0
Rev. Date:
Original Date: 5/3/95
Approval: DHS
Subject: New pending contract quality requirements analysis

1.0 **Purpose** To provide a means (upon request from estimating or marketing departments) for quickly determining the quality requirements of a new contract or a potential contract as a first step in the quality planning function at the ABC company.

2.0 **Application** Relates to new and pending business and involves the marketing contracts and quality departments as required.

3.0 **Associated materials**

3.1 New or pending contract quality requirements analysis: Form No. 3.1. 1–1.

3.2 Design review participation: quality procedure X.1.2.

4.0 **Procedure**

4.1 The marketing contracts department of ABC is responsible for providing the quality department with copies of new contracts and information regarding pending contracts.

4.2 The project manager evaluates the contracts and pending contract information to assess the impact the new business will have on quality assurance functions.

4.3 As a result of the analysis, the new or pending contract quality requirements analysis form shown in Figure 3.1 1–1 is to be prepared by the marketing contact person. It is to be filled out as follows: (1) name of the customer or prospect, (2) contract number, (3) contract type, (4) description of the product or products being ordered, (5) start date of the contract, (6) end date, (7) number of units ordered, (8) not applicable, (9) check-mark indication if this contract is identical to or similar to any previous contracts, (10) if identical or similar, then an identification of that previous business, (11) check-mark indication as to the contract's clarity in specifying quality requirements and then a series of statements relative to any special or unusual quality-related requirements that the new business will impose. These statements are broken down in terms of (12) summary statement, (13) advanced technology techniques, (14) special inspection equipment, fixtures, or gauges, (15) special test equipment, (16) special or unusual skills, (17) workload, and (18) other. The complete report is (19) signed and dated by the analyst and (20) signed and dated by the analyst's supervisor following a review.

4.4 This form will be filed with the quotation and placed in the job folder if a purchase order is issued.

4.5 The project manager is responsible for monitoring compliance to the tasks, assignments, and dates related to acquiring the new quality resources.

4.6 If design reviews are conducted in relationship to a new or pending contract, see QP X.1.2 design review participation.

FIGURE 3.1 1–1

New or Pending Contract Quality Requirements Form

Subject New or pending contract quality requirement analysis	Effective Date	Number
	Revision and Authorization	Page

Customer or Prospect (1)	Contract No. (2)	Contract Type (3)

Product Description (4)

Start Date (5)	End Date (6)	Quantity (7)	Maximum Rate/Mo. (8)

Identical to or similar to previous contract(s): Yes___ No___: Ident. No.___: Similar___: No___ (9)

If identical or similar, explain (10)

Are quality terms clear? Yes___ Difficult to interpret?___ Unclear?___ (11)

Identify special or unusual quality-related requirements
(Use extra sheets if necessary)

Summary statement: (12)

Advanced technology techniques: (13)

Special inspection equipment, fixtures, or gauges: (14)

Special test equipment: (15)

Special or unusual skills: (16)

Workload: (17)

Other: (18)

Analysis made by: (19) Date:	Reviewed by: (20) Date:

RECORDS REQUIRED BY ISO 9001

Plan (ned)(s)(ing)

1. Plans that identify the responsibility for each design and development activity (4.4.2).
2. Design and verification activities shall be planned (4.4.2.1).
3. Identify and plan production processes that directly affect quality (4.9.1).
4. Identify and plan installation processes that directly affect quality (4.9.1).

Document(ed)(s), Documentation, Written

1. Document the quality policy (4.1.1).
2. Document the objectives for quality (4.1.1).
3. Document the commitment to quality (4.1.1).
4. A documented quality system (4.2).
5. Contract requirements are adequately defined and documented (4.3.a).
6. Organization between different groups shall be documented (4.4.2.2).
7. Technical interfaces between different groups shall be documented (4.4.2.2).
8. Design inputs shall be documented (4.4.3).
9. Design outputs shall be documented (4.4.4).
10. Document design verification (4.4.5).
11. Design changes shall be documented (4.4.6).
12. Purchasing documents (4.6.3).
13. Documented work instructions defining the manner of production and installation, where the absence of such instructions would adversely affect quality (4.9.1.a).
14. Criteria for workmanship shall be stipulated in written samples or by means of representative samples (4.9.1.a).
15. Documentation that dispatched product has satisfactorily completed all activities specified in the quality plan or procedures (4.10.3).

16. Where no calibration standard exists, the basis for calibration shall be documented (4.11.b).

17. Document the validity of previous inspection and test results when inspection, measuring, and test equipment is found to be out of calibration (4.11.g).

18. Documentation of nonconforming product and notification to the affected functions (4.13).

19. Documented plan for internal quality audits (4.17).

20. Documented results of internal quality audits (4.17).

Record(s)

1. Records of any product quality problems (4.1.2.1.b).

2. Records of management reviews of the quality system (4.1.3).

3. Records of contract reviews (4.3).

4. Records of design reviews (4.4.5.a).

5. Records of acceptable subcontractors (4.6.2).

6. Records of subcontractor's demonstrated capability and performance (4.6.2).

7. Records of purchaser-supplied product that is lost, damaged, or otherwise unsuitable for use (4.7).

8. Records of identification that are required to establish traceability (4.8).

9. Records for qualified processes (4.9.2).

10. Records for equipment required for qualified processes (4.9.2).

11. Records for personnel performing qualified processes (4.9.2).

12. Records to identify incoming product that was released for urgent production and to allow its recall in the event that a nonconformance is identified (4.10.1.2).

13. Records that give evidence that the product has passed inspection and/or test with defined acceptance criteria (4.10.4).

14. Calibration records for inspection, measuring, and test equipment (4.11.2).

15. Records as evidence of control of test hardware (4.11).

16. Records as evidence of control of test software (4.11).
17. Inspection records (4.12).
18. Records of authority for the release of conforming product (4.12).
19. Records of nonconformity that has been accepted and/or repaired (4.13.1).
20. Service reports (4.14.b).
21. Records of changes in procedures resulting from corrective action (4.14.2).
22. Records of retention times for quality records (4.16).
23. Records of training (4.18).

THE 22 PROCEDURES REQUIRED BY THE ISO 9001

1. Procedures that document the quality system in accordance with the standard (4.2.2).
2. Procedures for contract review and the coordination of these activities (4.3).
3. Procedures to control and verify the design of the product (4.4.1).
4. Procedures for the identification, documentation, review, and approval of all changes and modifications (4.4.6).
5. Procedures to control all documents and data that relate to this standard (4.5.1).
6. Procedures to identify the current revision of documents in order to preclude the use of nonapplicable documents (4.5.2).
7. Procedures for the verification, storage, and maintenance of purchaser-supplied product (4.7).
8. Procedures for identifying the product from applicable drawings, specifications, or other documents during all stages of production, delivery, and installation (4.8).
9. Procedures to ensure that special processes are met (4.9.2).
10. Procedures to prevent incoming product from being used until inspected or otherwise verified as well as to allow the urgent release and tracking of material (4.10.1.1).

11. Positive recall procedures for products released under paragraph 4.10.1.1 (4.10.2.3).

12. Procedures for final inspection and test (4.10.3).

13. Procedures to complete evidence of conformance of the finished product to the specified requirements (4.10.3).

14. Calibration procedures (4.11.3).

15. Procedures to protect nonconforming product from inadvertent use or installation (4.13).

16. Procedures to define a corrective action system (4.14).

17. Procedures for handling, storage, packaging, and delivery of product (4.15.1).

18. Procedures for identifying, collecting, indexing, filing, storing, maintaining, and disposing of quality records (4.16).

19. Procedures for internal audits and follow-up activities (4.17).

20. Procedures for identifying the training needs and improving training for all personnel performing functions that affect quality (4.18).

21. Procedures for performing and verifying that servicing needs are met (4.19).

22. Procedures for identifying adequate statistical techniques to verify acceptability of process capabilities and product characteristics (4.20).

Generating a Checklist

In this appendix we present our reader thoughts on how to generate a good checklist. Our intent is to give a broad view of the ISO 9001 so that all industries may use this approach. The *QSA* acts as the official checklist for the QS-9000 requirement, and there is no need to generate a supplementary checklist.

We are also providing the reader with four distinct items. The first, a generic list, forms the basis for generating the questions for the checklist; the second identifies some specific considerations for a laboratory; the third is a generic list of possible documentation records; and the fourth focuses on the software industry. None of the items is exhaustive; rather they all provide the impetus for generating questions in specific areas in preparation for an ISO audit. The QS-9000 auditor does not have much flexibility to form questions during the audit because the *QSA* document serves as the checklist.

GENERIC LIST

The team may consider the following items to generate a comprehensive checklist for the organization about to be audited for ISO certification.

General

1. Management participation in the program.
2. Authority and responsibility of those in charge of the quality assurance (QA) program are clearly established and documented to show lines of communication for individuals and groups involved.
3. QA organization responsibility includes review of written procedures and surveillance of activities affecting quality.
4. Person or organization responsible for defining and measuring overall effectiveness of the QA program is designated, is independent from pressures of production or testing, has direct access to responsible management, and reports regularly on the effectiveness of the QA program to management.

5. QA manual includes statement of policy and authority of the QA manager, indicates management support, and calls for periodic review of the QA program by a level of management higher than the QA manager.

6. QA manual covers all applicable requirements of referenced standards.

7. QA manual revision control system is defined.

8. Provision is included for review and approval of the QA manual to assure that it is current and that there is evidence of this approval.

9. Identification of the activities, services, and items to which the QA manual applies.

10. QA procedures are available to personnel as required.

11. Provision is included for submission of a controlled copy of the QA manual and the proposed revisions to ASME (American Society for Manufacturing Engineers) for acceptance.

Design Control

12. Adequate review and comment by applicable groups to assure correct translation of design or test specification requirements into specifications, drawings, procedures, and instructions.

13. Design or test reviews and checking performed by individuals or groups other than those who performed the original design or test.

14. Management of responsible design or testing organization reviews report.

15. System for handling design or test changes provides for acceptance by the organization that performed the design or test.

16. System for communicating design or test changes that affect form, fit, or function to the operators.

Procurement Control

17. Procedures for qualifying suppliers/vendors by survey or appropriate third-party registration:
    a. System to periodically evaluate and revise accepted supplier/vendor list for materials, items, or services being purchased (or alternate approach).

      b. System for removal of suppliers/vendors from list.

      c. Suppliers/vendors identified by name, address, and scope of work or product.

      d. Survey and audit documentation.

      e. Source surveillance/inspection including report system.

      f. Audit frequency.

      g. Corrective action system.

18. Measures to control issuance and approval of purchase documents, including review by QA to assure inclusion of appropriate quality provisions.

19. Receiving inspection.

      a. System providing for use of applicable specifications, purchase orders, drawings, etc.

      b. Procedures to assure all required characteristics are reported with recorded results.

      c. Status indicator system and procedures for identification, segregation, and disposition.

      d. Nonconformity control system.

      e. Documentation reports and records to be forwarded to required recipients.

20. Criteria for determining that required activities have been satisfactorily accomplished are included; objective evidence of each accomplishment must be available.

21. Measures established for identification and control of materials and items to assure use of accepted materials and items only.

22. Identification maintained on items or records traceable to item marks or travelers not detrimental to item.

23. Provide for document number and revision to which tests are made, sign-off, and date.

24. Control features of referenced procedures and instructions for quality systems are included in the QA manual.

25. In-process and final examinations and tests established.

26. Review, approval, and revision system documented.

Note: Whenever possible the organization should deal with suppliers as opposed to vendors. In a supplier relationship everyone operates in a win-win mode , but in a vendor relationship the win-lose attitude prevails.

A customer works closely with a supplier for the benefit of both organizations, but in a vendor relationship both parties are interested in getting their own "best deal."

Document Control

27. Measures established to assure revisions and approval are performed prior to release.
28. Issuance of documents that prescribe activities affecting quality is performed by designated personnel using procedures that include accountability, as necessary.
29. Control of revisions and replacements to assure use of current revision and to prevent misuse of obsolete documents.

Control of Processes

30. Process Control
    a. Preparation and control of traveler, process sheet, checklist, etc., in use.
    b. Provision on traveler, etc., for establishment of hold points.
    c. Provision on traveler, etc., for signature, initial, or stamp, and for date by QA customer representatives for activities witnessed.
    d. Critical processes including welding, heat treating, NDT (Non-Destructive Testing), forming, and bending accomplished according to referenced specifications and standards using qualified personnel; control for certification of equipment where required.
    e. Provision for accomplishing activities under suitably controlled conditions: appropriate equipment, correct environmental conditions, and prerequisites satisfied for given activity.

Indoctrination and Training

31. Indoctrination and training program for personnel performing activities affecting quality.
    a. Program description.
    b. Personnel involved.
    c. Documentation records.

Inspection

32. Regular first-line examinations will be verified with quality assurance checks by persons other than those who performed the work or test being inspected.

33. Checklists prepared include document number and revision to which examination is to be performed, provides for recording of results, sign-offs, and dates.

Test Control

34. Written test procedures incorporating or referencing requirements and acceptance criteria from design or testing documents.

35. Test procedures provide for meeting prerequisites, adequate instrumentation, and necessary monitoring. Prerequisites include

    a. Instrumentation calibrated.

    b. Personnel trained.

    c. Adequate test equipment and items ready to be tested.

    d. Data accumulation techniques.

36. Test results documented and evaluated including issue and date of test specification to which test is performed.

Control of Measuring and Test Equipment

37. Measures established and documented to assure use of proper tools, gauges, instruments, and other equipment affecting accuracy quality.

38. Documented procedures established to assure that measuring devices are calibrated and adjusted at specified periods to maintain accuracy.

39. Calibration traceable to national standards or designated if national standards do not exist.

40. Control methods for identifying test equipment and calibration status.

41. Nonconformities in examination and testing equipment.

    a. Equipment identified and findings documented.

    b. Required corrective action.

    c. Materials and items checked since previous valid calibration, identified and considered unacceptable until acceptance established.

    d. Corrective action documented.

Inspection, Test, and Operating Status

42. Measures established to control items per established instructions, procedures, or drawings.

43. Procedures reviewed and approved.

44. Examination and test status control system.

    a. Provides for identification of conforming and nonconforming items.

    b. Provides for control of status indicators.

    c. Indicates authority for application and removal of status indicators.

Nonconformance Control

45. Nonconforming materials or items.

    a. Approved procedures developed for identification, documentation, segregation, and disposition.

    b. Review procedure established for nonconforming items to determine acceptance, rejection, repair, or rework.

    c. Procedures established for accomplishing designated disposition of nonconforming items.

    d. Responsibilities and authority designated for control of nonconformities.

    e. Procedure provides for review by responsible individual or group.

    f. Provision for documentation of disposition and procedures followed in correcting nonconformity or otherwise disposing of items.

    g. Quality records indicate clearly the status of nonconformities.

46. Corrective action.

    a. System provides for prompt identification of nonconformities and determination of recurring nonconformities.

    b. Management awareness and involvement.

    c. Problem, cause of problem, and corrective action implementation documented.

    d. Corrective action program applicable for manufacturer and subcontractors.

Quality Assurance Records

47. Written procedures established to ensure a quality record system.

48. Required records determined early and list developed to serve as index to the document file.

    a. Existence of control documentation.

    b. Existence of master file.

    c. Retrievability of files.

49. Quality program and procedure identifies responsibility for and location of records.

50. System provides suitable protection of records from deterioration and damage.

51. System provides for retention of required records—permanent and nonpermanent—for times specified.

52. Records are reviewed for completeness and review is documented.

Quality Assurance Audit

53. Quality procedures require performance of scheduled audits to assure maintenance of the quality system.

54. Audits are performed to written procedures or checklist applicable for area audited.

55. Audit checklists address areas related to item(s) and system(s) of subcontractors.

56. Management reviews are performed and documented to verify that the QA program is functioning.

57. Audit findings and management reviews are documented and reviewed and specific responsibility for corrective action and reaudit is assigned.

58. Reports indicate problems, corrective actions, and show that reaudits verified correction of nonconforming conditions.

59. Personnel performing audits are qualified.

60. Personnel performing audits do not have direct responsibilities in area audited.

Equipment Failure, and Malfunction Analysis

61. A system shall be established for handling malfunction and failure reports.

62. A system shall be established for reporting changes to equipment to all purchasers of like equipment.

CERTIFICATE OF ACCREDITATION (LABORATORY)

The audit team shall consider the following areas when auditing a laboratory applying for accreditation to test to a specific SPPE (Safety and Pollution Prevention Equipment) standard:

Quality Assurance Program

Program documentation.

Elements of a quality assurance program.

Organization.

Control of testing procedures.

Test reports.

Control of measuring and testing equipment.

Audits.

Control of subcontracted services.

Nonconformances.

Records.

Laboratory Requirements

Organization.

Staff.

Physical plant.

Test equipment required to comply with standard.

Supporting equipment requirements.

Calibration equipment requirements.

Equipment handling requirements.

Report reproduction and processing equipment requirements.

Storage of records.

The laboratory requirements in each of the above areas are given in Section LA-3000 and LA-4000 of *ASME/ANSI SPPE-2, Accreditation of Testing Laboratories for Safety and Pollution Prevention Equipment Used in Offshore Oil and Gas Operations.*

DOCUMENTATION

The audit team may look for the following documentation (not an exhaustive list), and accordingly it may generate questions for its checklist:

Inspection check sheets	Control charts
Pareto charts	Data collection forms
Quality audit forms	Drawings
Inspection standards	Quality manual
Procedures and policies	Instructions
Flowcharts	Standard operating procedures
FMEAs (design and process)	Capability studies
Inspection results	Test results
Control plans	Inspection instructions
Training documentation	Forms of records
Quality planning	Corrective action documentation
Deviation documentation	Supplier records
Purchasing records	Design review records
DOE results	Calibration records
Material certifications	Preventive maintenance records

AREAS OF POSSIBLE QUESTIONS FOR THE SOFTWARE INDUSTRY

Basic Concepts and Principles

How do you classify defects?

What is your plan for eliminating defects?

Do you have a zero-defect tolerance program?

How do you define reliability?

How do you determine your software quality indicators?

How do you identify system errors?

What is your quality system and control?

What is your policy on testing?

Do you track the results of testing?

Bugs

How do you categorize bugs?

Do you measure bugs?

Do you evaluate the results?

Do you use statistical analysis for predicting and costing bugs?

Testing

How do you structure the testing methodologies?

How do you differentiate the testing between phases?

What is the hardware test environment?

How do you determine the appropriate tools and techniques for testing?

> Bottom-up tests versus top-down tests.
>
> Test drivers.
>
> Test management tools.
>
> Test data (transaction) generators.
>
> Test-bed data generators.
>
> Test-script and test-case generators.
>
> Manual versus automated detection of errors.
>
> Comparators.
>
> Software complexity matrices.
>
> Database-driven testing
>
> Functional reviews.
>
> Automated testing.

Test Planning

How do you set the objectives?

Is your testing structured or flexible?

How do you develop your procedures for testing?

How do you define test responsibilities?

How do you test for interdependencies?

Do you estimate test time and cost?

How do you evaluate the testing results?

Do you use the results as a benchmark to improvement?

How do you know when you are finished?

Unit and Integration Testing

Do you use the following techniques? If so, how do you document them?

White-box versus black-box testing.

Base-level and modular testing.

Path and transaction flow testing.

Input validation testing.

State, graph, and matrix testing.

Decision tables

Provably correct design and code.

Sequencing of tests.

Unit and integration testing.

Testing of system functionality.

Specification reviews.

Module testing.

System complexity considerations.

Debugging methods.

Integration test methods.

Systematic Testing Techniques

Do you use the following? If so, how? Is there an evaluation based on the results? Is there documentation?

Techniques for identifying test cases.

Configuration testing.

Backup and recovery testing.

> Switching to "hot" backup.

> Disaster recovery drills.

Performance and stress testing.

Security and controls testing.

Systems "auditability."

Cyclomatic complexity.

Regression testing.

Traceability.

Test data sources.

Acceptance Testing

Does the customer play a role in the following?

User involvement in testing.

Conversion testing.

Usability and ergonomic (human factors) testing.

Software package installation testing.

The role of auditors.

Parallel testing.

Conditions for system acceptance.

How do customer requirements enter your acceptance testing? Is there appropriate documentation?

Test Strategy and Procedure

Minimizing redundant retesting.

Ensuring complete coverage.

Setting priorities.

Use of automated or manual test beds.

Test sequencing and interdependencies.

Top-down versus bottom-up testing.

White-box versus black-box testing.

Test procedures.

Test logs and documentation.

Follow-through on fixing and retesting.

Progress measurement and reporting.

Conversion, Maintenance, and Package Testing

Are conversion testing, auditing, and management compliance within standard parameter(s) and/or customer requirement(s)?

Are documentation and auditing requirements appropriate?

Is maintenance testing appropriate?

Is there a procedure for testing external systems packages?

Effective Working Relationships

Goals, perspectives, and concerns of

Systems developers.

Systems maintainers.

QA professionals.

Users who are responsible for systems acceptance.

Sources of conflict in testing.

Procedures for conflict resolution.

Structured Walk-Throughs and Inspections

How do you define, document, and evaluate the following?

Objectives, roles, and responsibilities.

Time and resources requirements.

Who should be involved.

Supportive environment.

The role of the quality assurance.

Checklists

In this appendix we provide the reader with a three-part checklist. The first part is a complete checklist for an ISO 9002 audit of an international company that leases tank containers. The second part is a generic checklist for the design, review, and service clauses of the ISO 9001. The final part is a generic conceptual checklist for the BS 7750 standard. These checklists are neither universal nor exhaustive, and they are presented here only as examples.

AN ISO 9002 CHECKLIST

I.   Introduction (Section 1.0)

    A.   Does company XYZ document its quality policy?

    B.   Does a quality council oversee continuous improvement efforts?

    C.   Does the quality manual refer to ISO 9002?

II.   Distribution List (Section 2.0)

    A.   Obtain the most current copy of the manual distribution list.

        1.   Review the manual distribution list to ensure that the appropriate personnel are included (i.e., managers and above).

III.   Control of the Manual and Changes (Section 3.0)

    A.   Obtain the most current copy of the continuous improvement manual from the senior vice president for corporate reporting.

    B.   Obtain correspondence related to all changes to the manual from the senior vice president for corporate reporting.

        1.   Randomly select a sample of continuous improvement manuals in the possession of personnel on the distribution list to ascertain that each copy is current and complete.

        2.   Review changes to the manual and ensure that they were approved.

IV.   Continual Improvement Manual Compliance with ISO 9002 (Section 4.0)

    A.   Obtain all ISO 9002 standards and review the quality manual to ensure that the manual includes standards 4.1 through 4.18.

        1.   Review each standard and its corresponding section in the manual to make sure all points of each standard are included in each section.

V.   Management Responsibility (Section 4.1)

    A.   Determine if the responsibility and authority of those who do the following is defined and documented:

        1.   Manage work affecting quality.

        2.   Perform work affecting quality.

        3.   Verify work affecting quality.

    B.   Determine who has documented authority to

        1.   Initiate action to prevent the occurrence of product nonconformity.

        2.   Identify and record any product quality problems.

        3.   Initiate, recommend, or provide solutions through designated channels.

        4.   Verify the implementation of solutions.

        5.   Control further processing, delivery, or installation of nonconforming product until the deficiency or unsatisfactory condition has been corrected.

    C.   Determine if the independence of those performing verification of activities from those having direct responsibility for the work being performed has been documented.

        1.   Document who is responsible for verifying procurement plans and who is responsible for initiating the procurement of equipment.

        2.   Determine if the above two persons are adequately independent of each other.

    D.   Document the name of the person assigned to be the management representative.

           1.   Obtain any documentation regarding ISO 9002 in his or her possession that shows management commitment to continuous improvement (e.g., memos, new procedures).

    E.   Request minutes of meetings from the management representative and ensure that ISO 9002 was specifically discussed.

           1.   Document the findings of any reviews (excluding internal quality audit) such as reviews conducted by outside parties or management teams.

           2.   Determine if those findings have been addressed.

VI.   Continual Improvement System (Section 4.2)

    A.   Describe how the quality system is documented.

           1.   Document who is responsible for the preparation and maintenance of each section of the documentation hierarchy.

           2.   Determine if there have been any changes to that area of documentation (e.g., work instructions and procedures) and whether or not the responsible person approved of the change and/or had the current information documented.

    B.   Determine who decides what training is necessary and determine if the training includes adequate ISO 9002 or some similar continuous improvement reference in the training course.

    C.   Verify that there is a process for updating and improving techniques for production and verification (e.g., meetings, flowcharts, reviews).

VII.   Contract Review (Section 4.3)

    A.   Determine if the contract review procedures provide a clear indication of who shall participate in the process and the expected inputs and outputs.

    B.   Select a random sample of units, and for each unit ensure that the contracts department has the appropriate documentation on file. This documentation should include a lease agreement, amendment (if applicable), and/or an addendum.

    C.   Determine the depot from which the tank originated and ensure that there is a current depot agreement on file.

    D.   Select a sample of purchase orders from the procurement department. Make sure that an addendum (if applicable), authorization sheet, placement telex, and a signed invoice (if applicable) are on file for each purchase order.

    E.   Randomly review the specifications attached to the purchase orders selected above to see which approvals must be on file and verify that the documentation is on file in the tank department.

    F.   Obtain a list of third-party accreditation agencies and ensure that a sample of inspections are performed only by those agencies.

VIII.   Document Control (Section 4.5)

    A.   Determine if procedures and instructions for the control of documentation have been established, documented, and maintained.

        1.   Determine who prepares, approves, issues, and modifies all quality documentation. (e.g., purchase orders, customer contracts, new procedures, technical bulletins).

        2.   Determine if these procedures ensure that pertinent documents are available to personnel at all locations.

        3.   Determine if there is a master list providing visibility on the current revision status of all control documents.

IX.   Procurement/Purchasing (Section 4.6)

    A.   Obtain the list of criteria for manufacturer selection.

        1.   Select a sample of manufacturers, review XYZ document to ensure that all criteria are met.

    B.   Obtain the criteria for selecting a depot.

        1.   Review a sample of current depot agreements to ensure that they meet the criteria specified by management.

    C.   Based upon the sample selected in Section VII (Contract Review), perform the additional steps.

1. Examine for signature(s) of approval.

2. Determine if the purchase order properly describes the equipment delivered by comparing the units in EMS to those listed on the purchase order.

D. Select a sample of units, ensure that the appropriate documentation is on file, and verify the accuracy of the repair documentation as follows:

1. Obtain a sample of equipment interchange reports and repair estimates (EIR) and review to ensure that they are complete.

2. Examine the EIR to ensure that an inbound inspection was performed and signed by the customer's driver and depot personnel.

3. Determine if the repair estimate noted the same damages as the EIR.

4. If there were rebillable damages, review the estimate noting customer signature.

5. Obtain depot invoices and compare them to final repair estimates.

6. Obtain depot invoices and compare them to the information in EMS.

7. Determine if the calibration chart is legible.

8. Review previous tank interchange reports and make sure chemical tanks were not used to transport food by looking at the last cargo section on the EIR.

9. Ensure that tanks failing tests were not used again.

X. Company Supplied Products (Section 4.7)

A. Determine where spare parts are stored.

1. Obtain bills of lading.

2. Obtain parts inventory listing. Select a sample and physically verify.

3. For a sample of part numbers, verify parts description in manufacturer book.

4. Follow up on the results of last stock audit and review to see if findings have been addressed.

XI. Product ID and Traceability (Section 4.8)

A.   Review the purchase order log for numerical sequence. Determine if the procedures for creating new unit numbers are adequate.

B.   Review a sample of units to ensure that XYZ's unit numbers correspond to manufacturer unit numbers listed on the purchase order.

   1.   Determine if the unit is designated properly as a finance lease (if applicable).

C.   Randomly select a sample of units and trace the history of each unit in EMS and compare the history to documentation kept on file in the tank department.

   1.   Determine if modifications were performed and obtain a tank modification report from technical services (if applicable).

   2.   Determine if a birth certificate is on file for units over six months old.

XII.   Process Control (Section 4.9)

A.   Randomly select units accepted into the fleet and obtain the corresponding inspection report to ensure that the tank was inspected before acceptance.

   1.   Review inspection report to ensure that it contains an approval signature by the proper personnel.

   2.   Obtain equipment specifications and determine if equipment met those specifications at the time of acceptance.

   3.   Determine if any nonconforming equipment was accepted into the fleet. Obtain documentation (EIR) showing approval of acceptance from the regional office.

B.   Randomly select off-hired units to ensure that they were properly inspected and repaired before becoming available for on-hire.

   1.   Obtain EIRs and compare to equipment estimates to determine if necessary repairs were performed.

   2.   Review documentation in the regional office or tank department for signatures authorizing repairs.

3. Determine if a post-repair inspection was performed.

4. Determine if repairs were in accordance with IICL and XYZ standards. How?

XIII. Inspection and Testing (Section 4.10)

A. Verify that a cleaning certificate was attached to the EIR to determine if a tank was accepted without a cleaning certificate. Review the cleaning certificate on file.

1. Determine if the cleaning certificate shows the last product carried in the tank and whether it was chemical or food grade product.

2. Determine if the cleaning certificate states the solvent and method used to clean the tank.

3. Ensure that the cleaning certificate is less than 30 days old, and if it is more than 30 days old, ensure that there is a written statement denying the reloading of cargo.

4. Ensure that a third party performed the cleaning.

5. Ensure that the tank was cleaned after each repair before being transferred to the available stack.

B. Determine if repairs were performed on the tank after it was off hired in EMS.

C. Randomly select units with an on- or off-hire status and review their files in the tank department to ensure that they were tested in accordance with the two-and-a-half-year and five-year test regulation.

1. Obtain a test certificate signed by an accreditation agency representative to ensure that tank was properly tested.

2. Ensure that the test certificate originated from an accreditation agency list on XYZ's directory of accreditation agencies.

3. Obtain the most current list of tanks due and overdue for testing and see if customers have been notified in accordance with XYZ procedures.

4. Determine if tanks were tested on a timely basis by the appropriate authority.

       5.   Ensure that there is a cleaning certificate on file for each tank that has been accepted as new equipment.

XIV.   Inspection, Measuring, and Test Equipment (Section 4.11)

    A.   Determine if XYZ is responsible for any inspection, measuring, and test equipment?

XV.   Inspection and Test Status (Section 4.12)

    A.   The following are required per our company policy, and were tested in other sections of this audit.

       1.   Hard copies of the inspection and test data relative to the acquisition and acceptance of new equipment into the fleet (DOT approvals and third-party certifications). See Section VII Contract Review.

       2.   Hard copies of certificates of periodic inspections (two-and-a-half-year and five-year certificates). See Section VIII Inspection and Testing

       3.   Hard copies of cleaning certificates. See Section VIII. Inspection and Testing.

XVI.   Control of Nonconforming Equipment (Section 4.13)

    A.   Obtain acceptance reports from procurement and compare them to the purchase order to determine if nonconforming equipment was accepted into the fleet.

       1.   If nonconforming equipment (equipment that does not meet the specifications) is shown as available, review section 4.12 page 2 of 3 in the continual improvement manual to ensure that utilization decision guidelines were followed.

    B.   Randomly select units and compare interchange reports to computer records to ensure that equipment in need of repair is not shown in the system as available for on-hire.

       1.   If nonconforming equipment is shown as available for on-hire, review section 4.12 page 2 of 3 in the continual improvement manual to ensure that release decision guidelines were followed.

    C.   For units identified in step A, ensure that third-party and XYZ surveyor authorizations were given.

XVII.   Corrective Action (Section 4.14)

A.   The credit and collections department, tank department, regional offices, and/or tank marketer may be responsible for addressing customer complaints and implementing corrective action.

1.   Obtain documentation from the appropriate offices describing any problems and the corrective action implemented.

2.   Review documentation proving that corrective actions were successful.

3.   List any problems that are repetitive to determine if there is a trend or if root causes have not been addressed.

4.   Does a certain area receive all problems requiring corrective action? If not, determine if there is a need to have this requirement.

5.   Determine who, if anyone, signs off on corrective action to be taken.

6.   Determine if a method exists for reporting corrective actions to the tank department for appropriate distribution.

XVIII.   Handling, Storage, Packaging, Preservation, and Delivery (Section 4.15)

A.   Is XYZ responsible for the handling of equipment?

B.   Do we inspect depots to ensure that they adhere to XYZ's guidelines?

C.   Is XYZ in a position to lose money from any dilemmas concerning the handling of equipment in the depot?

D.   Is XYZ responsible for the storage of equipment?

1.   Select a sample of units at the depot and scan RICS and EMS to ensure that the units are in the system.

2.   Randomly sample units recently off-hired and ensure that they are actually in the depot.

E.   Determine if any tanks require packaging.

F.   Select a sample of units, review their history in EMS, and look at the activity sheets to determine units recently repositioned.

       1.   Obtain appropriate documentation to ensure that approvals were given to reposition a sample of these units.

  G. Read the regional office written instructions to depot operators. During the visit to the depots selected for testing in Section IX, look for any nonconformities that might negatively impact customer service.

XIX.   Records (Section 4.16)

  A. Review procedures for documentation retention in each department and ensure that documents are kept on file according to the time listed in the procedures.

       1.   Choose a sample of quality documents and check the files of different departments to determine that the documents are kept in accordance with retention requirements.

       2.   Determine who is responsible for the identification, preparation, and retention of quality records to ensure that continuous improvement efforts have been documented.

       3.   Ensure that documents available for customer review are properly kept.

XX.   Internal Continuous Improvement Audit (Section 4.17)

  A. Obtain the previous year's audit report and determine if findings were addressed.

  B. Review the last few audit reports (and corresponding changes to procedures) to ensure that the company is continually improving its service.

XXI.   Training (Section 4.18)

  A. Obtain section VG in the corporate policies and procedures manual.

       1.   Review to ensure that it is not in conflict with the continuous improvement manual.

  B. Obtain the personnel training records.

       1.   Randomly sample newly hired personnel. List their position, type of training necessary, and type of training received.

       2.   Include any seminars or orientation classes they attended.

3.   Randomly review the training records to ensure they have been updated annually.

4.   Review individual training records to ensure that they have been signed by the employee.

C.   Obtain a sample of annual reviews from human resources.

1.   Ensure that the assessment was performed annually.

2.   Ensure that the assessment was signed b the employee's immediate supervisor.

3.   Ensure that the assessment addresses the employee's specific responsibilities, performance goals, and overall performance.

4.   Ensure that future goals were documented to show desire to improve performance.

XXII.   Service (Clause 4.19)

A.   The auditor is interested in whether you comply with the service objectives your organization has set for servicing the customer. As a consequence, the flow of the investigation and questioning will be dependent upon the policy of the organization and the service contract that the organization and the customer have agreed upon.

B.   The tone of all the questions in reference to servicing should be based on the following question: Has servicing, where required by contract, been performed in accordance with established procedures for performing and verifying that the service meets specified requirements?

XXIII. Statistical Techniques (Section 4.20)

A.   Determine if XYZ is responsible for controlling key manufacturing processes with the assistance of charting techniques.

1.   Ensure that statistical techniques are used.

2.   Ensure that trending is utilized.

3.   Ensure that decisions are made on data-driven facts.

4.   Ensure that improvement is monitored, evaluated, and communicated throughout the XYZ company.

AN ISO 9001 GENERIC CHECKLIST
FOR DESIGN REVIEW

In dealing with design control (section 4.4), there are really nine areas of concern.

1. General design concerns.
2. The design and development planning.
3. Organizational and technical interfaces.
4. Design input.
5. Design output.
6. Design review.
7. Design verification.
8. Design validation.
9. Design changes.

The task of the auditor is to focus on these nine areas and probe the designers (or anyone else authorized, responsible, or knowledgeable) about the design activities. The auditor's interest is only conformance to the policies and contractual agreements and how the policies and contractual agreements are being met.

Because design activities are so diverse it is very difficult to produce a single checklist. Each organization with design activities has to be evaluated individually so that all appropriate and relevant design considerations are addressed.

A good design checklist should incorporate the following questions:

1. Does the design have special constraints specified by the customer? If so, have they been implemented? Is there a record of such implementation?
2. Is value engineering conducted in the planning stages? If so, how are the changes being implemented? Do the changes affect
   Reliability?
   Function (performance)?
   Cost?
   Maintainability?
3. Has the initial design and development stage identified unique (special, critical) processes or tests? How are these special processes or tests recorded? Does the customer become aware

of them? Is there a contractual requirement for such reporting?
How do these special processes or tests affect

    Environmental conditions (dust, noise, temperature, humidity, etc.)?

    Vibration?

    Shock?

4. Are design standards or special codes identified? Examples:

    Drawing standards.

    Material selection.

    Specific test and or design.

5. Does the design identify safety requirements? If so, does it include

    Hazard analysis?

    Criticality analysis?

    Fault-tree analysis?

    Failure mode and effect analysis (FMEA)?

    Classification of the problem (based on the above four analyses)?

    Provisions for guards, labels, etc.?

    Noise, including high frequency vibration?

    Human error?

    Exhaust gas contamination?

    Pollution concerns?

6. Does the design provide mean time to failure, mean time to repair, etc.? Does the design provide for maintainability considerations, such as

    Preventive and corrective maintenance?

    Accessibility of components?

    Interchangeability of parts?

    Ease of repair?

        Minimum use of components selected on test?

        Minimum use of special tools?

        Minimum requirements for routine maintenance?

    Ease of diagnostics?

Ease of removal for broken parts?

Ease of disposal?

7. Is the current design part of the product plan and design plan? If so, how did the product and design plan come about?

Quality function deployment?

Benchmarking?

Customer requisition?

Market forces?

Internal research and development?

8. How is design reliability demonstrated?

9. How are the reliability tests selected?

10. Are reliability test results analyzed or evaluated?

11. Do reliability constraints control materials, components, and processes?

12. Does the design have a current failure report, problem report, or both? If so, does the report have full documentation of the design? For example,

Full identification of the design.

Complete description of the problem or failure.

Conditions under which the problem or failure occurred.

Analysis of the problem/failure.

Is there a real probing for the root cause? If so, can it be demonstrated?

Cause of the problem/failure.

Corrective action.

Preventive action.

Appropriate authorization.

Distribution of the failure report to all interested and appropriate organizational departments and or personnel.

13. Are the drawings checked for

Dimensional interference?

Tolerancing?

Completeness?

Ambiguity?

Capability of being measured?

      Compatibility with other drawings?

      Control documentation?

      Producibility?

      Proper identification?

      Special notification for special processes?

      Appropriate reference to test procedures?

14. Are the components from suppliers appropriately checked? If so, how was the system developed?

15. Are purchasing documents checked for accuracy of specification? If yes, how? If not, why not? How do you make sure that you receive what you purchased?

16. How does the designer make sure that the requirement has been established?

      Are there design reviews?

      Has the content of the design been reviewed for accuracy and relevancy by the appropriate personnel?

      Is the documentation for such an agreement available?

      Have all the known warranty conditions been agreed to and all legal implications been considered? If yes, how? If not, why not?

17. Are the packaging considerations in accord with the customer and environmental requirements?

18. Is the packaging design appropriate for the item? How do you know?

19. Is the design ergonomic?

20. Is the design environmentally friendly?

CHECKLIST FOR BS 7750 AND ISO 14000 ENVIRONMENTAL STANDARDS

The BS 7750 and ISO 14000 are standards that focus in the environment. However, quite a few of the clauses are very similar to the ISO 9001. Because of the similarity, we recommend that the reader review the other checklists in this appendix. We believe that the questions are quite appropriate, and perhaps with some minor modifications, they can indeed apply to individual organizations trying to meet the requirements of the BS 7750 and ISO 14000 standards.

In addition to the similarities between the ISO 9001, the BS 7750, and the ISO 14000, there are some very unlike elements. This checklist identifies these differences in a generic form to help the reader develop a specific checklist.

I.   General.
     A.   Does the company have an environmental policy?
     B.   Is the environmental policy in tandem with the quality policy?
     C.   Is the environmental policy distributed throughout the company?
     D.   Is there an environmental manual? Is it controlled?

II.   Environmental issues.
     A.   Is there a record of all environmental issues?
          1.   Legal requirements.
          2.   Product dispensing.
          3.   Noise.
          4.   Trees, amenities, landscape, and wildlife.
          5.   Use of materials.
          6.   Energy.
          7.   Waste.
          8.   Toxic waste.
          9.   Emissions.
          10.   Effluent discharge.
          11.   Transportation.
          12.   Health and safety.
          13.   Packaging.
     B.   Is there a document for the register of regulations?
          1.   Is there a description of the regulation?
          2.   Is there an approval?
          3.   Is there an authorization?
          4.   Is there a provision for change?
     C.   Is there a document for environmental effects?
          1.   Is there a description of the regulation?
          2.   Is there an approval?
          3.   Is there an authorization?
          4.   Is there a provision for change?
          5.   Is there a provision for corrective action?

Miscellaneous

TABLE G-1

Comparison of Audit Processes

Item	Internal Audits	Second-Party Audits	Third-Party Audits
Definition	Auditing one's own organization using a planned schedule and trained auditors. May be the result of customer feedback, problem areas, or management requisition.	Audit initiated by the client, the organization, or auditee. May be conducted as part of a supplier assurance program.	Audit by independent organization or regulatory body. For ISO 9000 certification, this is the appropriate audit.
Person responsible for planning	Person managing internal audit program. May be the quality manager or the ISO facilitator.	Person managing corporate audit program and/or supplier quality. May be the quality manager or the purchasing manager.	Lead auditor assigned to the specific audit
Checklist	Quality manual Departmental procedures Work instructions Customer feedback Previous audit results	Performance records Contract order specific Agreed quality plan	Detailed audit plan
Opening meeting	Very informal	Informal to very formal depending on the relationship	Very formal
The audit	Interviews Observations Reviews of documentation	Interviews Observations Reviews of documentation	Interviews Observations Reviews of documentation
Findings	Reach agreement	Reach agreement	Communicate findings
Closing meeting	Very informal	Informal to very formal depending on the relationship	Very formal and mandatory
Audit report	Informal; based on procedures set by the organization. Often reported on an official form or corrective action report.	Informal to very formal; based on agreement with the client. Often reported on a form or a corrective action report.	Very formalized and standardized report
Person responsible for identifying corrective actions and closure dates	Manager of the area	Auditee's responsibility (the auditor may have input).	

TABLE G–2

Example of Notification Letter

August 6, 1995
Mr. Cary Stamos
President
The Scorpion Farm, Inc.
1029 10th Street
Quality Town, USA 00002

Mr. Stamos:

An audit of The Scorpion Farm's quality assurance system is planned for the 29th and 30th of September. The dates and preliminary arrangements have been discussed with your QA manager, Mr. S. D. Pots. The purpose of the audit will be to evaluate the compliance and effectiveness of The Scorpion Farm's quality system against the ISO 9001 standard. The scope of the audit will be limited to the systems relevant to your facility in Quality Town.

The audit team will consist of T. D. Hots, lead auditor; C. D. Tots; D. H. Bricks; and C. J. Sands. They will be arriving at your facility in Quality Town at 8:00 AM to meet with you and your staff for a brief preaudit conference. The postaudit is scheduled for 5:00 PM on September 30.

If you have any questions on this audit, you may direct them to Ms. V. A. Philis at 1-800-555-1212.

Sincerely,

N. A. Gall

Neal A. Gall
Lead Auditor

TABLE G–3

An Audit Schedule

Day	Time	Team 1	Team 2
Monday	8:00–8:45	Opening meeting	Opening meeting
	8:45–10:30	Review of quality manual, procedures, and instructions	Review of quality manual, procedures, and instructions
	10:30–12:30	Contract Department	Manufacturing Department
	Lunch		
	1:30–3:00	Purchasing Department	Manufacturing Department
	3:00–4:30	Handling, storage, and delivery	Engineering Department
	4:30–5:30	Packaging and Labeling Department	Engineering Department
Tuesday	7:30–9:00	Laboratory	Training Department
	9:00–10:00	Laboratory	Training Department
	10:00–12:00	Quality Assurance Department	Document Control Department
	Lunch		
	1:00–2:00	Receiving Department	Management responsibility
	2:00–3:30	Servicing Department and nonconforming material (holding area)	Internal auditing and corrective action documentation
	3:30–4:15	Preparation for closing meeting	Preparation for closing meeting
	4:15–5:00	Closing meeting	Closing meeting

TABLE G-4

An Audit Plan

Audited organization	The XYZ Company
Purpose of the audit	To verify compliance and effectiveness of the company's quality system to a specific ISO standard.
Scope of the audit	Management systems relevant to the production of ABC product in facility AAA.
Requirements	The specific ISO standard and any other pertinent standards.
Activities to be audited	The areas to be audited.
Identification of auditee personnel	The individuals who will host the audit team.
Identification of the audit team	The individuals who will actually perform the audit.
Applicable documents	All appropriate documents for a thorough and unbiased audit.
Date and place of the audit	The date and facility for the audit.
Schedule of the meeting held	The detailed schedule of all the meetings in reference to the audit.
Schedule of the audit	The actual schedule of the audit by department and the approximate the time of the visit.
Confidentiality requirements	If there are issues of confidentiality, they should be identified and cleared before the audit.
Audit report and distribution	Who will receive the audit report?
Equipment needed	What, if any, equipment will be used for the audit?
Additional resources needed	What, if any, specific resources are needed for this audit?

TABLE G–5

A Typical Checklist Form

<table>
<tr><td colspan="4" align="center">Example of a Process Audit Checklist</td></tr>
<tr>
<td align="center">Area of
Audit</td>
<td align="center">Question or
Concern Item</td>
<td align="center">Check
Item</td>
<td align="center">Comments</td>
</tr>
<tr>
<td>Disposal
of trash</td>
<td align="center">21</td>
<td>Proper measures are established for removing stains, dust, and trash in and around the manufacturing equipment, workbench, parts and products containers, and floor.</td>
<td>Procedures and instructions were in place. However, they were not followed.</td>
</tr>
<tr>
<td></td>
<td align="center">22</td>
<td>Possibility of powder and dust from hands and gloves being transferred to the parts and causing defects is minimized.</td>
<td>No problems were found.</td>
</tr>
<tr>
<td></td>
<td align="center">22</td>
<td>Arrangement for controlling the adhesion of foreign matter to the jigs or cutting tools is satisfactorily established.</td>
<td>None found.</td>
</tr>
</table>

FIGURE G-1

A Form for the Checklist

Manual Reference	ISO Clause	Key Elements	Remarks	Status*		
				AD	UN	NA

* AD   Adequate
  UN   Unacceptable
  NA   Not Applicable

Training Curriculum

Training has been identified as an indispensable characteristic in the documentation and auditing process. Because of this importance, we are identifying a generic curriculum for both documentation and auditing that is appropriate for the ISO series. The curriculum is not a prescription for every organization; rather it provides the sequence for appropriate training. Each organization has to assess its own environment and then plan accordingly.

We also want to remind the reader that some organizations may need more training in other areas as well, for example, project management, teams, employee empowerment, general quality training, and specific quality tools (brainstorming, cause-and-effect diagrams, process flow charts, FMEA, DOE, QFD, SPC, etc.).

ISO 9000 INTERNAL AUDITOR TRAINING

This two-day training sessions explains why auditing is an essential component of every quality assurance system and how to carry out audits to comply with ISO 9000 and ISO 10011 requirements. It is diverse enough to be applied across all industries. Any training in auditing should include role playing for the auditors as well as exercises to enhance audit and communication skills.

I.   Quality and quality assurance
       A.   Quality defined
       B.   Quality assured
       C.   Quality controlled

II.   Quality audit
       A.   Definition
       B.   Rationale
       C.   Overview

III.   Auditing to the standard
       A.   ISO 9000 theory and structure
       B.   Documentation review
       C.   ISO 9001 explained

IV.   Audit process
        A.   General information
        B.   Types of audits
        C.   Characteristics
        D.   Participants
V.   Audit administration
        A.   Lead auditor training qualifications
        B.   Auditor training qualifications
        C.   The use of lead auditor versus auditor
        D.   Maintenance of qualification records
        E.   Appropriate audit records
             1.   System analysis
             2.   Checklists
             3.   Tools
             4.   Working papers
        F.   Evaluating the evaluators
        G.   ISO 10011 requirements
        H.   Sampling
        I.   Planning for the appropriate resources
VI.   The auditor
        A.   A position of trust
        B.   Auditor qualifications
        C.   Auditor traits, knowledge, and aptitude
        D.   Ethics
VII.   The audit
        A.   Types
             1.   Scope
             2.   Purpose
        B.   Audit preparation
             1.   Define the scope of the audit
             2.   Define the resources of the audit
             3.   Define the time of the audit
             4.   Schedule the audit
             5.   Prepare a checklist

      6.   Prepare an audit plan

      7. Send (if appropriate) the notification letter

VIII.   The functional audit

     A.   Preparation

     B.   The opening meeting

     C.   The actual audit

     D.   Documenting nonconformances

     E.   Team meetings

     F.   Exit meetings

     G.   Communicate results of the audit

     H.   Inform auditee of certification status

IX.   Audit closure

     A.   Reports and follow-up

     B.   Act on corrective action requests

X.   Workshops

     A.   Several activities to enhance the understanding of the actual standards

     B.   Audit role play

     C.   Simulation

ISO 9000 LEAD AUDITOR TRAINING

This five-day training session prepares the participant to conduct and lead (if the participant meets all the other requirements) an ISO 9000 audit. The very extensive and concentrated training requires from 12 to 15 hours daily. Team work is expected, and after-hours work is mandatory.

Day 1   Welcome and introductions

         Quality and QA

         What is ISO 9000?

         Who runs the program?

         Definitions

         Quality management systems ISO 9000

            Analysis of the individual clauses

            Requirements of the ISO

            Documentation

           Quality manual
           Procedures
           Instructions
           Forms and tags
    Certification and assessment
    Workshops
           Extensive exercises on the entire set of the standards
           Read a quality manual for discussion next day

Day 2   Questions about the company represented in the quality manual
    The assessment/audit system
           Types
           A perspective on first-, second-, and third-party assessments
                Scope
                Objective
           Quality assurance manuals
           Plan the audit
           Prepare a checklist
           Evaluate the checklist
           Prepare a notification letter
           Prepare an audit plan
           Prepare an audit schedule
    Workshops
           Extensive workshops on preparing a checklist, notification letter, audit plan, and audit schedule
           Prepare a checklist based on specific clauses of the standard from the sample quality manual

Day 3   Present and discuss the checklist and general preparation for the audit
    Feedback
    Opening meeting
    Carrying out the audit
    Nonconformances
           Found
           Recorded

Workshops

    Mechanics of the audit

    Writing and presenting noncompliances

    Prepare action items from the quality manual and case studies

Day 4   Present and discuss the noncompliances as well as the action items

Feedback

Closing meeting

Reporting the audit

Corrective action

Follow-up and surveillance

Workshops

    Role playing

    Extensive writing practice on reporting noncompliance items, corrective actions, and follow-up requirements

    Review material for next day's examination

Day 5   Present and discuss the writing exercises

Feedback

Summary

Review of the training

Examination

Selected Bibliography

_____ (November 1992). "A Strategy for Standards and Quality." *Quality at Work Newsletter*. Yarsley Quality Assured Firms Ltd., p. 4.

_____ (July 1993). "ISO 9000 and Inspection." *Continuous Improvement*. Alto, MI: National ISO 9000 Support Group, pp. 2–4.

_____ (July/August/September 1993). "Environmental Leadership." *Leaders*, pp. 46–49.

_____ (August 1993). More Questions about ISO 9000." *Continuous Improvement*. Alto, MI: National ISO 9000 Support Group, pp. 2–4

_____ (August 1993). "The Environmental Standard - BS7750." *Continuous Improvement*. Alto, MI: National ISO 9000 Support Group, pp. 1–3.

_____ (September 1993). "The Environmental Standard - BS7750." *Continuous Improvement*. Alto, MI: National ISO 9000 Support Group, pp. 2–3.

_____ (October 1993). "How to Prepare for ISO 9000." *Continuous Improvement*. Alto, MI: National ISO 9000 Support Group, pp. 1–3.

_____ (December 1993). "Tips on Streamlining Your ISO 9000 Certification Process." *Continuous Improvement*. Alto, MI: National ISO 9000 Support Group, pp. 2–4.

Block, M. R. (March 1994). "ISO/TC207: Developing an International Environmental Management Standard." *The European Marketing Guide*. Atlanta, GA: SIMCOM, pp. 5–6.

Bobbit Jr., C. E. (October 1993). "Conduct More Effective Audits." *Quality Progress*. Milwaukee, WI.

Byrnes, D. J. (November/December 1993). "ISO 9000-Style Eco-Audits." *PI Quality*. Carol Stream, IL: Hitchcock Publishing, pp. 14–15.

Cook, N. P. (July/August 1993). "Quality System, Poor Products?" *ISO 9000 News: The International Journal of the ISO 9000 Forum*. Geneva, Switzerland: ISO Central Secretariat, p. 2.

Durant, A. C. and I. Durant. (October 1993). "The Role of ISO 9000 Standards in Continuous Improvement." *Quality Systems Update*. Fairfax, VA: Irwin Professional Publishing, pp. 14–15.

Dzus, G. (November 1991). "Planning a Successful ISO 9000 Assessment." *Quality Progress*, pp. 25–27.

Dzus, G. and E.G. Sykes Sr. (October 1993). "How to Survive ISO 9000 Surveillance." *Quality Progress*, Milwaukee, WI. pp. 32–35.

Eade, T., Byrnes, D. J. (September/October 1993). "Documentation per ISO 9000." *PI Quality*. Carol Stream, IL: Hitchcock Publishing, pp. 4–6.

Earnshaw, D. (November 1993). "The EC's Eco-Management and Audit Scheme." *The EC Marketing Guide*, pp. 4–5.

Garavaglia, P. L. (October 1993). "How to Ensure Transfer of Training." *Training and Development*. Alexandria, VA: American Society for Training and Development, pp. 46–49.

Grounds, R. (October 1993). "Employee Involvement: A Major Change in Direction. *Quality Digest*. Red Bluff, CA: QCI International, pp. 19–22.

Guzzetta, S. (September/October 1993). "How ISO 9000 Changed Supplier Quality Assurance." *PI Quality*. Carol Stream, IL: Hitchcock Publishing, pp. 6–8.

Hayes, R. H. and S. C.Wheelwright. (1984). *Restoring Our Competitive Edge: Competing through Manufacturing*. New York: John Wiley & Sons.

Hovermale, R. A. (February 1994). "ISO 9000 - Continual Improvement." *The European Marketing Guide*, pp. 8–10.

Howe, K. R. and K. C. Dougherty. (December 1993). "Ethics, Institutional Review Boards, and the Changing Face of Educational Research." *Educational Researcher*. AERA, pp. 8–10.

Jeffrey, N. (January 1994). "Waste Not . . . Minimizing and Disposing of Hazardous Waste Requires More Than Lip Service." *American Printer*. Chicago, IL: Maclean Hunter Publishing, pp. 52–53.

Kinni, T. B. (October 1993). "Preparing for Fast-Track ISO 9000 Registration." *Quality Digest*. Red Bluff, CA: QCI International, pp. 19–21.

Kinni, T. B. (January 1994). "Reengineering Primer." *Quality Digest*. Red Bluff, CA: QCI International, pp. 26–31.

Kochan, A. (October 1993). "ISO 9000: Creating a Global Standardization Process." *Quality*. Carol Stream, IL: Hitchcock Publishing, pp. 36–37.

Kromrey, J. D. (May 1993). "Ethics and Data Analysis." *Educational Researcher*. AERA, pp. 24–27.

Lamprecht, J. L. (1994). *ISO 9000 and the Service Sector: A Critical Interpretation of the 1994 Revisions*. Milwaukee, WI: Quality Press.

LeDoux, T. J. (December 1993/January 1994). " ISO 9000: What You Don't Know Might Hurt You!" *Continuous Journey*. Houston, TX: American Productivity and Quality Center, pp. 3–4.

Marash, I. R. (February 1994). "ISO 9000 and the Medical Device GMP." *The European Report on Industry*, pp. 6–8.

Mehta, P. (1994). *ISO 9000 Audit Questionnaire and Registration Guidelines*. Milwaukee, WI: Quality Press.

Schmauch, C. H. (1995). ISO 9000 for *Software Developers*. Revised. Milwaukee, WI: Quality Press.

Skrabec Jr., Q. R. (January 1994). "Integrating Quality Control into Your TQM Process." *Quality Digest*. Red Bluff, CA: QCI International, pp. 66–70.

Stamatis, D. H. (September 1993). "FMEA Fulfills Prevention Intent of ISO 9000." *Quality Systems Update*. Burr Ridge, IL: Irwin Professional Publishing, pp. 16–17.

Stamatis, D. H.; Epstein, I.; and R.P. Cooney. (June 1993). "Documenting Personnel Qualifications." *Quality Systems Update*. Burr Ridge, IL: Irwin Professional Publishing, pp. 21–23.

Wayman, W. R. (January 1994). "ISO 9001: A Guide to Effective Design Reviews." *Quality Digest*. Red Bluff, CA: QCI International, pp. 45–48.

Wilson, L. A. (1996). *Eight-Step Process to Successful ISO 9000 Implementation*. Milwaukee, WI: Quality Press.

INDEX